I ONLY WANTED TO LIVE | ARIE TAMIR

Producer & International Distributor
eBookPro Publishing
www.ebook-pro.com

I Only Wanted to Live
The struggle of a boy to survive the holocaust
Arie Tamir

Contact: tbcarmi@gmail.com

ISBN 9781694929365

I dedicate this book to the memory of my parents, Wilhelm (Nicknamed Wilek) Wimisner and Eva Dorf, my sisters, Gizia and Sarenka, and dozens of cousins, uncles and aunts.

My dear readers, remember the millions who were murdered and were not given the chance to live a full, happy life.

I dedicate this book to my sweet 5 grandkids: Tom, Liran, Shelly ,Ben and Itamar who, when the time is right, will be able to read the stories about our family.

I ONLY WANTED TO LIVE

The Struggle of A Boy to Survive The Holocaust

ARIE TAMIR

ACKNOWLEDGMENTS

Thank you my beloved wife, Ariella, who was patient when I suddenly decided to 'play' at being an author, for the advice, the corrections and the encouragement.

Thank you my lovely daughters, Orit and Liat, who were moved by my stories about the holocaust when we visited Krakow.

Thank you my cousin Miriam Milgrom Nitzan, who devoted many hours to using her vast professional experience to improve the book in its early stages, and, most importantly, encouraged me to keep writing when I was about to collapse.

Thank you many friends who bothered to read the book in its early stages, made helpful comments and encouraged me to continue.

Thank you Ayelet Maria Mitch, my talented editor, who edited, improved and made the book more interesting and readable.

Thank you Tali Carmi and eBook-pro team.

Lastly, thank you all the good people who at one point or another helped me to save my life, some of whom are Germans.

INTRODUCTION

Why did I suddenly remember to write my story?

I was about 7 years old when World War II broke out. We were a happy family with three children. My sister, Gizia, was three years older than me and my sister Sarenka was about five years younger (she was a year old when the war began). I was nicknamed "Leosz" which stood for my formal name – Leon. My mother took care of the house and kept busy with all sorts of social activities. I remember her as always being beautiful and radiant, dressed in the best of taste, and always concerned about her appearance. Like every good Jewish Pole she was very proud of her children and would habitually boast about our amazing exploits. Financially, we were in the upper middle class. The horrific war burst into this good and happy life and after an unbearable six years of going through all the levels of hell, my whole family – parents, sisters, 16 aunts and uncles and 23 cousins – were all murdered, and only I survived.

Like many Holocaust survivors, I didn't talk much about what I experienced. After I was liberated on May 5, 1945, from the Mauthausen concentration camp, I repeated my story hundreds of times in various circumstances. About a year later, though, I gradually disconnected myself from my past. This break lasted for about 50 years. Few of my friends knew I was a survivor; they thought that I was at least a second-generation Israeli. Even my children didn't know. I didn't hide it, and I wasn't ashamed of being a Holocaust survivor – I just wasn't interested in telling anyone. For me, it was like I had been reborn in Israel and started my life over again here on the kibbutz. However, ever since the Holocaust, it has been like a sad cloud always hung over me. It's hard for me to feel free, to be happy with all my heart, or even to go wild.

Around 16 years ago I started getting more interested in the history of the Holocaust and World War II in general. I did have one cousin of my father's who had survived, Gina Milgrom. She had immigrated to Israel in 1946 and had had three children who were parents themselves at that point. Since we were the only relatives the two of us had in Israel, we were very close. Gina passed away in 1994.

In May 2010, my family decided to go on a trip back to my roots, so we went to Krakow, Poland, where Gina and I were born. My wife, Ariella, and two daughters, Orit and Liat went, as did Miriam Nitzan, Gina's daughter, with her husband Meir and three children – Michal, Eran and Einat. This trip was mainly meant for the "children," the second and third generations – who at this point were in their twenties and thirties. For five days we visited the "Kazimierz" Jewish quarter, the Jewish ghetto, the Plaszow concentration camp on the edge of Krakow, and the Auschwitz concentration camp.

I was surprised by the "children's" interest in everything I told them about the Holocaust and my family. I'm not one of the world's great story-tellers, but I still felt that they listened to my stories with a growing thirst. Sometimes they wouldn't let me end a story; they immediately asked me to keep going and tell the rest of it. One evening, we sat in our hotel, and – thanks to Eran's great initiative – we watched "Schindler's List," directed by Steven Spielberg. After the film was over, I related a story about one of the incidents in the movie that I'd had the "honor" of being part of In it: I and my friend Jezyk and several other kids organized an escape from a children's transport from Plaszow to Auschwitz. When I finished telling it, my family started peppering me with questions, mainly revolving around their desire to know what happened at the end to Jezyk. Unfortunately, I couldn't answer that. To my sorrow, I don't have answers to hundreds, even thousands of those kinds of questions: "What happened to them at the end." Events occurred at a dizzying pace, where I'd meet various people and then they'd disappear from my life. This trip back to my roots and the strong desire of the young generation to know ever more of my experiences during the war, was one of the causes of my writing down my memories.

As I read more about the Holocaust, my memories – long suppressed – began running through my mind once more. I started picturing each one of my relatives, and the friends with whom I had been significantly involved with. I started imagining how each one ended his life, if he'd suffered before he died, if she had cried, acted with self-respect, tried to fight. Maybe after I finish writing my memoir I'll try and search for the people whom I met during my six-year fight for survival.

I hope that the story that follows – as so many have done before – will act as a kind of memorial for my sisters and parents, aunts, uncles and cousins, and every single person I will mention in my memoir, even if I didn't remember their names with total accuracy.

CHAPTER 1

My Family

There were three children in my family: Gizia, my big, sweet and wonderful sister. She was a beautiful girl with big blue eyes and a noble, serious and quiet character. She was three years older than me and a wonderful big sister, showering me with all her maternal feelings. We played a lot together. As a boy, I had many trucks, trains, mechanical and cardboard construction sets. But with Gizia I played mostly with her dolls. We'd organize a school, and Gizia would repeat what her teacher said in class, while I joined the dolls as one of the students. We'd organize whole plays with the dolls, and apparently we did a good job, as Mom asked us to present it to guests as well. Gizia had all kinds of doll houses and castles that contained furniture and tiny figures that we would rearrange all the time. After my little sister, Sarenka, was born in 1938, when I was about five, Mom started allowing me to play in the street with the other children, relying on Gizia to watch over me.

When Sarenka came along, I went though the same crisis as all children who had been the baby of the family until then. Suddenly I stopped being the one who got most of the attention from relatives as well as the many guests who came to our house. Gizia fulfilled a very important role for me during this period, as she showed me a lot of love, showering me with hugs and kisses when my mother didn't. Besides my mother and nanny, Zosia, she was the only one I loved to have hug and kiss me…

Sarenka was a wonderful baby and everyone was crazy about her except for me. I was angry at her for stealing my status and was jealous of her. But I didn't express my feelings by showing any hatred or aggressiveness. In time, I found my "big brother" feelings starting to develop and grow.

My parents, Wilhelm (Nicknamed Wilek) Wimisner and Eva Dorf, were a happy and lucky couple. They grew up in the Austro-Hungarian Empire in the beginning of the twentieth century, on the cusp of World War I. They learned together in university in Vienna in the Twenties, which is where they apparently met. In university they absorbed the whole Austro-Germanic culture. At home they spoke German often, especially when they didn't want the children to understand – but that didn't work, because both my sister and I basically learned Polish and German at the same time. I didn't even differentiate between the two languages. (In Krakow, where we lived, the Jews didn't speak Yiddish, and I was only exposed to it much later.)

Krakow is in western Poland in a region called Galicja. I was a second generation Krakower, as my mother had also been born there. In 1936 or 1937 we moved to a new home in the city; our address was 17 Sarego Street. It was one of the most beautiful streets in the city; a small one nestled between the ends of two long boulevards with grass, trees and benches (called "Planty" in Polish). My sister was apparently the reason for the move, because it was only a few hundred meters away from the Hebrew school where she had just started to learn.

My mother ran the house and was socially very active. Like every Polish Jewish mother, she was very proud of her children. Since I was excellent in math from a very young age, every guest would ask me math problems that I would easily answer. Mom would look on and positively glow with pride and joy. I didn't understand why these grownups didn't know math by themselves and had to come over to my house to ask me… In general when guests came, we children would stand in a kind of "receiving line" with our parents, with Mom holding baby Sarenka in her arms.

My mother Ewa 1939

My mother was a lovely woman who always dressed beautifully. I was very conscious of her beauty and was very proud of her. It should be noted that my last memory of her was when she was in her early thirties, so from my current point of view I knew her when she was still a child...

Our building had an elevator, and our apartment consisted of five luxurious rooms. We even had a telephone – something rare in those days. We had a housekeeper who lived with us and took care of my little sister. She had her own room. My mother also had a maid who mainly cooked, cleaned and did other house chores, and a nanny whose job was to take care of the bigger children. Since Gizia already went to school, for three years I'd had the nanny to myself. Her name was Zosia, and she was young, under twenty years old. She was a university student and worked for us part-time. It should be remembered that in those days there was no such thing as organized day care, so she was like my pre-school teacher and I was very attached to her and admired her.

My father was part owner of a wholesale textile business. He supplied fabrics to most of the stores and sewing factories in Krakow and the surrounding area. One of his jobs was to import textiles from various factories around Poland and other countries, such as Austria, Czechoslovakia, Germany and even England. He frequently traveled for work and wasn't home a lot. The headquarters of the business was at 10 Stradom Street, less than a kilometer from our house. The head office took up the entire building, and they also had several other offices and warehouses.

My father Wilhelm

From this short description, it seems that we were quite well off financially, and if one compared it to today's economy, we would be considered among the wealthiest people of the city. I was well taken care of but not spoiled, as my parents took care that there would be discipline in the home – in every sense of the word. We had to talk quietly and politely; nothing would be gained by crying or yelling. I remember crying very rarely even during the war... Even when I would "get it" from Dad, I'd accept my punishment quietly and with self-respect. Strict table manners were enforced; we ate quietly and didn't get up from the table unless permission was granted. Our toys and books were always neat.

My extended family consisted of many aunts, uncles and cousins. I never knew my father's parents, who had died when I was very young or before I was born. The grandfather whom I was named for had four brothers and three sisters, whom I will presently discuss. And my father himself had one brother and three sisters. My grandparents on my mother's side were relatively young. When the war broke out, they were in their fifties. They lived in the ancient Jewish quarter, called Kazimierz, and were Orthodox, Sabbath-observant Jews. They had five children; three girls including my mother, and two sons. None of their children were religious as adults.

We were a very warm and close family. Most of our relatives lived nearby, in walking distance, and we'd meet on birthdays, for bar mitzvas, weddings, anniversaries – there were always reasons for celebrating. Almost every weekend there was a party. Most of our relatives didn't have particularly big apartments, but that wasn't a problem. Dozens of adults and children would crowd into someone's home and it would be very joyous...

The aunt who was most important and closest to me was Aunt Rozia, my mother's youngest sister. According to a population registry I found, she was 17 in 1939, so she seemingly finished her

tests that year. Of course, I remember her as being
and older. When I'd go to Grandma's house, I essen-
.o her. She'd tell me stories and teach me things. In my
ordeɪ ˍ iority, after Zosia, Mom, my sister and father, she was the
most important and beloved person in my life. Rozia understood me
and knew how to answer the "hard" questions that I would pepper
her with. For example, it greatly interested me to know where I was
before I was born, and so she constructed for me a whole world in
Heaven and taught me the concept of "God." According to her, before I was born I was in God's palace up in the sky. He was the king
of heaven and earth and loved me very much; I would sit at his feet.
Once she told me that God loved me as if I was his son, while I had
learned from Zosia that Jesus the Christian was the son of God. So
what I drew from this was that I was Jesus' brother! I remember that
when I told her this revelation, it both embarrassed her and struck
her as very funny, and she used to tell others about my "discovery."
Aunt Rozia also told me many stories about angels who were the
messengers of God, how they'd come to people who had done good
deeds and give them gifts. These angels had wings like birds and
flew everywhere. I liked this job description of angels very much – it
looked like a lot of fun. I asked Rozia if I could learn to be an angel…

Mom's little brother was called Kuba; I estimate that he was a year
older than Rozia. I loved his sense of humor. Among the cousins he
was known as "the funny uncle." The second brother who was older than my mother, Juzek, was "the serious uncle." He was a lawyer,
wore glasses, was always dressed fastidiously and radiated authority
and respectability. I found out later that he had earned a doctor-
ate. He lived in Katowic, was married and had young children, and
would come every few months to visit the family. Every time he came
to Krakow, Uncle Juzek would take me to the toy store near Rynek
(Market/Square) and let me choose a gift. That was world-class fun!
Sometimes he'd leave me there alone for hours and I'd have the best

time wandering among the toys until one of the assistants would help me pick one out. In addition, he'd buy me a torte with several layers of colorful cream that I loved very much. In this way, Uncle Juzek became the stuff of myth and legend to me. (I have tried this method with my children and grandchildren, but don't think it works quite as well...)

Aunt Fela, Mom's second sister, was younger than her and very modest. I don't remember anything particular about her. She had two children, a baby and a son a bit younger than me called Bronek, whose nickname was "Bronush." Fela's husband disappeared in the beginning of the war. I'd invite Bronush over to play with me, and would give him some of my toys. I even remember asking my father to take him once to the store and get him a present. I remember him as a sad child who needed support and encouragement.

I didn't have much of a bond with my grandfather. He was very busy with his stationery store. It was a kind of wholesale business that sold merchandise to other stores as well as to the public. It was only natural that the games in my grandfather's house were almost all based on drawing and educational workbooks, construction paper, and all kinds of paints and coloring tools. Grandma would spoil me, making all my favorite foods.

I know very little about my grandparents on my mother's side, or previous generations. I only know that my great-great-grandfather was a rabbi of a synagogue, and that to a certain extent my grandfather went astray religiously; not to mention my mother and all her siblings, who threw their religion away almost completely. I vaguely recall that they spoke of an ancestor about five generations back who was a famous rabbi who made innovations in Jewish law. I also heard that Grandpa's lineage stretched back to some great rabbi whose family came from Spain to Amsterdam, and who then emigrated from Amsterdam to Krakow.

My father's family, the Wimisners, came from Tarnow. His father's name was Leib, which in Polish became "Leon." I was named for him, but everyone called me by my nickname, "Leosz." Grandpa Leib had four brothers and three sisters. Two of his brothers, Oskar and Abraham, and one sister – Esther – emigrated to London at the end of the 19th century, and established a very successful textile factory there. This branch of the family was very large.

My grandfather Leon on the right and his four brothers.
On the left "Little David", end of 19th century

Abraham's daughter, Gertie, moved to Israel with her husband after her two children (Marion and Ivor-Chaim) had preceded them. My father was Gertie's cousin. She lived in Jerusalem with her husband and died at over 100 years of age. Marion lives with her husband, Harry, in Haifa and has two children and several grandchildren. Ivor lives with his wife in Jerusalem: They have four children and many grandchildren.

My father had three sisters and a brother, David, in and around

Krakow. My father's uncle (Grandpa Leib's brother) also lived in Krakow. His name was also David. My father's brother was several years older than my dad, while their Uncle David was only a few years older than they were, so the family basically treated them all like brothers. I considered both Davids to be my uncles. Since my dad's brother was very tall, we called him "Big David." And since my great-uncle was short, we nicknamed him "Little David." These three – the two Davids and my father – were partners in the fabric business mentioned above. Big David had two daughters. The older one, Genia, was 18 in 1939 and had just finished her matriculation exams in the local Hebrew high school. Her sister, Lucia, was about 12 when the war broke out. Lucia was a sweet, gentle and cultured young lady who behaved aristocratically and loved little children. Along with all the other little kids, I loved and worshiped Lucia, who spoke and played with us a lot.

My uncle "Big David"

Dad's sister, Aunt Hela, also had two daughters – 14-year-old Dora and 11-year-old Eva. Eva was a wonderful redhead, as mischievous as a boy, who always played with the boys. Dora was a quiet, intelligent and aristocratic girl who died of some disease at the beginning of the war.

Another (younger) sister, Genia, had two sons, Leon and Jurek. Jurek was about four years older of me. Her husband had also disappeared at the beginning of the war, as did Leon about a year later. Jurek and I had a good relationship, and he taught me quite a few things, as I shall detail later.

My cousin Lucia, daughter of Big David at the age of 14

My cousin Genia, 1938

Little David was married to Aunt Mina and had two sons and a daughter. The oldest was the daughter, Gina, who was 17 when the war broke out, and the boys were twins, aged 14. All three of them survived the war, after which the twins went to England. One of them, Morris, lives today (as of 2011) in London with his wife, Jeanne. They have two children and six wonderful grandchildren. Their son, Paul Manor, emigrated to Israel and lives in Jerusalem with his wife Gila and three children. Their daughter, Simone, lives in London with her husband Ian and has three children. The other twin, Ziggy, was killed in a traffic accident in 1987. Gina, meanwhile, went to Palestine, arriving on an illegal ship in 1946. For the first two years she lived on Kibbutz Avuka in the Beit Shean Valley, marrying the love of her life, Shmuel Milgrom. They had three talented and wonderful children who were a great comfort after the loss of the rest of the family in the Holocaust. They worked very hard during the first years of the state, when the economic situation in Israel was difficult, to give their children every advantage. They were very proud and happy with their offspring's success. Both Gina and Shmuel died several years ago, but as of this writing they already have six grandchildren.

"Little David" my grandfather's brother

As a young child, I remember Gina as a beloved relative who had a special, motherly relationship with all her little cousins. And in Israel, even after I'd grown up some, she continued treating me like a mother does a small child... Since she was my only relative in the country, we were very close for many decades, and now, following her death and that of her husband, my relationship with her children and grandchildren grows ever closer.

Zygmunt, son of Little David and twin of Mauri

Mauri, son of Little David and twin of Zygmunt

As I mentioned above, we were a close family, and most of our social life revolved around the extended family. Since we were about 20 cousins in all, you could just imagine what went on when all of us got together. We'd divide up into various age groups: In one room a kind of nursery would be set up for the babies and very little ones, and the girls who loved children – like Lucia, Gina, and Aunt Rozia – would take care of them. The teens would take another room, from which would then emanate the sound of music, dancing, games and gossip. The in-between age group would go down to the street to play. I would like to note that at that time it was very acceptable to play in the street – mainly in the tiny side streets, like ours, which barely had any traffic on it. We'd take all sorts of things with us to play with, like bikes, scooters and balls, and take over the sidewalk and street. I had a lot of fun at these family meetings.

Aunt Gina 1938

CHAPTER 2

War Is Coming; The City of Lwow

As the threat of war drew nearer in the beginning of August, 1939, my father – just like many other Jews of means – decided to take the family away from Krakow, a city that was very close to the German border. Of course, I didn't understand anything, but I felt that something bad was happening. They told me that we were going on vacation, on a trip – things I was used to. But still, it wasn't the same thing. There was tension in the air; it wasn't the same happy atmosphere in the house as there always was before we went on vacation. Mom was very irritable and Dad had to calm her down all the time. My big sister, who apparently understood what was going on, didn't share her knowledge with me. We also didn't do the kind of packing we usually did for a trip; there were many more suitcases than normally accompanied us on vacation.

As usual, we traveled by train in first class to get to Lwow. It was a very big city, about 300 kilometers east of Krakow and about 400 kilometers from the German border. We came to a rented apartment that had apparently been organized ahead of time. After settling in and getting to know the neighborhood, Dad returned to Krakow and was supposed to come back to us a few days later. The nannies didn't come with us; our parents hired a local girl to take care of us as well as a maid who came every day to cook and clean.

As the days passed we started to get used to life in a strange city. We had taken along tons of toys and books, so we weren't bored.

Mother would take the older ones – that is, me and my big sister – to all sorts of fun places: we went walking through the city's wonderful parks, horseback riding, to the amusement park and the zoo. Every evening, when it would start getting cooler, the whole family would go for a stroll along the beautiful avenues of the city. Mom met many friends like us, who had "moved away from the front." My sister, Gizia, and I would play outside and we made many new friends.

One day, the holiday routine was disturbed when Janek suddenly appeared. He was one of the younger assistants in Dad's business, around 20 years old. I knew him from my visits to Dad's office and I loved him, so I was very happy he had come and fell on him with lots of hugs. But I noticed that Mom was not greeting him happily. For her it was a sign that Dad was going to delay his arrival. It turned out that Dad had indeed been scheduled to return that very day to us, but urgent business dealings were going to put off his arrival by a few days, so he sent Janek to us in his place. Mom really didn't like that because she was already quite impatient to have Dad back. However, Janek's arrival was a great pleasure for me. My sister and I started going out with him without our mother. He'd play ball and hide-and-seek with us, let us ride on the big horses, and said we could go on the rides in the amusement park that Mom had prohibited. Since we had many toys like balls, a scooter and roller skates, every place we went we always had a lot of friends to play with.

Then, on September 1, 1939, just after breakfast, we were getting ready to go out for some enjoyable activity or other when suddenly, with no warning or siren whatsoever, we heard explosions. Everything shook, the windows shattered and everything that had been on the shelves fell to the floor. Janek, Dad's assistant, said forcefully but quietly, "We have to go down to the shelter."

What did that mean, 'go to the shelter'? Mother apparently understood. Janek took my one-year-old sister in his arms and we went down to the shelter. That's how World War II and the Holocaust began for me – and it lasted for six long years, less four months.

CHAPTER 3

War Breaks Out; Escape to Lublin

When the war began, our "vacation" routine in Lwow was immediately disrupted as the Germans began shelling the city. I didn't understand what was happening, but for some reason the loud explosions didn't scare me; it was sort of fun and seemed like a game to me. As far as I can recall, until the war began and even after it started, nobody bothered to explain to me what was going on. The concept of "war" was not in my lexicon at all. I used to play with tin soldiers and I also heard romantic war stories from my nanny, so war and armies seemed to me to be lots of fun, with a lot of horses galloping, swords being brandished, and all kinds of terribly interesting machines, like cannons and rifles. I simply saw it as another game.

It seems that the first parts of the city to be shelled were the industrial area and the army bases outside the city. The thunderous explosions were pretty far from us. The first shells had landed without warning, but afterwards, we would hear a siren several minutes before the bombs fell, which was enough time to descend quietly to the shelter.

At Dad's business, Janek was the assistant to the technical support manager. He had brought several tools with him to Lwow, and after the first bombing he immediately began fixing the damage. I helped him, and this gave me tremendous pleasure. In a city under fire, one very quickly gets used to the situation and gets into a routine. When the shelling came more frequently, we would stay in the shelter for a long time. Of course, the shells were one big nightmare for the adults, but for the children it was simply fun and games. There were dozens of kids in the building's shelter between the ages of 5 and 12. The parents couldn't keep them in the shelter for an extended period of time; after every all-clear sounded, we'd go play on the street next to the house until the next siren.

After several days, Mom had apparently had it with the nightmare of sitting in the shelter and she decided – possibly after consulting with Dad by telephone – to escape Lwow to a place that wasn't being shelled. One night, we packed all our suitcases and went by taxi to the train station to go to a small city called Lublin. When we had come to Lwow several weeks earlier, this train station had imprinted itself on my memory: It was a beautiful station, completely covered with a glass roof. When we had arrived it had been a bright day and the roof acted as a prism when the sun's rays entered, breaking the light into colorful splashes. This lent the station an aura of magic and legend for me. When we went back that night, I was full of anticipation to see the wonderful station again. Janek told me that at night the station was lit up with many lights, there was live music and street performers. How disappointed I was when we got there and instead of finding a train station, we found ruins. The Germans had taken care to destroy the area. The whole glass roof was shattered in pieces all over the floor.

The trains didn't stop in the station anymore, but several hundred meters beyond it. We had to push and pull our luggage to the train through all the debris. It took a long time to get from the station to the train. Mom exhibited great fitness and adaptability; I noticed that for the very first time, she wore sneakers outside the house, not shoes with heels. Janek carried Sarenka close to his chest with one hand and dragged two suitcases behind him with the other. Gizia and I dragged one suitcase and my mother alternately dragged and carried a suitcase and a big bag. Usually there were many porters in Polish train stations who begged to help carry the luggage, but this time they had vanished. After a strenuous journey of an hour or more, we got to the train. But we didn't drag the suitcases alone all the time. After we'd made only a little progress with the bags, Janek went and found two young men who helped us bring them to the train. I have no idea how Mom knew which train to get on; it could be that she really didn't know, and simply entered the first train she could. The main thing was to escape Lwow. What was certain was that at the end we did get to Lublin. This wasn't a luxurious journey in first-class, but one of refugees all crammed together in the train-car.

When we got to the station in Lublin, it was working normally, with all services intact. The city hadn't been shelled yet and it was quiet. As usual, porters with carts arrived and we rented two of them to load up all our bags and packages. They sat Sarenka and me on one of the carts and took us to the area where the carriages waited. It should be noted that at that time, most of the transportation in Poland's cities was via electric trams. Carriages were usually reserved for special trips. Car rides were very rare. After a short ride, we got to a nice house. It could be that it was actually a hotel, because we had a small apartment and most of the people in the building were refugees like us from western Poland. We were in that apartment for a very short time, because two days after our arrival, Lublin started getting shelled. This time, the Germans bombed the residential sections of the city. It was a very small city, so in the very first shelling the house was hit badly and it was impossible to return to our apartment. We spent a few days in the shelter, when suddenly Dad appeared. How could he possibly have found us? Possibly the trip to Lublin was co-ordinated with him and he knew what hotel we'd be in.

A huge hullabaloo ensued when we saw him; we cried and laughed...Everyone in the shelter shared our joy. Mom cried and hugged Dad and yelled at him, "How could you abandon us at such a terrible time!" As usual, I asked him, "What gift did you bring me?" I saw the whole tragedy of the war as a vacation and adventure, although a bit of a strange one...The first second Dad had appeared I suddenly imagined that we had been playing hide-and-seek with him and he had found us...

After Dad came we continued living for a few days in the shelter. The shelling lasted for relatively short periods. Usually it started about ten minutes after we heard the sirens, the bombs would drop for a few minutes, and then the all-clear would sound. Sometimes hours passed between one bombing and the next. The routine was that between the bombings, Gizia and I would go out with Janek to play outside, while Mom and Dad stayed in the shelter with the baby. Sometimes our parents dared to go out and get some fresh air with her. Dad would sometimes leave to buy food, make calls and run all kinds of errands. Several days after his arrival, Dad told us that we'd be going to a new place that very night.

So on a magical and wonderful night with a full moon up in the sky, a number of farmers' wagons rolled up to our hotel. Dad had rented them together with a few other families who were with us in the shelter. We loaded up the wagons with all our suitcases and the things we'd managed to save from the destroyed apartment. We left Lublin in a long line of farmers' carts to go to the surrounding villages. Our goal was to be "hosted" by a farmer "until the crisis was over." There was no shelling at night and we had a quiet journey. I don't know how Dad and the others had managed to rent the wagons, nor how they found places to live in the villages. All I remember from that night was that I was very happy to get in the wagon. I got to sit next to the driver, just as I did in the carriages in the city, and he even let me hold the reins. When I got tired, they lay me down to sleep on the suitcases and I woke up the next late morning in the farmer's house.

The farmer's family cleared out of their house for us and they and their three children went to sleep either in the barn or with neighbors. The village was a wondrous and completely new world for me. Like many other agrarian countries, Poland's farmers had a very low and primitive standard of living. Only a few knew how to read and write, and the children barely went to school. Most went for only a short time, just enough to learn a little bit of math and their letters. Nonetheless, they were very relaxed, goodhearted and naïve people. They worked very hard, from morning until night, and even young children had to help with the work. Already back in Krakow I had somewhat understood the concept of what "farmers" were, since they would come to the city from the surrounding villages to sell their produce. Every morning they'd come with milk, cheeses, fruit, vegetables, etc. Their language – primarily in eastern Poland – was very strange. It was a kind of mixture of Polish and Ukrainian, but just like all the kids, it was very easy for me to pick up their dialect and slang.

CHAPTER 4

Life in the Village;
Our First Meeting with Germans

Coming to the farmer's house in the village was a fantastic experience for me. For the first time ever, I saw a farm and learned where our milk and eggs came from. When they let me milk a cow I almost fainted from happiness and fear. I volunteered enthusiastically to be the geese-herder. Zosia, the farmer's little 7-year-old, was an experienced geese-herder and she instructed me in this art. We would go out together to the fields with a few hundred of them. This Zosia was the second Zosia in my life, after Big Zosia – my legendary nanny. Little Zosia was a wonderful child, blonde, with blue eyes. It took a little time before we understood each other; she didn't understand my accent and my "sophisticated talk" and I didn't understand *her* accent, the special dialogue, and most of all – the farm slang. But in only a few days we were speaking freely in what was really a mishmash of "languages," and my mother yelled at us that she didn't understand what we were saying, and how I was turning into a farmer...

Zosia went around barefoot; she didn't know what shoes were. And after several days I also started going out barefoot with her. She would walk on stones and thorns without it bothering her a bit. It turned out that it was completely natural for the kids in the village to walk around this way. The soles of their feet would develop muscles, the skin thickened and hardened, and so a kind of natural shoe would grow on them. Of course this process takes years, and I would always get hurt... They made me special shoes out of cloth but I absolutely refused to give up the wonderful experience of going barefoot.

Geese-herding is a special expertise. Geese don't follow you until they've gotten used to you – and this takes a long time. In the beginning they were scared of me and would run away. They knew and loved Zosia, though, and it was an amusing sight to see how the geese would crowd around her to get a hug and a pat, and fight to get near her. She would hug and kiss them. She explained to me that the geese were her daughters and she was their mother. As time passed, Zosia started hugging and kissing me as well. I wasn't so enthusiastic about that; it reminded me of my aunts who'd come to visit and shower me with kisses. It should definitely be noted that – as opposed to girls – boys usually don't like to be kissed. When I asked her why she's kissing me, since she's not my aunt or my mother, Zosia explained that I was like her son and she loves me like the geese... I will note here that even though I didn't love to kiss I did love Zosia with all my heart, because of her simple spontaneity and her beauty. I missed her terribly for a long time after we left their home. We would go out to fields that had just been reaped and the grain gathered, and the geese loved to eat the leftovers. Zosia would lead the flock, with the geese marching behind her and me acting as the "sheepdog" at the back, running around and making sure the flock didn't scatter. I also acted as a guard and ensured that foxes, jackals and other carnivores wouldn't come near our charges. I had a long, threatening staff for this purpose. When we would return from the pasture, my big sister, along with one of the older boys, would help us get the flock into their pen. I was very jealous of my sister, because they let her milk cows for real, and go out to the pasture with horses.

Together with the farmer's wife and her older daughter, Mom would do chores around the house, prepare meals and we would eat with them. The wife was very proud that "Pani Eva," the esteemed mistress from the city, worked beside her in the kitchen. For the first time, I saw my mother working in the kitchen and getting her dainty hands dirty. I had the feeling that she was enjoying the whole thing; she was in an excellent mood and always joked around.

We would usually eat together with the farmer's family. The food was very simple: potatoes, bread, eggs, butter, and various drinks similar to cocoa and coffee. Sometimes, in our honor, they would kill a chicken or goose. It should be noted that the farmers considered meat to be a luxury and would only permit themselves to eat it on holidays or special occasions. This joint meal was a unique experience for me. They had a big table that they would usually take outside and set with simple wooden bowls and spoons, and one knife for the whole table. There wasn't enough room for everyone around the table and in the beginning the farmer's children would sit on the ground. After a few days of that, my sister and I rebelled and demanded to eat on the ground along with them and for me and my sister it was a great pleasure to eat on the ground. I assume that Dad paid the farmer well for hosting us. Dad would disappear during the day, going out to do all sorts of errands, or traveling with the farmer to the nearby town.

This stay on the farm was one big holiday for we children and I think that our parents also enjoyed it and forgot the war a bit. Unfortunately, it didn't last long. About two weeks after we arrived, we started hearing the firing of cannons, and planes began passing over our heads. A day or two later, these signs were joined by the sight of Polish soldiers retreating, wearing dirty and torn uniforms, begging for food and drink. Most were on foot; a minority traveled by wagon or on horses. These soldiers radiated misery and wretchedness and aroused our pity. Then, a day or two after the worn-out Polish soldiers passed by, the German soldiers arrived.

They came on the main road, heading east. There was no skirmish between the Polish and German armies in the village or around it.

Of course we children ran to stand on the side of the road to see the Germans soldiers and wave to them. They really did look like the lead soldiers I played so much with in the house – just a lot bigger... Tanks, armored personnel carriers, trucks and cannons all went by – in short, wonderful toys... All the kids stood open-mouthed at the sight of all these huge toys. The soldiers were happy and nice; sometimes they threw candies and sweets to us. They were not at all like the Polish soldiers who had come through earlier. I immediately decided that the new soldiers were very nice, good and handsome.

After the armored vehicles passed by came German soldiers in all kinds of jeeps and trucks. The latter would also enter the village and ask for water, as well as buy fruits and vegetables. Once they came to our farm. Dad hid in the house, and Mom went outside to greet them. They came in two trucks and a jeep. The trucks stayed out on the road, and the soldiers got off them and came to the house on foot. The officers, who were in the jeep, came right up to the house. The farmers didn't know a word of German, while my mother knew the language fluently.

The moment the soldiers came to the house they lined up in two rows and only the officers went over to speak to Mom and the farmers. All the kids stood around and rubbed their eyes. The German officers were very polite. They were surprised by the elegantly dressed city lady who spoke German. I will note that my mother was about 30 at this time and was a beautiful woman who paid great attention to her looks. I understood from the conversation that my mother was telling them how we'd come to be there. When she spoke of the bombing of Lublin, they apologized, and promised that if they would ever get to Krakow they would come visit us.

After a few minutes of polite chitchat, the officers asked for water and then if they could buy some fruit and vegetables. There was a well in the yard with a hand pump. The farmers brought over a wooden bucket and some wooden and metal cups, and the soldiers lined up and each one in turn got a cup of water to drink. It seemed that their water had been rationed and they were very thirsty. Many asked to drink again and again, and the whole drinking "ceremony" took a very long time. It seemed a bit strange to me that each time a soldier got a cup of water he'd say "Danke schoen" (thank you). The farmer and his wife brought out potatoes, beets, cabbage, carrots, apples and pears. The officers took out from their jeep cans of fish and meat and offered them in exchange; they also paid the farmer some money. They were German marks, and the farmer was very embarrassed because he didn't understand what they were and had no idea that something else existed besides the Polish zloty. There was one young German officer who knew a bit of Polish and he apparently acted as their translator, but since he wasn't needed here he played with the children and gave out sweets.

This was the only time the Germans ever entered our yard but they would pass by from time to time in the village and the children would run after them and see similar sights at other farmers' houses. I continued living in a dream; it all still seemed to me to be an adventure that was part of our long vacation. So my first impression of the Germans was a long line of fascinating vehicles, carefully kept uniforms, and interesting weapons that proclaimed power, order and good manners. One time (not in our yard) they even let me hold a "Schmeisser", the German submachine gun. My parents explained that these soldiers came from a different country and I really admired these interesting "uncles" from a foreign land.

A few days later, the war ended. No other interesting things happened in the village. The Germans became permanent guests, and we children ran from place to place to get more candy from them. Meanwhile, I made some progress in geese-herding: The flock started to like me and follow me. I think that this was where I had one of my first original ideas: In order to make it worth their while to follow me I began taking with me a handful of seeds and would drop several at a time every so often. The geese would then run over and stick to me. Zosia watched me admiringly; she didn't understand why they were suddenly make love with me...Meanwhile, thanks to my sister I got permission to milk the cows. I was deathly afraid of being kicked by them but overcame my fear and everyone was impressed by how brave I was. It was one of my very first lessons in how to overcome fear – or in other words, how to hid the fear and pretend to the outside world that I was self-assured. Later on, in my fight for survival, this became one of my most important weapons.

One day, Dad came to the farm and notified us that we'd soon be returning to Lublin. When the day came, I ran to tell the news to my geese and said goodbye with tears in my eyes... it was early in the morning, and we loaded our bags onto the farmer's biggest wagon along with boxes of vegetables and screaming geese and chickens. We parted from the farmer's family and a neighboring family quite emotionally; Zosia and one of her brothers wailed, and the farmer even had tears in his eyes. We promised to come back to visit. Zosia hugged me – this time without kisses. Finally, we left for the city. The farmer had hitched two horses to pull the wagon, and for the first time I got to hold the reins of pair of horses. I was in seventh heaven...

We passed through several German checkpoints on our way, so I got to meet our nice foreign "uncles" again, who always asked for "papiern" (papers). Ours were apparently in order, as we got to Lublin safely. Several days later, the Germans announced that everyone was free to travel anywhere they wanted within the German Occupation Zone. (Before that you had to get special permission and Dad had spent days in line to get it.)

We didn't go back to Krakow by train. For some reason Dad decided to rent a car. It was a very big one, more like a mini-bus or van, with several benches and a big trunk. We left before dawn and reached Krakow late at night, as it was over 300 kilometers away and the ride was slow and very tiring. All the roads were paved with stones; there were almost no paved roads. Here, too, we had to pass through many checkpoints and at several they demanded to search the car and luggage. This was always done very politely, with "bitte schoen" and "danke schoen" said constantly. We went into villages to buy food and also ate once in a restaurant, and everywhere we went people treated us very respectfully. Sometimes they made us get off the road to let a military convoy pass. At one checkpoint, we took on two young German soldiers who wanted to get to Krakow. They were very nice and helped us tremendously to get through the checkpoints easily by testifying that we have already been searched at the previous checkpoint.

When we got to Krakow we first brought the soldiers to their base, which was on the outskirts of town. It contained tents and shacks they'd erected, as well as a few houses they'd confiscated. When we stopped at the gate, the soldiers explained what we'd done for them. A short time later, an officer came out and thanked us for the favor we'd done the German army, and to ensure that nobody would bother us for the rest of our journey, he gave us a motorcycle escort. We came home like a general with such an escort...

When we opened the door to our house we were met with quite a surprise: The house wasn't empty! While we were gone, Grandma, Grandpa and one of Mom's sisters, Aunt Pela, with her two little children had "invaded" the apartment. For all the happiness at our reunion, I felt that Mom wasn't altogether pleased from their "settling" into our home. They had made a huge mess, and since they hadn't expected us they hadn't cleaned or made order so it all looked terrible... They left the next day.

After our return from the East, which took place in either November or December 1939, several relatives who'd been an important part of my life disappeared and I never saw them again. First of all, my wonderful nanny Zosia, who'd been the main person in my life for the last three years. (It could be that my parents didn't even know what happened to her themselves.) Aunt Rozia and her brother, Uncle Kuba also disappeared. So did Uncle Juzek and Aunt Dora (who didn't live in Krakow). My parents never told me what happened to them. When I tried asking they put me off with the answer that they'd gone far away – and they told me to stop asking these questions. It may be that they escaped to Russia or maybe they changed their identities and started living as Christians. Perhaps they'd tried escaping abroad and had been caught... A year later, my cousin Leon also disappeared and I didn't hear from him again. After the war I still had hope that specifically those who'd disappeared at the start of the war had perhaps survived and would reappear. But unfortunately, this never happened, except in my dreams... I still have no idea or even a hint as to what their fate was.

During this whole stage of the war, I lived completely in my own bubble of fairy tales and imagination. I didn't understand what was going on around me and didn't care. I knew how to read by this point, and spent my time reading children's books and living in those worlds. Apparently with the intention of keeping me safe, neither my parents, sister nor other relatives told me about the war or anything that was going on. My parents tried to make up my loss of my beloved Zosia, and my mother started paying me more attention. It was hard for me to get over her loss; I thought and dreamed about her all the time. I also asked my sister to read me all the stories Zosia had read to me, and I'd close my eyes and imagine that I was hearing Zosia's voice instead of hers. I also asked her to tell me stories about Jesus (like Zosia did). For some reason I was very attached to that good uncle called Jesus, whose job – Zosia said – was to be a messenger and the son of God and to guard children and give them gifts. Once, Mom listened in on one of these stories that my sister told, of a boy who'd gotten lost in the woods and was about to be killed by a bunch of wolves – but he crossed himself and at that second a shepherd appeared with a stick and scared away the wolves and took the boy out of the forest. Of course, who had sent the man? Jesus. Mom wasn't happy with this story; she came from a religious Jewish home and such stories were certainly unacceptable to her. Wisely, however, she didn't say a word, though it could be that she spoke to my sister about it afterward.

A very pertinent question to ask is if I knew at this point (early 1940) that I was a Jew, and if I understood what that meant under German occupation. The answer is: My parents never clearly explained to me in an orderly way – even though even by age five I was certainly able to understand. I was a very curious child and asked questions all the time. However, the things that interested me were technical, physical, about nature or fairy tales. Art and subjects like that didn't interest me at all. I saw and felt that we were a little different and special; we didn't celebrate Christmas, a holiday that I knew a bit about. My mother's parents lived in the "Kazimierz", the Jewish quarter, and were Sabbath observant. Mom would also light candles on Friday nights, put a kerchief on her head and bring in the Sabbath with a prayer, but since this was the routine ever since I was born I saw nothing special or unusual about it. Our Sabbath meal was also a very traditional one, with fish and chicken soup – but we didn't keep the Sabbath. We only went to synagogue on the High Holy days – and we certainly had a Passover *seder* on the first two nights of the holiday...

CHAPTER 5

First Round of Decrees Aimed at
the Jews of Krakow

The German conquest brought with it the slow strangulation of the Jewish community in Krakow, with the Jewish decrees coming out gradually. They would appear as notices put up everywhere, always entitled "Obwieszczenie," loosely translated as "Announcement and Order." At the end of the notice it always said that the punishment for disobeying was death. One of the first decrees was to prohibit Jewish children from going to school, so all Jewish schools were closed down. Another forbade the Jews from owning businesses, and all the big companies were confiscated; however, Jews were allowed to continue working in the companies under new German owners and management. Jews were also not allowed to own bank accounts. When I visited my father's business, I saw a German sitting in the director's chair while Dad was sitting on a chair on the side. This German was a resident of the part of eastern Poland that had been taken from Germany and annexed to Poland after World War I, and the Germans who had lived there continued to do so under Polish rule. When the Nazis seized the country, these people, called "Volksdeutsche," were granted all the rights accorded to regular German citizens. My father had a great relationship with this new director, who came to our house often and became a family friend. Even after we moved to the ghetto, Dad continued working in the business along with his brother and uncle.

The Poles and Germans were allowed to beat Jews, and there was no-one to whom the Jews could complain about it. They could also confiscate any Jewish property without offering any kind of compensation whatsoever. Jews could no longer stroll in the parks, enter cafes, or ride on the trams. They were forbidden from walking on the sidewalks of the main streets of Krakow, and had to walk in the gutters. It was a terrible sight to see the few Jews who still dared going outside, walking in the gutters to the occasional catcalls and jeers of Polish passersby. As yet, there were no mass murders, however.

Jewish teachers organized small, private classes in their homes. There were many teachers, since all of them had been fired from the schools in which they had worked. All Jewish professors had also been fired from the big university in Krakow. My big sister started going to these "private schools," and I joined her toward the end of 1940. I don't think the German disturbed these private classes.

In the spring of 1940, a decree ordered 45,000 of the 60,000 Jews who lived in Krakow to get out. They gave out about 15,000 permits to stay in the city. (There were an additional 15,000 Jewish refugees in Krakow at the time as well). My father and his brother managed to obtain these permits for the entire extended family. This accomplishment was the result of connections that my father had developed with the Germans in various ways, mainly through his fabric store. Many Germans came to shop there with their families, among them high ranking officers in the Occupation forces. Many of them would visit our home, kiss Mom's hand and talk to my parents as friends.

(It should be noted that Krakow was the capitol of the "General Government," the entity that was German-occupied Poland. All German centers of authority were concentrated in the city – so thousands of Germans came to live there with their families. All the foreign diplomatic missions were located in Krakow as well, including the American embassy. Perhaps this was the reason that at this stage the Germans weren't acting openly violent against the Jews.)

CHAPTER 6

Breaking the Illusion

As I mentioned above, we lived at 17 Sarego Street, which nestled between two stately boulevards. The people who lived there were mostly of the middle- and upper-class. The Germans cleared out almost all its Polish Christian residents, but strangely, most of the Jews were allowed to remain, including us. Two other Jewish families also remained in our building, with Germans taking over everything else. I have no idea why they let us live among them....

Opposite our house was a very large and ornate building that was divided into three blocks of six stores each. It was called "Dom Wola," or "Wol's House." Before the war it was the biggest and most splendid house in all of Krakow. Of course, the Germans occupied almost all of it – but a few Jews remained, including my sister's friend Dora and a friend of mine.

There was one caveat to being allowed to keep one's apartment: All Jews were asked – or forced – to host Germans who had come to Krakow without their families. Until we were forced into the ghetto in March 1943, we always had German boarders. Our first one came in the beginning of 1940, and he got a room to himself. He would eat breakfast with us, and sometimes supper as well. We were very friendly with him. In addition, most of the kids I played with outside were now Germans. They would come to my house to play, and I'd go to their homes too. We got a new nanny, whose name was Posta. She was no substitute for my legendary Zosia...

During those first months of 1940, I continued living in my dream world and wasn't conscious of what was happening all around us. My parents insulated me as much as possible from the terrible reality that was inexorably being woven around us. Our relatives rarely visited anymore, as there was usually a German sentry near the house checking everyone who came in and it wasn't pleasant for a Jew to come over. Our relationship with our German neighbors was normal; I didn't feel that there was anything special in the way they related to us. In fact, the German housewives in our building wanted to be friends with my mother, and would come to visit. In a way, all the awful humiliations and decrees against the Jews all around us didn't touch us; we were protected by our Germanic environment.

One of the new German families in our building had a boy approximately my age, called Hans. His father was the director of a food supply company. I became friendly with Hans and we played together very often. His mother was very neighborly with my mother. His father owned a car that he would park in the lobby of our building (there were two parking spaces there). We'd play in the car, moving it by working the starter. At first I was afraid to do it, but Hans promised me that his father had given him permission. Once, the guard of the building called his father, who came down to us. It turned out that he had allowed Hans to sit and play in the car, but not to move it!

This was my chance to see German discipline: The boy stood for long minutes at attention with a lowered head while his father showered him with a string of harsh reprimands. After that, he told Hans to look him in the eye, whereupon he delivered a series of slaps to his face, during which his child didn't move a single millimeter. I dreaded what he would do to me, but that terrible father told Hans to ask my forgiveness for including me in a forbidden game, and to ask that I please let him continue playing with me...

At the time I didn't see this incident as being anything special. It seems that Hans' parents felt guilty that their son had enticed me into doing forbidden things... His mother came to apologize to my mother, and even brought with her some kind of present of appeasement. In the days following this whole incident, I heard my mother telling the story to her friends, who were all agog over it.

This whole story of our lives among the Germans must sound strange in light of all that we know of the Holocaust. My intuitive explanation for this is that most of the Germans weren't anti-Semitic by nature, and seemingly were not really convinced by Hitler's racial theories. Otherwise, how could they prefer to live among Jews – and even in their homes – rather than among Polish Christians? After all, Jews were supposedly filthy, disease-spreading con-men and thieves. Of course, the Germans also hated and feared the non-Jewish Poles...

My happy life in this German bubble took a sharp turn on the day the Germans conquered Paris and France surrendered in June, 1940. The Germans declared a holiday and a victory party of sorts began on our street. Both adults and children went wild with joy, dancing in circles outside, giving out treats, alcoholic drinks and sandwiches. Stages were set up and all kinds of people made speeches. Most of the children were dressed in the uniform of Hitler Youth. My sister wouldn't come down to the street with me, so I went with Hans and other German kids. Hans offered to give me a Youth Hitler uniform as well, but for some reason I refused to wear it. However, in the middle of the party, someone put one of their brown shirts on me anyway. Many girls kissed me, people gave out Nazi symbols, pins with Hitler's picture on them, and miniature military medals for children. The Germans took their radios out to their balconies and windows, for everyone to hear the constant military marches that were being played. At one point in the afternoon, Hitler gave a speech on the radio, and you could hear it from every direction. The crowd went wild, screaming "Heil Hitler" over and over, "Hitler is God," "our beloved Fuehrer." I finally went home late in the afternoon, all happy about our having captured Paris, sweated all through with the Hitler Youth shirt studded with pins of Hitler in various poses, swastikas, miniature Iron Crosses, and all kinds of other decorations.

The first one to see me was the nanny, who gave a start and yelled out, "Pani Eva!" My mother appeared, and I saw the horror on her face. She took me to my room, took off the shirt and all the decorations, and put me in the bath. After a thorough wash, she told me to go to the room and play. My father and sister weren't home. At supper they still didn't say a word to me. I kept trying to tell them about the party I'd been in, but Mom and Dad didn't react; they just looked at each other, with their eyes saying volumes. Meanwhile, my sister kept trying to hint to me to stop with all my stories.

After supper, my father called me into the living room. This room was different than the living rooms of today. A long table with chairs all around it ran down the middle, while along the sides stood sofas, bookcases and china cabinets. My father would usually call me in there for a "conversation" after I had done something wrong. It was actually more like a trial that would end with a conviction, a short exhortation on ethics, and a punishment. Dad was the one who taught me that one must be honest and fair, and that the biggest sin was to lie. Over time, telling the truth became an axiom of my life. To be honest and fair was the most important lesson I ever learned from my parents and it is an quality I have prided myself on my entire life.

I asked my father why he was angry with me, and if I had done something wrong. He answered me in a roundabout way, saying that if you do something wrong but don't understand that it's bad, then you're not to blame. Over the course of our conversation, he asked me if I remember why we read the Haggada on Passover. I didn't really know what to say, so he started explaining the Exodus from Egypt, about how God chose us from all other nations and that He loves us very much. I said that I knew that from Aunt Rozia, because she'd told me how before I was born I was in Heaven and also that God loved me very much… Dad continued talking about how after we had left Egypt with God's help, we became one group, that this group was called the Jewish nation, and that the Jews were scattered among people who weren't Jews. These people were called "goyim" and we have different beliefs and customs than the *goyim*; and in Krakow there are both Jews and goyim and we are Jews.

This was the most serious and important conversation I'd ever had with anyone in my whole life. I asked a lot of questions, and Dad answered every one of them. I was suffused with love and admiration for my father for explaining all these things in a way that I understood. I treated every word of his with serious attention.

Then my father explained that sometimes the *goyim* hated the Jews, and now there was one *goy* called Hitler, who was king of the Germans, and he hates Jews a lot and wants to punish us.

I showered my father with more questions. "But the Germans I know are very nice," I said, "and I don't feel that they hate us and are doing anything bad to us!"

Dad then told me about the laws that the Germans had made against us, that Jews couldn't travel on the trams, that they'd taken all the Jews' businesses away from them, that they had caught Grandpa on the street and had beaten him, and that most of the Jews had been expelled from Krakow.

"If the Germans are so bad, why do we continue living with them?" I asked. "Maybe we should go live near Grandpa, because there are no Germans there?" I think that Dad tried to explain that we were trying to survive by living with and among the Germans, but I didn't understand what he said at this point. I had read stories about other countries, but only dimly understood what "another country" meant. Still, I asked my father why we don't go live in another country where there are no Germans. (I don't remember if he answered; it is also reasonable to assume that he had no answer at this point…)

Over the next several days I received quite an education, and grew wiser as well as more mature. I remember my father praising me to my mother for accepting the things he was telling me like a much older child. When I talked with my sister about the things I'd learned, I found out that she knew everything already. When I asked why she hadn't told me anything, she "snitched" on our parents, who had told her not to talk to me about the Germans because I was too young.

CHAPTER 7

Life Among our German Neighbors

During this period I hardly left the house. I stopped playing with Hans altogether, and was left with one Jewish friend who came over to play. Then I asked my mother if I could go visit my cousin Jurek, who was 13 years old. He lived in a small apartment with his mother, Aunt Genia. It was a very sad home, because his father had disappeared at the beginning of the war and his brother Leon disappeared few weeks ago.

Now, we had a big, beautiful globe at home, as well as a huge atlas full of maps of Poland, Europe and the entire world. I knew that there was such a planet called "Earth," which turned up in space, and this was why we had day and night, winter and summer – but it all confused me greatly and I couldn't figure out how we could walk or travel on a ball that itself turns; why we don't fall off when we're on the bottom; why they draw countries on flat paper if we live on a ball; why do I only see a level plane when I'm outside, etc. I would bother everyone with these kinds of questions all the time.

However, certain questions I had were clarified when I saw Jurek. He explained to me lots of things about the war, about what countries were fighting, who was good and who was bad. For the first time, I learned concepts like Nazism, fascism and anti-Semitism. Not that I really understood what he was saying, but it was definitely clear to me that Nazism was something very, very bad.

I asked Mom if Jurek could visit, and he would come with his mother. I had many more lengthy and deep conversations with him, peppering him with countless questions. From his answers, I began making order in my head, piecing together the reality of our situation. And I understood that something very bad was happening. Jurek also made me happy by praising my father highly, telling me how he was helping his sisters by providing them with money and proper papers for their families.

Even though Jurek told me a lot, I would still go to my father night after night and ask him the same questions over and over: Why do the Nazis hate the Jews? Why don't we explain to them that we haven't done anything wrong? I also asked if the German who lived with us and ate with us was also a Nazi and hated us. Dad kept repeating that we had to be strong. I didn't quite understand what it meant to be strong; after all, I was little and Gizia wasn't powerful either, so how could we be strong? Dad explained that being strong didn't necessarily mean to have a lot of muscles, but to be disciplined, know how to endure, and act wisely.

My father was considered a great expert in textiles. Despite the fact that officially his company had been confiscated by the Germans, he and his brother and uncle were the ones who really ran everything. The German director was fine with this, since he didn't have a clue how to run such a complicated business. Everyone treated Dad and his brother like they were the real directors, and the German sat in his fine office and didn't do much. Dad continued traveling to order fabrics, and even went to Czechoslovakia and Austria. Sometimes he would go with the German director; he had special authorization as an essential worker. Many times I saw him presenting his papers to German policemen, who would stand at attention and salute. The Germans were in awe of stamped documents, "*papiern*."

Dad accepted the humiliations and repression as a fact of life and worked to support the family. In contrast, Mom sank into despair. She was ashamed to go outside with the Jewish star on her armband and suffer all the humiliations and restrictions that Jews had to contend with. Sometimes she'd go out with her German neighbors without the armband. She constantly complained of headaches, would lie in bed a lot, ask for doctors and in general be very miserable. My big sister apparently understood her and would be very supportive and encouraging, as was my father. I, on the other hand, acted and thought according to my father's dictum that "we have to be strong." I wasn't ready to understand or forgive my mother for not demonstrating fortitude and strength. Although she would occasionally recuperate, this deeply despairing and suffering state of mind did not change – until we were forced into the ghetto. Then, when she had to fight for her life and the lives of her family, she recovered and started battling. For years – and really, to this day – I feel guilty for not having supported her during this difficult period.

Living among Germans protected us and let us live almost normal lives. Polish thugs couldn't come in and harass us, we had servants almost like before the war, we had plenty of the basic foodstuffs and never felt hungry. There was a definite shortage of luxuries we used to have, like oranges, bananas, chocolate, coffee, tea and spices, not to speak of any kind of meat. But our German tenant could and did get meat for us…

When I started playing again with Hans and the German children who came to his house, I began feeling how different I was. I constantly checked if they were treating me in a special way, but I don't remember ever feeling something amiss. I noticed that Hans' mother treated me especially well. This came out in many little things, like when she brought us food she'd specifically ask me what I wanted to eat, and when we would go outside to play she'd take care to give me a cap. Hans' father also treated me with affection. The fact that I was a Jew was never mentioned in their home.

I would often invite Hans to come with me and my sister to the park to play. Of course, we always went with our nanny. Hans' mother had no problem with this, only asking if this nanny was reliable.

In June I celebrated my eighth birthday in a very quiet way. My father gave me a present and my mother hugged and kissed me, and then started to cry. She said that she was crying out of happiness that she had such a mature son and that she was so proud of my behavior. (After a long period of being focused completely inward, she had started hugging and kissing me often.)

My grandparents on my mother's side lived at the time in the Kazimierz[1] neighborhood, the ancient Jewish quarter that contained dozens of synagogues. Before the war almost 20% of the Jews of Krakow lived there. They hadn't visited us since our return from the East, but we would go to see them in a horse-drawn carriage. My sister, nanny and I would also often go visit them on foot.

The war had brought so many changes to Kazimierz, the neighborhood was practically unrecognizable. Before the war, the streets there were humming with people. Crowds of men, women and children streamed all around in a huge tumult and it was always happy there. In the center of the neighborhood there was a large market – which is still there today – where large numbers of women shopped with their baskets over their arms. When we went now, it was almost dead. Very few people walked in the streets, even near the synagogues that used to always have throngs of Jews around them. Now some of the synagogues were closed down, and some were being used by the Germans for other purposes; one had been converted into a barn. Most of the Jews of Kazimierz had been banished in May 1940 to other towns in the area, and the dimensions of the Jewish quarter were reduced.

---

1   *In 1535 the town of Kazimierz was established near Krakow, the Capital of Poland, specifically for the Jews, by King Kazimierz the Great. In this little town Jewish life flourished for the next 400 years, both culturally and religiously* (More about the history of Kazimierz see chapter 24, side note 1)

Aunt Fela (whose husband disappeared) and her young children lived with Grandma. We often brought them food parcels. I sensed the sadness that hung over the neighborhood in general and in Grandma's house in particular, but when we came, Grandma's face shone with joy.

Practically speaking, from the beginning of the German occupation until the spring or summer of 1941, official Nazi policy toward the Jews was to harass, plunder and humiliate them in order to cause them to leave the area under German control. Because of this policy, any Jew who could get a visa to any country not under German occupation could emigrate with their blessing. Our tragedy was that very few countries were willing to accept Jews. In contrast to the whole "enlightened" world, like Switzerland, Sweden and the United States, only the Soviet Union allowed Jews to enter the country almost without restriction. As a result, a large part – and perhaps even the majority – of Polish Jews who survived were those who escaped to Soviet Russia.

There were hundreds, if not thousands, of kinds of official documents, authorizations and stamps in occupied Poland. For example: Permission for a Jew to ride on the train, the tram, or in a taxi; a certificate stating the level of your essentiality as a worker; authorization allowing one to be out after curfew, etc. Because of this, a flourishing business began in forging documents of such high quality that the Germans were helpless to stop it. To make it harder for the forgers, the Germans kept releasing new certificates and stamps that were more and more ornate and complicated. However, even before they had managed to dispense them, perfect forgeries would appear. (For example, before the major deportation from Krakow in May 1940, the Germans gave out about 15,000 authorizations to be able to stay in Krakow. Several weeks later, they found out that the Jews had about 30,000 such certificates…)

I finally asked my friend Hans if he knew I was a Jew. He said yes, but that he loved me and was happy to play with me. Once – it was already the fall of 1940 – Hans came to my house in the afternoon dressed in his Hitler Youth uniform. He had come directly from some activity of theirs. When I opened the door, he wouldn't come in. Instead, he stood in the doorway and told me that they had taught everyone that it was forbidden to play with Jews, and he couldn't play with me anymore. I remember very well that he looked sad, and that I tried to comfort him… I told him that I had enough friends to play with, and that surely he'd find another close friend for himself. Then, later that same day, before I'd had a chance to tell my parents about it, Hans appeared again and with great happiness he said that his father had told him that he actually could play with me. He asked if I was willing to continue playing with him. I said, "Come on in, we're pals again…" When I think about it today, it surprises me how little significance I attached to this incident. I was neither insulted nor hurt, and completely forgot about it, just as children usually do when arguments with friends are over. I only told my parents about it several days later.

I was quite a thoughtful child and spent quite a lot of time mulling over concepts like "being strong," "you can't lie," "we fight in order to survive," "being honest and fair," and "being loyal." I struggled over each principle, what it meant and how I could act according to each one. I considered myself to be extremely cowardly; I hated to get into arguments and fights with other kids – something that was very acceptable at my age – and always tried to make peace instead. I was the kind of kid that would be called a "wimp" or a "nerd" today. I asked my father how I could make myself not be afraid if I was frightened. He explained that fear is a natural feeling but that I have to learn to overcome it, not to show that I'm afraid, not to let fear control me and dictate my actions. In Polish children's literature there were many stories of wolves as the bad guys, and how to be careful of them. I asked Dad what to do if a wolf catches me and asks me if I love him. If I tell him "no," surely he'd eat me; but if I tell him "yes," then I'm lying. Here is where I managed to get out of my father that in certain cases it's allowed to lie – like in this one. And if the wolf would ask me where my grandma lived, I should give him the address of a witch, so he eats her instead of Grandma...

In order to be as strong as Dad said, I asked my cousin Jurek to teach me how to fight as well as how to protect myself. It was a common pastime among Polish children to have mock fights as games. There were clear rules to such fighting. When boxing, for example, you weren't allowed to wear rings, and you couldn't hit the other fellow in the head, neck, stomach or private parts. Wrestling was another game, in which you couldn't bite, catch someone by his private parts, or catch him by the head or neck from behind. To win, you had to fell your opponent, preferably laying him out on his back. Jurek taught me that to land a really hard blow, one has to swing one's fist with the power of one's whole body behind it. In my room, I hung a small mattress over a tiled oven as a kind of dummy and practiced hitting it. I also made a dummy out of old clothes to hit as well.

I loved and admired my older sister, Gizia, with all my heart. I was devastated that she wasn't interested in my games. I had many, and most shared a single theme: trains. I had 4-5 engines, driven by springs that would have to be set afresh each time they ran out of power, dozens of train-cars, meters upon meters of tracks, all kinds of train stations, water-filling stations, coal-loaders, etc. I didn't have enough room to keep them all set up, so every time I'd have to reassemble them. Of course, I dreamed of being a conductor...

I also had all kinds of toy cars, all driven by springs as well, and loved any kind of construction set. I had a tricycle, a bicycle and a scooter (my sister had one too), and we both played with balls. I adored flying toy planes, either making them out of cardboard or buying the kind that had a propeller that could be wound up with a rubber band. Gizia had many dolls and dollhouses, doll-sized medical equipment and school accessories. One of her favorite games was to play "School" with her dolls. She'd set up about 20 of them in a "class," speak to them, ask them questions, and in general mimic her teachers. She could copy every one of her teacher's voices. I would play "Doctor" with her, where we would make up little plays, like pretending one of the dolls was very sick, and my sister would call me (the doctor) on the phone to come quickly. I'd answer, "I can't come right now, because I'm in the middle of an operation..." And then I'd arrive in a car or by train. I had a whole doctor's kit which I'd pack into my car to bring to treat the sick doll. We'd include our little sister, Sarenka, in these games, as she was already two years old if not older.

Another great interest of mine was reading. Ever since I can remember, I treated books with reverence. I saw them as wondrous objects that I could sink into and sail away in my imagination to other worlds, meet friends, live through wonderful experiences. Gizia started going to school when I was four years old and I started learning from her books with my wonderful nanny, Zosia. As far as I can tell, I began reading her school books and other children's books by the time I was five. I had a very organized library, arranged according to topic. Every time I got a new book, Zosia would read it to me first, and then I'd read it for myself. I would read my books over and over again.

I remember that my sister had a class called "Martwa Natura" (Inanimate Nature) from third grade on. Essentially it was physics for children, and I was crazy about it. I asked Zosia to help me find more books to buy on the subject, even those for older children, as well as workbooks. (My parents never put a limit on these kinds of purchases.) I was really blessed with a wonderful trait – I loved to learn. Everything interested me and I was never bored. The advantage I had due to this character trait became ever clearer in my later years.

A thought that really bothered me at that time about the Germans was why they had ever come to our country. Didn't they have what to do in their own land? They seemed to me to be so nice, polite and impressive – and suddenly I find out that they're evil and killed so many people. What is war? Is it only a game or is it really people killing each other? What are they fighting for, and what does the victor and the vanquished do? Is it like when we children fight, where afterward we simply shake hands and make up? Why did the Germans defeat the Poles – after all, the Poles – that is, we – are much stronger and braver than they are. What does it mean to die? After all, according to Aunt Rozia and my nanny, after we die we go to Heaven. But how do we get there – in a plane, or in a boat? Aunt Rozia said that when good people die an angel comes and takes them to Heaven. According to the pictures of angels that I'd seen I built an image in my mind of a creature that looked like a man, but with wings. But how could he hold me when taking me up to the sky – why, I could fall! Perhaps he'd tie me to him with a rope… With all these thoughts tumbling about in my mind and then being vocalized constantly, I was what one would call an "insufferable child" who pesters and asks unanswerable questions. They told me that my father's parents were already in Heaven, so I asked why we don't go visit them, and maybe we could call them! Go figure an answer out to that one…

It was now Autumn of 1940 and it was starting to get cold. Our German tenant left and "Fraulein" Gerta took his place. Fraulein Gerta was a young German woman in her mid-twenties, very erect, blond and blue-eyed, pretty – and very conscious of it. During her very first conversation with my mother, they each complimented the other on their beauty. Fraulein Gerta was a very social and noisy type who loved to chatter. In our first dinner together, she told us all about herself and asked many questions about us, our families, and our friends. She was a university graduate and found many topics of mutual interest with my mother. They became great friends and I think it was a genuine friendship. My mother's mood greatly improved when Fraulein Gerta moved in, and she began smiling again.

In the mornings, Fraulein Gerta would make her own breakfast, with my mother sometimes keeping her company. Occasionally she would join us for dinner, and from the conversations, I learned that Fraulein Gerta was a member of the Nazi party. She had a pin on her shirt collar that proved it. One of the absurdities during these meals was how she would try to justify the Nazi regime to us with all the well-worn mantras: How the Nazis helped both German pride and the economy recover, how the Nazis and Hitler hadn't wanted war but just to get back their rights, that it was France and England that had declared war on Germany and Hitler was trying to stop the war against England. Oh – and she had many Jewish friends and she disagreed with the anti-Jewish policies of the Nazis. She worked in the Foreign Office or the Propaganda Department, and it really seemed that she would forget to whom she was speaking, as she would complain to us about how hard it was to explain the German position to the world. Perhaps she got confused and thought that she was talking with her Nazi friends… or perhaps she did this on purpose, to hear our reactions. I noticed that my parents were greatly baffled by it and always tried to turn the conversation to non-political subjects like art, German literature – which they knew very well – the weather or the theater. They often talked about Vienna; apparently Fraulein Gerta had also spent some time in that city.

Many times after supper, we would have a musical evening. We owned a piano which the whole family could play, but my mother and sister were the real experts. As Gerta also knew how to play, the three of them would put on a show for us. My little sister would dance and we would have a party. These musical evenings didn't interest me very much, although Mom would try and involve me – unsuccessfully. Another German neighbor who also apparently loved music would join the little group as well. Since we had a gramophone with many records, it, too, would play its part during these parties. Those were happy times for my mother, and as little as I was, I noticed this and was happy for her joy.

Gerta would also take my mother to have a good time in the city, with Mom taking off her armband with the Jewish star before leaving the house. They apparently relied on no-one daring to arrest a German party member. Sometimes one of the German neighbors would join them and they'd all return loaded down with packages, including gifts for my sisters and me. Sometimes they'd go to Dad's store and return with fabrics that our seamstress would work overtime to turn into the clothes they wanted. (At that time in Poland, even before the war, it was customary for many people to have their clothes made by hand. We were always calling our seamstress to come to our home.)

Fraulein Gerta lived with us until the beginning of 1941. A short time before she left, she introduced us to a friend of hers who was an officer; I believe he worked in Intelligence. He came in civilian clothes and introduced himself, but I don't remember anything about him. Both sides felt uneasy, and conversation was stilted. However, he was apparently very taken with my sister Gizia and talked with her quite a bit. At one point he asked her what school she attended, and in all innocence she replied that she doesn't go to school. Mom hurried to clarify that it was forbidden for Jewish children to go to school, and he was completely taken aback. Gerta explained something to him and there was great embarrassment all around. At the end, he said that he was very sorry that this was the case. To this day I wonder if his words held a touch of real regret and friendship or if they were a meaningless politeness.

When we moved into the ghetto, Fraulein Gerta visited us with her boyfriend at least once, and I know she kept in contact with my father. At some point in the beginning of 1941 she moved to Paris, stayed there for a short while, then returned to Krakow.

Our third tenant was from the Gestapo, and apparently he held a high rank there. He worked in the Polish Section and didn't deal with Jews. We had a correct relationship with him but nothing more. Like every undercover policeman, he rarely spoke. He didn't eat breakfast with us; he'd only prepare himself a cup of coffee. On rare occasions he'd eat supper with us, but he never told us anything about himself.

CHAPTER 8

A Hard Winter

The winter of 1940-41 arrived, and gloominess pervaded the house. Fraulein Gerta left and Mom lost her only opportunity to go to town without being humiliated. One German neighbor remained loyal and would visit us often. Dad would go out early each morning and return in a carriage (the taxi of yesteryear). I would wait for him on the balcony. He would usually be loaded down with packages that mainly contained food and gifts.

A short time after Gerta left, my mother went for a walk in the city with Gizia and me. It was a snowy, bright winter's day, and the city was decorated for Christmas. At one point in the middle of town, we passed a bakery and I saw a torte in the window with several layers of cream – my absolute favorite kind of cake. We went in and Mom asked for the cake. The saleslady yelled at her, "We don't sell to Jews!" From the shock of it, and in her confusion, Mom kept standing there, still as stone. One of the shoppers then said, "I'll buy it for you," and the saleslady answered, "You shouldn't." Mom recovered, took us both by the hand and we left. We walked home in almost complete silence. Mom did not leave the house again until we had to go into the ghetto.

It was very cold that winter, and there wasn't much coal, so we would walk around the house in two layers of sweaters. The gues-troom was warmer than the rest of the house, so my parents moved my desk and bookcases in there, putting them next to the big oven. This oven was made of brick and was covered with white, smooth, sparkling tile. It was about 60 centimeters (two feet) wide and about 1.5 meters (5 feet) high. That area became a kind of social center. My mother, sister and even the maids would come in from time to time to lean on the back of it to warm up a bit. The maids would shoot admiring and surprised looks at me, with all my books. One has to recall that usually maids in those days barely knew how to read or write, and writing script seemed almost like magic. I remember how one of them used to whisper, "Pan Leosz bedzie pisazem" (Master Leosz will be a writer).

Though we didn't go outside much, my sister and I never failed to walk with our nanny at least once a week to our grandmother's house to bring her food. I always made sure to bring toys and a candy to my cousin Bronek, as well as money to my grandfather, from my father. My sister, who loved to draw, would get drawing pads from him, as well as other office supplies. These visits brought great joy to our grandparents, Aunt Fela and her two children.

There were several ways we could choose from to get to Grandma's house; it was about a kilometer away. On one of our walks to their home, a strange thing happened: We were walking along Gertruda Boulevard toward Stradom Street around 10AM. At the corner of Stradom and Gertruda there was a cafe, and a few dozen meters from it we saw a group of young teenaged boys, about 13-15 years old. As we neared them, we saw that they were looking at us and there was something threatening about them.

I don't know why I said it, but I told my nanny not to speak. My sister started talking with them very naturally and nicely, not arousing any suspicion that we might be Jews – except that in her naiveté, she told them that we were going to Kazimierz to see our grandmother. Non-Jews did live in Kazimierz, but it was well-known as a Jewish part of town. The group grew suspicious and one of them asked if we were Jews. My sister recovered and said, "Of course not!" while the nanny said, "Are you out of your minds?!" and crossed herself. They were not convinced, and one said, "Fine. Give us your packages and we'll let you go." I had a feeling this was not going to end well. I already knew from experience that all the German police, their militias and undercover agents had to do to call for help was to blow on their whistles. What did I do? I had a whistle in my pocket, so I took it out and emitted several loud blasts.

The boys were very surprised and stood frozen in place. Two policemen from the cafe, one in uniform and one in civilian clothes, ran up to us. I went forward a couple of paces, with my head held high and oozing self-confidence. In my best German children's slang – learned from playing with all my neighbors – I told the policemen, "We live on Sarego Street (which was known as an area in which Germans lived). We have a Polish nanny and this gang is trying to rob us."

The men were apparently convinced that we were German children. The one in civilian clothes praised us for calling for help and told me to tell my father that I was a clever boy. They caught hold of two of the teens (the others had run away) and handcuffed them. This was the last time we used that route to get to Grandma's...

We swore our nanny to secrecy. I wanted to tell my father about it and hear his praise – or his rebuke for pretending to be a German – but I was afraid that he would limit our trips to Grandma's house. I really had had no problem acting and talking like a German kid after playing so much with the neighbors. I even had some of their clothing, like the brown shorts and knee-length socks (which I hated). I also still had all of those Nazi symbols and decorations, though Dad forbade me from wearing them. I hadn't planned it in advance at all, but acting like a German child had come almost instinctively when I confronted that Polish gang.

Until we went into the ghetto, we always hid our Jewishness when we left our house. My sisters and I didn't have to pretend anything since children up to age 12 didn't have to wear the armband with the Jewish star. We were also almost always accompanied by our Christian nanny. Many times we also took our German friends along on our walks. when Mom had gone out with Fraulein Gerta, she also pretended to be a German. Going around openly as a Jew in the city would be risky and entail humiliation of one kind or another: The police could arrest you or send you off to a labor camp; gangs of Polish youth could rob you; Poles would demand pay-offs; at the very least, they would jeer and mock you. But it should be noted that there were also other kinds of Poles and Germans. I witnessed situations when older Poles protected a Jew from the teenaged gangs, and even German soldiers intervening to help a Jew who was being beaten by boys from the Hitler Youth.

When they went out, Jews would protect themselves in various creative ways. First, there were people like us, who hid their identity – but this was quite dangerous. Another way would be to hire a Polish bodyguard; I saw many Jews going around with a young Polish tough at their sides. Small stores like that owned by my grandfather were not confiscated, but if Jews stayed on as the owners they had many restrictions and special laws they had to obey. They could also be robbed or vandalized without having the right to complain to the police. So the Jews would play it smart and take on a Polish partner, registering the business in his name instead. My grandfather did this, and all sides were satisfied by this arrangement.

There were many sectors in the Jewish population: About half consisted of the established Krakow Jews, who were mainly of the middle and upper class. The next group was made up of professionals, small businessmen, clerks and laborers. There were few poor Jews, comparably speaking, before the war, and all children went to school. However, when war broke out, about 15,000 Jewish refugees streamed into Krakow and their economic situation was very bad. To help these Jews in need, the Judenrat taxed all the Jews in Krakow (with German permission). They also got donations from the wealthy Krakow Jews, from Jews in America, the Red Cross, etc. They established orphanages, old age homes and soup kitchens. They also provided a roof over everyone's heads, even if the apartments were old and neglected, with no running water or electricity. Jews didn't starve to death at that point. Like my father, many of the wealthier Jews supported relatives who weren't as well off.

The Germans demanded that the Judenrat[2] supply a few thousand Jews a day to clean the streets, and especially to shovel snow during the winter. All male Jews had to do this kind of work several days a month, except those who had official papers saying that their jobs were essential for the war effort.

The Judenrat solved this problem very creatively: Any Jew without such papers could get out of doing this work by paying about 20 zloty (worth about four loaves of bread) for each day they wanted to be released from street cleaning. Of course, this was in addition to the regular taxes that everyone had to pay the Judenrat. They would then use this money to hire unemployed Jews – mainly the refugees – to do the work, paying them 8 zloty and two warm meals in the soup kitchen. Even as a young boy, the sight of these Jews saddened me greatly: In the freezing cold of winter, they were dressed in rags, had no real coats to speak of, were dirty, miserable, were barely able to stand, had overseers who sniped at them constantly and were subject to the curses and jeers of all the passersby. I have to say that there were some – both Poles and Germans – who intervened on their behalf. I once saw a Polish woman take a stick and chase away children

---

2   *From the start of the German Occupation a Jewish administration called the Judenrat ran the Jewish community. Until June 1942 the members of the Yudenrat were men of principles and did everything to ease the lives of the Jews.* (More about the Yudenrat see chapter 24, Side note 2: The Yudenrat)

who were throwing snowballs at a Jew shoveling snow from the sidewalk. And another time, I saw a Polish woman bring a warm bowl of soup to a Jew who was clearing snow near her house.

My sister, nanny and I would prepare slices of bread and butter and put them in bags with some sugar cubes to hand out to these poor street-cleaners. Doing this gave my sister and me great pleasure, but we didn't think overmuch about the significance of the whole issue. Today, when I think about these things – my father helping his extended family, all the aid the Judenrat arranged for thousands of Jews – it seems that it wasn't all chance, and fortunately there's something in the human gene in general and Jewish genes in particular that causes people to help those in need.

There was one more German child I became close with through playing together out on the street. His name was Wilhelm, like my father's. While people called my father Willek, however, this kid's nickname was Willy. Willy was tall and athletic and was an excellent soccer player. He lived opposite us, in the Wolf House. Many highly respected Germans lived in that palatial house, mainly high ranking officers of the German army and police. Willy's father was high up in the Gestapo (I don't remember how I knew this). I once suggested that Willy come with us to the main part of town. A few days later he told me that his parents had given him permission, but that he couldn't go into anyone else's home but ours. What was interesting was that during the months that we played together, either outside or in my house, he never once invited me into his house and I never met his family.

One beautiful winter day, after it had snowed all night, Gizia, the nanny and I went for a walk to the center of town. I invited Willy along. The central square, called Rynek in Polish, was a fun place to play. The name had been changed to "Hitler Platz", and of course Jews weren't allowed there anymore. As we passed by, a number of

Jews were shoveling the sidewalks and a group of Hitler Youth went up to them. I'd guess they were about 12 years old, and they came up to one Jew in particular and started teasing him, calling him names, and throwing snow on him. One even began hitting him with a stick. In the meantime, a group of adults gathered, with some helping the boys torment the Jew and some trying to defend him. My nanny tried to pull us away from there. I saw that the Jew was simply covering his face with his hands and crying. In the years to come I witnessed horrific scenes of murder and torture, but this picture of an older Jew standing surrounded by a rabble and sobbing became deeply etched in my memory.

I don't know why, but Willy suddenly stood next to the Jew to protect him. It was an almost surrealistic scene: Standing up to his fellow Germans, with the pathos of a lawyer and a religious preacher, he started explaining to them that what they were doing was forbidden according to Hitler's doctrine, that his head instructor had said this. I didn't quite understand his claims, but they seemed to have an effect on the youngsters. Meanwhile, two policemen came and dispersed the crowd. When he came back to us we didn't speak about it; he simply commented that these kids were hooligans. We decided to buy a roll and cheese and give it to the Jew, but when we returned he was no longer there. We gave the sandwich to a different Jew, and didn't talk about it again. We also asked the nanny not to tell our parents.

From the first time I met Germans I saw them as being on a higher level than us. Deep inside I wanted to belong to them. I asked my father why we couldn't be Germans... It wasn't easy for him to explain our situation to me. I already knew that we were Jews, that we had a different religion, that we believed in God in a different way. But if the Germans had it so good, why couldn't we belong to their group? Dad explained to me a number of times that we are proud to be Jews. But why couldn't we be proud Germans instead of proud Jews? It was hard for me to understand why I had to be a proud Jew... My father was insistent that there were different kinds of Germans. Some were very bad, but there were also good ones. It's interesting that it was important to me that there were also good Germans. I asked my father if Fraulein Gerta was a good German, if our current tenant was a good one, and what about Hans, or Hans' father. After all, all the Germans we knew were good...

Although during all of 1940 terrible persecution and tragedies occurred in Krakow, we lived in our bubble of Sarego Street, protected by our German neighbors. Dad worked day and night and used every trick he knew in order to keep his family safe and provided for. Until we had to go into the ghetto, the greatest tragedy he protected us from, of course, was the huge deportation from Krakow that had begun back in April. (This was when 60,000 of the 75,000 Jews in Krakow were systematically expelled from the city to the surrounding small villages and my father had managed to get permits for all our relatives.) For a few months, the Germans even allowed those who were expelled to take all their belongings with them, and even to leave by train or wagon. But starting in August, if they found Jews in Krakow without the proper papers, they expelled them with great cruelty and brutality.

The Germans started hunting Jews down in the city streets or by breaking into their homes. Those who were to be expelled were first crowded into closed-off areas, then packed into cattle-cars and taken hundreds of kilometers from the city. They would stop the train in the middle of nowhere, get the Jews out and simply tell them to start walking. It wasn't yet annihilation, but these people suffered terribly. Many got sick and died, or were robbed or murdered by Poles. Some of them managed to get to small Jewish villages and were taken in. Some got as far as the borders of Romania, Hungary or the Soviet Union and either settled in those countries or succeeded in getting even further away, thereby saving their lives. It should be noted that until the beginning of 1941, German policy was to expel – and thereby rid themselves of – Jews, and if Jews had an appropriate visa they could get permission to leave. Expulsions like this took place on and off until the ghetto was built.

Ever since the Occupation began, the Germans were allowed to confiscate any Jewish property they wanted. There was no way to oppose or resist this, to complain or appeal to anyone. Our family didn't escape unscathed in this regard, either. This is the story of my parents' bedroom:

Mom and Dad's bedroom set had been bought a few months before the war and was really outstandingly beautiful. I remember the many guests who came to our home to see it, and with what pride my mother showed it off. One morning several people showed up with two policemen and presented Mom with a written order to confiscate the set. Even though it wasn't true, my mother claimed that the bedroom was being used by our German tenant, who worked for the Gestapo. They agreed to wait and let Mom call our tenant. After a short while "our" German came and started talking to the men. In the meantime, Mom also called Dad, who came quickly with another German acquaintance whom he got to help us. There was a lot of discussion back and forth between the two sides, and a lot of phone calls. After a while, our German tenant took my parents to another room and explained that the order of confiscation came from extremely high up and it was impossible to cancel it. I didn't hear his exact words, I just saw my mother leave the room crying. My parents emptied the drawers and closets and the Germans took the whole set with them. However, they returned with a different set that very day. I don't know where they got that furniture from; it could be that it had belonged to that same high-ranking German for whom they had confiscated ours.

CHAPTER 9

The Move to the Ghetto, First Stage

In February 1941 the Germans published a decree announcing that the Jews had to give up their homes and move to a ghetto. They called it "Zydowska dzielnica," which freely translated means "Jewish quarter." It was in one of the poor neighborhoods of Krakow, called "Podgorze" that was right across the Vistula River. One side was almost on top of the river, while another side bordered a hilly area of the city called "Krzemionki" Hill. The Ghetto was 600x800 meters in size, containing about 250 houses and 1,500 small apartments. Some of them were meant to be public buildings, like hospitals, orphanages, old age homes, offices of the Jewish Police, etc. Since 15,000-20,000 Jews were transferred there, this meant that usually more than five people had to crowd into each available room.

The Judenrat had the job of giving out the apartments. We got a small three-room apartment all to ourselves, when it was the norm for 2-3 families to share such a space. I assume that my father got it due to his connections, having friends in the Judenrat, and a lot of bribery. While most apartments didn't have running water and the bathroom was an outhouse in the building's yard, we had a kitchenette with running water in the sink and a proper bathroom with a tub. Before we moved in, we even managed to renovate it; the water and sewage pipes were replaced, the windows were fixed or changed, and it was painted as well.

Our building stood at the end of Juzefinska Street, where the street almost touched the Vistula. There were a few buildings on the side of the street that faced the river and the promenade that ran down its length. Our apartment was in one of these "atypical" buildings. Several months after we moved to the ghetto, a wall was built at the end of Juzefinska Street in a way that there were still two sides to the street. Therefore, the front of our building actually jutted out of the ghetto. In order to get into our house from Juzefinska Street one had to go around the wall and walk through an area full of the rubble of half-destroyed buildings and yards to be able to get into our house via its back yard.

For me, the whole process of moving to the ghetto was great fun. We transferred our furniture in a small truck which had to make several trips back and forth. I sat next to the driver and he let me switch the gears and hold the steering wheel from the side. On one trip I took my sister along and we sang and acted silly the entire time. Of course, for my parents – and especially for my mother – the move to the ghetto was a terrible tragedy. She had to leave a beautiful, grand street in the center of the city, and a five room apartment with servants, to live on a miserable street in a poor neighborhood in three small rooms with a tiny, pathetic kitchen. However, there were some advantages in moving. First and foremost, Mom could now leave the house freely and walk around the ghetto without anyone jeering at or humiliating her, and meet many friends and acquaintances. On Sarego Street we were enclosed in a German bubble that on the one hand protected us from harassment, but on the other hand it had isolated us and made it hard for us to meet relatives and have guests come to visit.

Our home in the ghetto became a social center, especially for our family and friends. Many whose luck had run out and who were left with nothing would come to us to get help of all kinds. In this way, our home also served as a soup kitchen of sorts, and people would come to us to eat. Helping others helped Mom recover her spirits, and she began finding interest and a purpose in life again. Soon I saw her smiling and active once more. This was another lesson to me: how in helping others you help yourself first. Dad kept going to work every day, running around and helping the extended family. Interestingly, one of our Polish servants, a young girl called Jasia who was very close to my mother, continued working for us for half a year after we moved into the ghetto, helping to cook, clean and look after my little sister.

Grandma, Grandpa, Aunt Fela and her two children were also moved into the ghetto. They received a two-room apartment on Limanowski Street. Dad's two sisters – Aunt Genia and her son Jurek, and Aunt Hela with her redheaded daughter – also came. Dad's brother, Uncle David, moved to the ghetto with his wife and two daughters, and lived in a three-room apartment together with the family of his wife's sister and her mother. Little David, Grandpa's uncle, came with his whole family as well, and they lived on our street, about 100 meters away. They had a two-room apartment to themselves. We grew very close to Little David's children, especially after David and his wife did not manage to escape the "Action" of mid-1942, which orphaned their three older teens. The daughter, Gina, was my mother's closest friend, and they could and did meet frequently. Some of our relatives who had disappeared in the beginning of the war never arrived in the ghetto and I never heard anything about them. These included my mother's two brothers – Uncle Juzek and his family, Uncle Kuba and Aunt Rozia – and my father's third sister, who hadn't lived in Krakow.

According to the law we were only allowed to bring to the ghetto the furniture that the Germans moving into our old home allowed us to take. We gave our apartment to our German boarder, who graciously allowed us to take whatever we wanted, but there was one problem: Most of the furniture didn't fit into our new place. About a week before we left, the boarder took us to a "second-hand furniture warehouse" – which was really a place where Germans stored furniture they had stolen from Jews at different opportunities (mainly during the major expulsions from Krakow). We got furniture there that fit our new small home perfectly. For example, we found a bunk bed for me and my sister so there was enough room for us to also have a large closet, table and hanging bookcase. My little sister, who was about three years old, slept in my parents' room on a cot. The third room in the apartment was the largest one, and my parents made it into a living room. The kitchenette was only large enough to hold a gas ring and an oven, with a piece of marble around the sink. There was barely enough room for two people to stand there. We also had the luxury of a bathtub with a separate "closet" for the toilet. The bathroom also contained a contraption that could heat a small water tank.

My description of our move to the ghetto seemingly stands in stark contrast to what is described in books and shown in movies, where the forcing of Jews into ghettos was accompanied by great cruelty and violence. Indeed, I described it slightly romantically... When I saw Stephen Spielberg's movie, "Schindler's List", which depicts the transfer to the ghetto as lines of people walking and carrying their worldly goods on all kinds of wheeled contraptions, surrounded by Christian Poles who jeered and mocked them while throwing stones at them – my reaction was: "Where did Spielberg get this description from? I'd never heard of such a thing." That is, until I saw a documentary about the expulsion to the ghetto and it showed the exact scene that Spielberg directed. It turns out that some of the Jews who lived in Kazimierz – mostly the refugees from other towns – didn't move to the ghetto during the period decreed by the Nazis. Two days before the deadline, the Germans forcibly removed those Jews from their homes and made them move to the ghetto on foot, taking along only that which they could carry with them at the time.

As I mentioned above, though, the whole move and the first few months in the ghetto was a happy, good time for me. As a young boy, moving to a small apartment in a run-down building in a poor part of town didn't bother me a bit. In contrast, I was freed from a life in a German bubble, on a street where I had to pretend every time I was outside that I was a German child.

9.1 – Improvised Schools in the Ghetto

As soon as we moved into the ghetto, small classes were set up in the homes of private teachers as a substitute for school. The children were not grouped by age, so, for example, I learned math, Hebrew and English with my sister as my only "classmate," even though she was three years older than I was. We would pay a half or a whole zloty per lesson. All the teachers were superb: I learned math from a former professor in the University of Jagelonska in Krakow, and Hebrew with a Dr. Kvitner, who was the Hebrew Language department head in the Hebrew high school of Krakow. This wonderful teacher was deported in June 1942 to the death camps. After I came to Palestine at the end of 1945, I went to Kibbutz Merchavia to meet his son and family, to tell them about him.

We learned physics (called "inanimate nature" in Polish) from a physics professor, geography from a professor of astronomy and geography... He had a small telescope and we used to come to him at night to look at the stars. I learned the simple engineering taught in primary school from a professor of engineering from a Krakow university; every class with him was a party. I also learned music, history and literature. My sister went to dance classes, was in a choir, and I went with her to an after-school acting class run by famous theater actors. As I loved to learn from an early age, these ghetto classes were pure joy for me. They lasted for almost a year... At the end of 1941 Germans began moving Jews into the ghetto from the whole region, pushing more and more people into each apartment, and there was no room to hold group classes anymore. By the beginning of 1942, there was more concern about food than studies, so I mainly had private lessons with my sister, sometimes sitting on a bench or at a table in some yard or other.

The ghetto was quite small, consisting of three main streets that were about 800 meters long: Juzefinska, Limanowski (the main road, where the trams ran) and Renkavki – the upper street that was several dozen yards above Limanowski. Above Renkavki Street loomed beautiful Krzemionki Hill, which was covered in green for most of the year, though encased in snow in the winter. A large part of it was within the confines of the ghetto, and on nice days it was the place to go to for a walk in nature. Speaking of winter, there were a number of small streets running perpendicular to these main roads that attached them all together. The ones that descended from Renkavki to Limanowski were on a sharp decline and they were excellent places to skate, ski or sled down in the snow, as was Krzemionki Hill itself.

Because their homes were so crowded, in nice weather almost everyone stayed outdoors. I quickly turned the ghetto into my own large playground. I could go everywhere freely and was in charge of my own schedule. My parents rarely restricted me anymore. I made many new friends all around me and could reach all of them, as well as my relatives and teachers, within minutes. One of the neighbors in my building was a boy a year older than me. His parents were doctors, Blau by name, and they worked in the ghetto hospital. They called their only child Wojciek, but he told me his name was "Srulik," which was a diminutive of "Yisrael." His parents had changed his name to one that sounded more Polish because they were planning to escape with him from the ghetto.

I had another friend, named Voichek, who was called Voich. He was a very talented boy who loved to learn and owned many books, just like me. We'd go together to private lessons. The Jews opened several dozen stores, factories, bakeries, a post office, etc., in the ghetto, as well as a book store. We could buy all our schoolbooks there, as well as reading books. We could even order a book they didn't have from a catalog of publishing houses in Krakow. My grandfather transferred his store to the ghetto and to the best of my memory it was the only office supply business there. Cafes, clubs, and theaters opened, with the latter presenting mainly satirical plays, dancers and singers. I am describing here an almost idyllic life of a happy Jewish village and it is very different from all the horrifying pictures and stories told about ghetto life. The Krakow Ghetto also had its horrors, murders and tortures later on, as I will soon describe, but from March to December 1941, the situation was pretty comfortable and in this I do not exaggerate. One should remember that Germany was not yet at war with the United States and the Germans were trying to present to the world a picture of a seemingly autonomous Jewish lifestyle under their rule. The tragic and ridiculous thing was that on every Jewish store, the Germans forced the owners to write all the names and advertisements in Hebrew...

9.2 – Making a Living in the Ghetto

Besides the few store owners, how did the Jews in the ghetto make a living? The Germans confiscated all the property that Jews owned: businesses, factories, real estate. Jews had been fired from all institutions in the city, like schools, hospitals and the municipality. For example, about 50% of all doctors, lawyers and teachers in Krakow were Jews – and all of them lost their jobs. On the other hand, many Jewish businessmen, like my Grandpa, registered their companies in the name of Polish or German "partners" and kept working in them. But one of the most important reasons that Jews survived financially was that most of the Jewish population in Krakow was well off and they took care to always have cash, gold and valuables ready in case of need. Meanwhile, those who did not have savings were helped by a broad range of organized aid. First of all, there was family. I already mentioned how my father supported his two sisters, their families, his wife's sister, and my grandparents. So every wealthy family supported several poor ones. In addition, since the start of the Occupation, the Judenrat had established a whole system of social services for the needy, including establishing and running hospitals, old age homes, orphanages, and soup kitchens. Many high-quality people worked for the Judenrat and they did their jobs very well for the first three years of German rule. (In June 1942, however, the Germans appointed collaborators to head the Judenrat, and they only took care of themselves.)

As stated above, other ways the Judenrat got money was from taxing the wealthier Jews and by getting donations from abroad. I want to expand a bit on this point: Money, food and clothing came in from the Red Cross, the "Joint" in America, and other foreign charitable organizations. They worked through their respective embassies, which were in Krakow because it was the capitol of occupied Poland. Because they came in and out of the ghetto, they could report on conditions there to their governments – and the Germans had an interest in showing them that the Jews' condition wasn't so bad. It should be especially noted that the ghetto hospitals were very well equipped. They had x-ray machines, sophisticated operating rooms, and there was no shortage of medicines.

I would often stand near the Judenrat's warehouses and see how cars and trucks would arrive, with the names of their organizations and the flag of their country of origin on them. They would unload crates of food, winter clothing and various supplies. In addition, thousands of Jews got packages and money from their relatives overseas. You could see many happy people regularly coming out of the post office on Limanowski Street with packages in hand. The Germans didn't contribute a penny to the social services, but on the other hand they didn't object or disturb the Judenrat from raising the necessary means and getting help from abroad.

My Aunt Clara (nee Hollander), wife of Big David, used to get packages from her brother, who managed to escape Krakow before the war and reach the United States. They contained rare items like cocoa, chocolate, tea, coffee, and dried tropical fruits. There was a thriving black market in the ghetto for such foodstuffs, and tea and coffee were also a better means of bribing Germans than money. We would sometimes go to my uncle's house to enjoy these treats, and drink real tea or coffee. Aunt Clara was in touch with her brother and got these presents until the end of 1941. (In 2007, a wonderful book called **Every Day Lasts a Year**[3] was published by University of Cambridge Press. It tells the adventures of Clara's brother until he reached America and became a citizen, and contains an exchange of letters between him and his sisters. Hollander's son, Richard, had found the letters thrown carelessly in the attic and put them into the book.)

Despite the terrible overcrowding and primitive sanitary systems in the ghetto, no epidemics broke out as could be expected in such conditions. Great attention was paid to maintaining a decent standard of cleanliness: Garbage was collected daily in trucks and carts, yards and sewers were sprayed by exterminators, and health checks were made in every home. The German occupation authorities apparently believed their own propaganda about how Jews spread diseases – especially the SS, who were in charge of the Jews. They were extremely frightened of catching something, so they made sure the streets were clean and that medical treatment was available.

---

3   *Thousands of books have been written and tens of thousands of testimonies have been given regarding life under German Occupation in in the ghettos. In my opinion, one of the best testimonies ever written about the Krakow Ghetto is Tadeusz Pankiewicz's "Apteka w Getcie Krakowskim" (A Pharmacy in the Krakow Ghetto).* More about the this subject see Chapter 24, side note 3: Testimonies Regarding Life in the Ghetto

The ghetto also had its own Jewish Police force in charge of public order, the Ordnungdinst. Its offices were near the other end of Juzefinska Street. They and the Judenrat were in charge of all civilian matters, including tax collection, sanitary oversight and hospital administration, as well as having their well-known role as the community's link to the German Occupation authorities.

9.3 – Playing in the Ghetto

As mentioned above, around the area of my building, between Juzefinska and Limanowski Streets, there were dozens upon dozens of half-ruined houses that nobody lived in, in an area of about 100 meters by 80 meters. They became a wonderful playground for hordes of children. Among the hundreds of rooms, alcoves and basements, kids organized themselves into small gangs and took over certain apartments as their bases. The sign of "ownership" was making some sort of door with a lock for their place, and scrawling on it the name of their group. Often, the names were of Indian tribes taken from popular books. One particular "tribe" that included several tall children was called "Land of the Giants." Other names were "the Seven Dwarfs," "the Jolly Pirates," etc. My group consisted of me, my sister, my friend Voichek, two girls about my sister's age, and one older boy named Maciek. We got Maciek to join us by using various enticements: We told him that we had the best food, the prettiest girls, and a lot of money, as well as promising to make him our leader. Maciek's primary advantage was his height, muscles and ability to scare others. We needed him to be our military commander for all the war games we played. Later on, another boy joined us, His name was Jezyk, and he became one of my closest friends. His parents were extremely poor; his mother was disabled. He had a little sister whom his parents had given to a Christian family even before entering the ghetto, and he missed her terribly. Jezyk was about a year older than I was but he was very small – about my height, in fact, and I was very short. My nickname was Malutky, or Maly, which means "Shorty."

Each gang in this "children's country" took pains to decorate and equip their hideout according to its specific character. We had a pretty big apartment, albeit being partially in ruins, with the ceiling even having fallen in one of the rooms. But there was a lot of furniture around the ghetto that people had simply thrown away, so we found everything we needed. It was enormous fun making the place "livable" (to our standards). We even built a secret room that only our group knew how to enter. In it, we stashed everything we had of value and that would be in danger of being stolen from us. We had a whole swearing-in ceremony, declaring our loyalty to our gang and promising to keep its secrets.

We were not the only (semi-) organized group of kids in the ghetto. There were thousands of children running around and playing in the nice weather. The various youth movements continued their activities in the ghetto as well, though I personally did not encounter them. I was too busy in our "country," as several gangs would often gather in one place – sometimes as many as 30 children – to play, sing or play music together. One of the girls in our group knew how to play an instrument (I believe it was the clarinet), and Jezyk found a broken accordion somewhere, which we somehow managed to patch up. Obviously, my sister was very musical, playing the piano so well, but she also knew how to sing beautifully – as well as parody the opera singers of the day. Maciek knew how to tell rude jokes that nobody understood but we would all laugh anyway.

My loyal friend Jezyk was my military and P.E. instructor. He taught me how to use knives and beat an opponent in wrestling. He was also talented in sports and organized a soccer team out of our local "regiment." Actually, there were three soccer teams, and the regiments were organized around them... I loved to play the game but wasn't chosen for our team. We all worked very hard to clean up and level a few yards to turn them into a soccer field and play area in general. Of course, we also played other kinds of ball games, like dodge ball, rugby, etc. The girls played hopscotch. This was all in addition to our frequent war games, where we would try to conquer the hideout of another gang.

At the entrance to our house on the ground floor was a garage, which would be opened every day via a gate that was actually outside the ghetto. I was a regular there, becoming very friendly with the two mechanics who let me help them fix cars. I'd clean parts, screw and unscrew bolts, work the lift to raise the cars... They even sometimes let me move the cars. I was extremely happy there, but Mom was less so, so I tried to get as little dirt on myself as possible. Mom then sewed two work overalls for me like all mechanics wore, and I felt like a king.

They closed the garage at the end of 1940. I remember well how they took out all the equipment and loaded it onto trucks, while I stood there in my overalls and tried not to cry. After that, the outside gate never opened again.

This personal tragedy of mine, of the garage closing down, crushed me. I was so sad... Dad then compensated me for my loss by buying me a big, beautiful two-wheeled bike (that I had to share with my sister). Very few children in the ghetto had such a bicycle; most rode on scooters. It made me a very popular boy as everyone wanted to be my friend, and of course I let my circle of friends and Gizia's friends have rides.

Although the impression I'm giving is of playing all day, our schooling was actually supposed to take precedence. We had lessons on and off from morning until night, which didn't leave us much time to play – but we'd often "cut class" and go to our friends instead. One day, we had an important game and didn't go to English class. After the game, late in the afternoon, we went home – and to our shock, there was our teacher, sitting at our table, eating potatoes with sausage and cabbage. We were dirty and messy, and certainly didn't look like children who were coming back from school.

"What happened? Where have you been?" asked Mom, who was alternately happy and angry. I had already learned the simple wisdom that in such cases the best thing to do was say nothing and let others apologize and explain... My sister understood the situation, and squeaked out, "Przepraszam, mamusiu" (Sorry, Mom), but then she said the best and most truthful words possible: "We had a very important game and in this game we had to defend our home." Our teacher was an older man, over 40, who lived with his wife (I never saw any children in his house, so I don't know if he had any). I don't remember his name. He spoke Polish with a strange accent, and was a very polite and strict person. He earned his living from his English lessons and apparently he didn't have many students.

I pitied him very much. I knew that he had come to our house more to eat and get paid than because he was worried about us. So I apologized to him, saying, "Sorry, excuse us." Mom was gratified to hear her son speaking English, and the professor actually beamed. Our lessons continued twice a week for eight months, until the end of 1941. Years later, the only things that I remembered from these lessons were the alphabet and a few isolated words. But I did come away with a big asset: a British accent and the ability to twist my tongue around the strange words correctly!

We did, however, pay a steep price for cutting class: Mom had an attendance notebook of sorts, and at the end of each lesson we had to have the teacher sign it. After this episode, whenever we had an "important game," Mom would let us go and would pay the teacher anyway.

Doctors were in the same bad financial situation as the professors who didn't have enough students to teach. While they used to practice among 360,000 residents – remember, 50% of all Krakow doctors were Jews – now only a small percentage of them found any work at all in the ghetto hospitals. We had several family friends who were doctors and would come to eat at our house from time to time. I only remember two of their names: Dr. Eihenholz and Dr. Alexandrovich. They used to leave with sandwiches in hand for their children...

My sister and I also used to invite friends over to eat with us – especially those who had barely any food at home. Mom would cook for them happily, finding both interest and a sense of purpose in such activity. I remember how these children would ask if they could also take some food home for the rest of their families. Helping friends came naturally and spontaneously for us, and for many others who were better off financially felt – even without understanding it completely – that to aid and give to others helped the giver as much as the receiver.

CHAPTER 10

Spring and Summer 1941; Establishing Life in the Ghetto

10.1 – The First Passover Seder

The snow finished melting as we moved into the ghetto in March, 1941. A beautiful spring began; all the trees and bushes started budding and then flowering. The vacations spot of the ghetto, Krzemionki Hill, soon became covered with shrubs and flowers. Then it was time for the Passover holiday. This was the first time since the war began that we began preparing to make a *seder* (the traditional meal on the first two nights of the seven-day holiday) at our house for all the relatives in the family. This was a very dangerous "operation," since by order of the Occupation authorities, it was absolutely forbidden for Jews to gather to perform any kind of religious ritual whatsoever. Even before we came to the ghetto, when the Germans found out that in some house or other people were having some kind of holiday meal or prayers, they would descend on the house and riot, which would end with blows and arrests – and in many cases also with deaths. Of course, the Germans knew that Jews in the ghetto were preparing for Passover, and the question was how they would react on the first Passover night. Of course there was no vacation from work, since the Germans were very strict about making all the Jews go to work on the Sabbath and especially on major holidays like Passover, Rosh Hashana and Yom Kippur.

There were over 20 people in my entire extended family, what with uncles, aunts, cousins and grandparents. It took over a week to get ready. Our Christian maid slept at our house for a few nights, and all the aunts helped my mother. Those days before Passover were horribly tense, and the suspense went up a few more notches on Passover eve. Usually the Germans didn't walk around the ghetto at night, and if they did come in, they would do so in large numbers. At night, only the main gate to the ghetto was open, so there was a very simple and efficient system set up to warn of a German approach: The ghetto was very small, and it was enough to have a few dozen people in eye contact with each other for the news of a German incursion to spread like lightning throughout the ghetto. They used the Indian "bonfire" method – that is, flashlights. In addition, you could hear the noise of the cars entering from anywhere you stood. The fact that we had 20 people in the apartment was not dangerous in and of itself, because there were plenty of apartments where that was the usual number of inhabitants. The problem was how to quickly hide all signs of the *seder* in case the Germans broke in. Since in every country except Israel, Jews celebrate the first two days as holidays at the beginning of Passover and not just one, with a *seder* each night, we decided to have our *seder* only on the second night, after seeing what would happen the night before.

To our great and pleasant surprise, the first night of Passover was completely quiet; the Germans did not raid the ghetto. We were very sorry that we hadn't celebrated the first *seder*. But the quiet of the first night really seemed suspicious; perhaps the Germans didn't intrude then in order to lull everyone into having a false sense of security, and they would actually come in during the second *seder*?

Indeed, during the day, rumors spread that the Germans would surely raid us that night. The three Wimisners – that is, my father and Big David, and their uncle, Little David – didn't go to work that day. Big David came over in the early afternoon to try and convince

Dad to give up on having the *seder*, as it would be too dangerous. The argument ended with Dad deciding to go ahead with it, and his brother deciding to make his own *seder* at home with his family and his wife's sisters. My sister and I enthusiastically volunteered to set up the *seder* table. Tension was again running high, with neighbors or acquaintances coming in all the time to ask what was going on and to tell us the latest rumors. My big sister and I treated the strain and uncertainty like the tension before a game, except this time, instead of another gang or enemy "battalion" attacking us, it would be the Germans. I asked Mom if we caught the Germans before they got into the house whether they'd be "out..." although we somehow felt that the game versus the Germans would be different. Mom asked us to treat the matter seriously. So we prepared for the German attack – and there's no more intense display of devotion and diligence than that of children preparing to play a game. I imagined myself as the guard in front of the house seeing the Germans entering and yelling to them, "I saw you, you're out..."

On our own initiative, my sister and I decided to prepare a room in the ruins of the "children's country" as a hiding place in case the Germans raided the ghetto. We got the keys from the gang that had taken over an apartment that was hidden much better than ours. It wasn't free; after some negotiations, we paid a bar of real chocolate and a sophisticated slingshot for it. The gang that lent us its apartment belonged to our regiment. (It was inconceivable that a group from a different regiment would give us its apartment...) This one was hidden well among the ruins and was only a few dozen meters from our home. We told our parents and the others that if the Germans came into the ghetto, we would all be able to go to this hiding place. I don't know if our parents took our plans seriously. Unfortunately – or perhaps fortunately – we didn't have to put our plan to the test.

For us kids, the pre-*seder* stress was one big, exciting and unique experience. Here we were, playing a game with our parents that was for real. I even told my father that we also know how to protect our home in case the Germans arrived, as we had weapons like sling-shots, sticks, and even knives. We didn't use the latter in our games, but perhaps in *this* game it would be appropriate to put them to use... I had no concept of what "the German raiding us" meant to the adults who talked of it. I imagined a kind of game where the Germans would come and want to take the food we'd prepared for the *seder*, and we would have to stop them.

On the second *seder* night, we sat down for the most emotional and tense holiday meal that is almost impossible to describe. Maybe it was the Passover *seder* most like the one the Jews celebrated that very first time, before they left Egypt... Grandpa sat in a festive white suit, wearing a *streimel* (special Hassidic hat). Truth to tell, I found it a bit funny – but I didn't dare laugh. It was the first time I'd ever seen Grandpa with such a hat on his head. With great formality and emotion, Grandpa began reading the Haggadah. We sang in all the right places with great emphasis and festivity. Each person read the Haggadah with theatrical ceremony and defiance that here, the na-tion of Israel lived. The three aunts whose husbands were missing and who were alone with their children, burst into tears each time they read from the text. As the son of the host, I had the honor of reading the first of the Four Questions (the *Mah Nishtana*) recited at the very beginning of the *seder*.

At one point, Dad saw fit to explain in Polish what the words "this night" symbolizes for us, and also to answer the questions raised in the text with additional explanations. He told us that just as in our exodus from the slavery of Egypt, we would also survive the Germans. Of course, I didn't understand back then what was the connection between Pharaoh, Egypt and the Germans. My big sister, who was the best singer of all the children, sang something with her cousin, Eva the Redhead, and my little sister, Sarenka. At some point Grandpa didn't feel well, so as the eldest of the Wimisners, Little

David shouldered the responsibility of leading the rest of the *seder.*
Little David, my great-uncle, was the children's most beloved uncle. First of all, this was because he loved children very much. He'd always play with us, and tell jokes and stories. After every section that he read in the Haggadah, he would give a special explanation of what it meant to the kids, in Polish. The general theme was "Przezyjemy Hitlerowcow," meaning: We will survive the Nazis. Little David had a good sense of humor and he had a wonderful personality. He managed to give a humorous and optimistic undercurrent to the reading. "Here we are, a year and a half under the German yoke and we're still sitting and celebrating," he said. He managed to instill in us a sense of happiness, and all our tension melted away. In effect, we forgot for a moment what kind of situation we were in. Among his explanations of the Haggadah, after reading about the plague of pestilence, he said that after the war all the men of the SS would be infected with this: Their bodies would be filled with pustules, the letters SS would be engraved on their foreheads along with the swastika, they would continue wearing white gloves, and on their chests would be written, "I am preparing to go to hell."

Reading the Haggadah turned into a release for us of all the frustration, degradation, fear and the spirit of revenge that we had absorbed under the Nazi occupation – and all this was before the deportations to the extermination camps. We sat until the wee hours of the morning in this celebratory and uplifted spirit. We also ate wonderful food – meat and fish the likes of which just wasn't seen during this period. It was the only Passover *seder* during the entire war where we had so many family members celebrating together.

Not a single raid occurred during the entire holiday. The Germans made no attempt to disturb the *seders.* We had a lot of food left over and the next day we invited many children – friends of mine and of Gizia – to eat at our house. It gave me a lot of pleasure to watch children who hadn't seen food like this for a long, long time, eating with joy.

10.2 – Having Fun in the Ghetto, Krzemionki Hill

There was nothing like the month of May in the beautiful weather of Krakow. I could wear shorts and the short-sleeved shirts I loved. The sun was pleasantly warm, everything was in bloom, and flowers scented the air. There was no better time to take a picnic to Krzemionki Hill, which was the vacation spot of the ghetto. Mom fell in love with the area and often, all the children went with her, as well as other relatives. Even Grandma and Grandpa would come.

We would climb the hill, pushing Sarenka in her special buggy, the one that could take the rugged paths. All around us would be hundreds of other families with the same idea of making a picnic. The women would quickly start talking with each other, while the kids organized games. Spending time in nature, on this hill, in wonderful weather, were some of our happiest hours in the ghetto. We went there dozens of times during that spring and summer, and I don't remember the Germans bothering us even once. Not far from the hill there was an airport, and planes were continually taking off and landing there. I could have spent hours watching them. I even got my hands on a simple pair of binoculars so I could see them even closer up.

As I mentioned earlier, there were several cafes, restaurants, bakeries and grocery stores in the ghetto – all with Hebrew signs on them, by German order. Perhaps this strange phenomenon stemmed from a German desire to lend the place the character of a Jewish village...

There was one cafe I knew well, which was located on the end of Limanowski Street. It actually touched the main gate of the ghetto. One could enter it both from the ghetto side and from the other side, without having to pass through the gate. That way, Poles and Germans could go in without having to present a ghetto pass at the gate. A small orchestra played in this cafe, both light music and dance music. In the evenings, couples would dance there, and there were also performances of operettas, stand-up comedy, and singers together with dancers. I personally never sat in this kind of cafe when I was in the ghetto, and I don't know if my parents did, either. However, I'd often sneak into cafes – including this one – with other kids, to see performances while standing in a discreet corner. We particularly loved this cafe because we found a way to get from our house to it via the ruins of our "children's country" so we wouldn't be in danger of being caught after curfew on Wegierska Street, which linked our street to Limanowski. (Whoever was out after curfew stood a good chance of being caught and arrested by the Jewish Police.)

It was well known that this cafe was owned by a man named Forster, who was a unique and mysterious person. He spoke only German, lived in the ghetto, but walked around without the Jewish armband. He was possibly Jewish, possibly German – but he worked for the Gestapo. Rumor had it that he also had an apartment outside the ghetto. In any case, Poles, Jews and Germans – in and out of uniform – all sat together in his cafe, and there was a very friendly atmosphere. Forster would wander between the tables and it was clear he was everyone's friend. He would sometimes tell a waiter to give us a sandwich or piece of cake. He never threw us out; he was always very friendly to all the children who showed up at his cafe, and we all loved him very much. Other patrons would also bring us things to eat. We were very much part of the scenery, standing in corners and along the walls. We behaved very well, never uttering a sound, and this may be why we were never thrown out.

According to various sources I found, the place was also used by the Gestapo to gather information – among others, about those Germans who frequented the cafe, and they used to follow them sometimes as well. There was also a young couple (in their twenties) who regularly worked for the Gestapo there. Their name was "Salinger." They would listen in on Germans' conversations and then report them to their bosses. Mrs. Salinger was a German Jew who had learned to read lips. My friends and I paid particular attention to her because she was very beautiful – she had the face of a doll – and she sat in the cafe very often. What also made her stand out was that she went to the bathroom frequently and stayed there for long periods of time. Apparently, she was writing down what she had overheard...

There were more than a few Jews in the ghetto who collaborated with the Gestapo and acted as informers[4]. One word from them was enough to arrest someone and make him disappear – either by being executed or sent to a concentration camp. The Gestapo never made much of an effort to corroborate an informant's statement. The arrest would come in the middle of the night, carried out by the Jewish Police. The person would be taken by the Gestapo in the morning, and never be seen again. These night arrests terrorized the ghetto.

In addition to spending part of my time playing in the "children's country" near my house, there was one other location where I played: Plac Zgody, or Zgody Square. Today it is called "Heroes' Square." It served as a playground for hundreds of children, and I often went there, especially after I got my bike and could show it off.

As my sister and I shared the bicycle, while one rode it to the square, the other would roll along on a small bike or use a scooter. Once there, we'd give out rides to our friends. But our favorite place of all was the post office, which was the only one of its kind in the ghetto. There were always a lot of grownups and children around it. Since people would leave the post office carrying parcels they had gotten from abroad, a market of sorts sprang up in the alleyways around, where brisk trade would ensue for at least part of the contents. Many sold the more exotic foods or goods in these packages

---

4   *In general, the Jewish informants and collaborators were the dregs of society and criminals who engaged in extortion, theft and acts of fraud even before the war (More about the Gestapo Collaborators see Chapter 24, side note 4)*

(tea, coffee, chocolate, dried pineapple, canned meats, etc.) for a very good price, enabling them to buy a lot of simple food like potatoes and bread. For example, they would take a 100-gram packet of real tea and divide it into tiny envelopes of 2 grams each, to make a greater profit. Two grams of tea was enough for one cup, or even a whole teapot for a family dinner.

I already mentioned the aid that arrived from other countries, to be distributed by the social services of the Jewish authorities in the ghetto. Cars would constantly arrive from the Red Cross of Switzerland, Sweden, Argentina, Mexico, etc. And the "Joint" operated through the American Embassy (until the end of 1941, when the Americans joined the war). It was fascinating to see these officials in their impressive (and sometimes funny) uniforms or suits, with their fancy coats and polished shoes, while in the ghetto people walked around in dirty, torn rags. My sister and I even got to speak with them sometimes. One told us he was from Sweden. Another time, a Red Cross official came over to us – I don't remember from which country – accompanied by a Gestapo officer. He wanted to ask us some questions, and we willingly acquiesced. He asked us what we ate, if we were hungry, if our whole family was well. We answered all his questions and a crowd soon gathered around us. We felt so important... The man wrote down everything we said. The Gestapo man told us we could say whatever we wanted. How did we know he was from the Gestapo? Their agents always wore long, polished, sparkling leather coats, brown gloves, a round hat and a badge on the lapel of their coats. (Of course, they also had black uniforms, and could wear civilian clothes too, as befits an undercover police force[5].)

---

5   *The Jewish police in the Ghetto fulfilled many tasks under the command of gestapo and SS. commander of the Jewish Police, Symche Spira, who was dressed like a South American general, all polished and sparkling.* (More about the Jewish Police see Chapter 24, side note 5

10.3 – The Card Club, War Developments

In the second half of June, 1941, war broke out between Germany and the Soviet Union. It was at this time that I began being extremely interested in what was going on in the war. My interest was primarily piqued because that's what the grown-ups were always talking about. There was a group of about six people, including two women, who came once or twice a week to play cards with my father (my mother wouldn't play). There were heavy drapes on the windows in the guest-room where they played, which gave a sense of being cut off from the world. I had a small desk in that room, and would usually sit there busying myself with one interest or another while they played, but at the same time listening intently to all that was being said over the cards. While dealing and holding, they would discuss all the problems the Jews were having in the ghetto.

They really talked more than they played; frequently, they'd stop altogether and just start debating – often quite forcefully. A lot of the time, the conversation was about families that had received foreign citizenship, or families that had left the ghetto to hide in some way among the Christian Poles, about what was going on in the war and the chances of survival. I made a mental note of what was said even if I didn't understand it all, and would ask my father to explain it to me later. In fact, most of the discussions I had with him began to be about the war. Dad made me swear not to talk to anyone about what was said in our home. At this stage I began to understand the danger entailed in informants telling the Gestapo about people who "spread rumors."

Survival was a prime topic of conversation during these card games. Jews who had relatives outside the Third Reich tried to obtain citizenship of those countries where their family lived, but this cost a great deal of money. Once, someone said, "I heard that the Rappaport family got an American visa and already went to a German port city to get on an American ship." Rumor also had it that every person who had foreign citizenship could get the right to live outside the ghetto and would be protected by the embassy of that country...

It was during one of these card games that I learned that Dad's brother, Big David, was about to get Nicaraguan citizenship for his family. I also learned about the method of buying a Polish Catholic identity and go live under that assumed name in a village where you wouldn't be recognized. The story was told of the Piotrovskys, who had vanished from the ghetto and went to live in some town or other in that way. Here, Mr. Bernstein, who had four children, opined: "It's very dangerous to live with your whole family under a false identity. The family should be separated so they won't all be caught together." The subject of giving up one's children to be adopted by Christians also came up, with names mentioned of people who did just that. Pani Bronia maintained emotionally that one shouldn't separate children from their parents.

These discussions[6] all took place with the sense that danger was far off. What most bothered them was the feeling of helplessness, that there wasn't anyone to protect us, there were no laws and the Germans could do whatever they wanted. "Hitler wants to annihilate all the Jews and nobody in the entire world is going to protect us."

After the war began against the Soviet Union, the card club discussed the war a lot. Despite initial German victories, they all agreed that at the end, the Germans would lose the war, the United States would enter, and that vast country would simply overwhelm the Nazis. Mr. Zuckerberg spoke of the war developments with great pathos, as if he had returned from the front at that very moment. He claimed, "It's true the Germans are winning right now, but they

---

6   How could we get the news: There were official news of the war from German newspapers like "Nowiny Krakowskie" (The Krakow News). The most reliable source was Via the BBC, Radio Free Poland. it managed to broadcast throughout the country. (More about the "Industry of News" in occupied Poland See Chapter 24, side note 23)

are suffering heavy losses. Every day thousands of Nazis are being wounded and killed. Churchill said that this was the first time in the war that Nazi blood is being spilled like water on the steppes of Russia." And Mr. Zuckerberg's face grew red with excitement.

I began to understand better the significance of what war was and that the Germans – whom I had so admired in the beginning – were truly evil and we desperately desired that they lose the war. My hatred of the Germans in general grew deeper, but here I would like to note that throughout the war, I never thought or felt that *all* Germans were bad, and that there were also "good" Germans.

There was another friend of Dad's who would come over from time to time, a Mr. Romek. He and Dad would sit together at the big table, spread out maps and discuss the progress of the war. Mr. Romek was the expert in military matters and would always bring us news. I would again sit on the side and drink in every word.

I also spent many hours studying maps of the world, and learned my atlas almost by heart. I especially loved the numerical statistics about the different countries: How big they were, how many people lived there, their economic power, how many natural resources they had like coal, oil, and iron, and their military might. I would also ask my uncles and older cousins to test me in geography. Once, one of my cousins mocked me in front of my mother, saying, "Little Leosz wants to be a general..."

There was no movie theater in the ghetto, yet throughout the summer and fall of 1941 I saw many films. How? At the end of Limanowski Street, across from the ghetto gate, there was a big square called "Plac Podgorski". After the war began with the Soviet Union, the Germans started showing propaganda films there almost every evening. They spread a huge white screen on one of the houses, and scattered loudspeakers around the square, because the movies usually came with Polish translations. The movies revolved around several themes. One had to do with news of the war ("The Germans are winning on every front"). They would show scenes of tanks rolling through Soviet fields and streams of prisoners going in the opposite direction; the population – apparently Ukrainians – welcoming the Germans with flowers, with the women kissing the soldiers; the head of Ukraine welcoming the liberators with bread and salt; thousands of Ukrainians joining the German army; thousands of Soviet planes, tanks and cannon lying destroyed and smoking on the ground; German submarines sinking British ships; Rommel's tanks thundering through the sands of North Africa; and many British prisoners.

Another theme in this Nazi Propaganda was incitement against Jews and Jewish Bolshevism. Here they'd screen anti-Semitic movies the Nazis made, such as "Jew Suss," as well as many shorts that were staged specifically for the Poles. These tried to convince the population that the Jews spread disease, trick Poles and steal from them. In order to protect the Poles from these evil disease-mongers, the Jews had been closed up in a ghetto. Whenever they showed Jews on screen, they always had lice and fleas on their clothes and in the background they showed scenes of rats coming out of sewers.

A third theme was how Germany saved Poles[7]. They showed areas of Poland that were liberated from the Soviets. In one case, they interviewed a Pole who had been freed from a Soviet jail. He said he had been arrested because a Jew had informed on him, and thanked his German saviors. At this point, they showed pictures of Polish detainees who had been murdered by the Soviets.

The movies tried to rewrite history and suddenly emphasize German-Polish friendship. They presented the pact signed between Poland and Germany after Hitler rose to power: Here was Goering,

---

7   *During the last five hundred years the relation between Poland and Germany was one of bitter enemies and full of wars. When the war between Germany and the Soviet Union began the Germans made great effort to persuade Poles to join them in this war.* (More of the Abbreviated History of Polish-German Relations see Chapter 24, side note 6)

one of the founders of the Nazi Party, on vacation hunting in the Polish forests; there he was, being received in very friendly fashion by the Polish government. In contrast, they presented the never-ending wars between the Poles and Russians. Great emphasis was laid on the war between Marshal Pilsudski, a leader who was adored in Poland, vs. the Bolsheviks toward the end of World War I, and his heroic victory. They showed the German honor guard that they set up near his grave in Krakow. They also presented scenes of Germans paving Polish roads, establishing factories, giving farmers gifts of tools and equipment and encouraging them to raise pigs. Then we would see the German army buying the pork for generous amounts of money.

At that time it wasn't a problem to get out of the ghetto, so I would sneak out to Podgorski Square with many other children to see these shows. There was no place to sit, so hundreds of Poles – mainly children – would stand and watch for hours. Others would bring chairs or boxes to sit on. The balconies around the square were usually full of people watching as well. There were also many Gestapo agents in the crowd, watching how the people were re-acting to these films. In general, the viewers did not react loudly; there was neither applause nor booing.

I loved going to see these movies and could stand for hours, for-getting the outside world. Before this, I had only gone to see one movie in my life, starring Shirley Temple. When I came back home, I'd tell my father what I'd seen – and then he would set me straight on the facts. I also heard one of my father's card-playing friends, Mr. Zuckerberg (who was also considered a bit of a war expert), ex-plain what was really happening: "Even though the Germans were winning right now", he said, and were advancing toward Moscow, "they were still absorbing heavy losses in the hundreds of thousands. Meanwhile, the Soviet army was learning how to fight the mighty Nazi war machine and was beginning to get aid from the United

States. The Soviets had also established a huge arms factory hundreds of kilometers east of Moscow, where the Germans couldn't bomb it."

One sunny day, surprise guests came to our "children's country": A senior officer in the department of the Gestapo that dealt with the ghetto's Jews, accompanied by another Gestapo agent and two Jewish policemen. They surprised us in our playground while several groups were playing handball. With our Jewish "chutzpa," (cheek) we didn't stop playing. They watched us for a minute, and then one of the policemen announced in a loud voice in Polish, "Sturmscharfuhrer, Kriminalsecretar Wilhelm Kunde wants to speak with you." We gathered round, Kunde passed out some candy, and started asking us very banal questions: Do we also play soccer, do we have enough food, what did we eat for breakfast.... One of the policemen translated our answers. Kunde then asked a few more questions and asked to see our apartment hideouts. My sister, who knew German well and was very good at public relations, was one of his guides. Kunde seemed pleased after his visit, and when we told our parents about it that evening, they didn't get excited at all.

Kunde was actually known as a Gestapo man who tried to be liked by the Jews under his control. He had an office at the Jewish Police station, and one could get in to see him to make requests, which in many cases he would actually fulfill. But he was "the devil in Prada." He appeared relaxed and courteous, while constantly gathering information and making sure to send "elements dangerous to the Reich" to their deaths. He was also in charge of the "civilian" department in the Jewish Police and ran dozens of agents, both in uniform and undercover. Later on he was revealed as a cold-blooded killer, of children as well as adults, and after Germany's defeat he appeared on the list of war criminals that the Polish government demanded should be jailed. (Unfortunately, he wasn't caught until the beginning of the Sixties, when he ran for the Bundestag, Germany's Parliament, in one of West Germany's states. At the end, he died while on trial there for his crimes.)

CHAPTER 11

A Sad Fall and Winter in the Ghetto, 1941

The autumn months of 1941 brought a lot of rain and windy, cold weather; it was no longer pleasant to play outdoors. In general, these were among the less enjoyable months in Krakow. There wasn't enough coal for heat, or enough electricity. They would cut the power to the ghetto for several hours each evening, so we made do with oil lamps. I was lucky to have an oil lamp of my own and could read and learn. But these were sad times. Many of our relatives frequently crowded in with us. We grew closer to Little David's family, as my sister and I would go over to play cards and games with the twins, Morris and Ziggy. They had an excellent sense of humor, and we were always making jokes and laughing. We had a great time whenever we got together. Their older sister, Gina, would keep an eye on us and her presence lent a serene atmosphere to their home. We'd sometimes arrange to have party games at our house, and then we'd invite all the rest of our cousins as well.

Meanwhile, I kept following the news of the war; it became so real to me it was almost as if I was living it. Mr. Romek kept coming to the house and exchanging whispered secrets with my father in the guest-room. But I would listen in, and hear things like: "The German army is still advancing to Moscow but its situation is getting worse. They're suffering from heavy losses and lack of supplies... Most hospitals in Krakow and other parts of Poland have been confiscated by the Germans to treat their wounded soldiers... The German army could not conquer Leningrad... Hundreds of Polish pilots are fighting the Germans out of Great Britain... Polish pilots participated in the bombing of Berlin... A partial draft has been declared in the United States, our savior is preparing to join the war..."

Mr. Zuckerberg came to play cards and spoke of the murder of the Jews in Ukraine: "Thousands – maybe even tens of thousands – of Jews have been murdered. Before that, thousands of Jews in Lithuania, Latvia and Estonia were killed." Mr. Rapaport said that such things were implausible, while Mrs. Bronia added that people always tended to exaggerate such things. After all, there are rules of war, and the Red Cross is everywhere, and surely it wouldn't let such things happen...

11.1 – Stealing Our Furs

One evening, either in November or the beginning of December, we saw from our window that faced the Christian side that many German policemen had surrounded the ghetto. This was a sign that something bad was about to happen. Indeed, early the next morning, hundreds of Germans and Ukrainians came into the ghetto and cars went up and down the streets announcing through loudspeakers that everyone had to come in person to the Judenrat and hand over every single fur they owned. Anyone who did not obey, or who would hide or damage his furs, would be shot immediately. After the first shock, Mom and Dad agreed to give up all our furs. We started taking them out of the closet and putting them on our parents' bed: two beautiful fur coats belonging to Mom, a long one and a short one of Dad's, one for Gizia and a padded one for me. We also had hats, a fox-fur that Mom used as a scarf, and leather gloves padded with fur. Gizia started crying, and when Sarenka saw her cry, she melted into tears as well. Mom had tears in her eyes and she was shaking in suppressed rage and despair, while Dad as usual was quiet and exhibited self-control.

At a certain point our parents asked us to leave the room, and when they were alone they took out all the money, gold and diamonds that were hidden inside them.

The whole family went together to give in the furs. We waited for about half an hour on line in a big hall with dozens of tables. German clerks and policemen sat at the tables. When it was our turn, the German clerk identified Dad by the documents he presented. There were huge containers for the furs, and as Dad gave them in, the clerk noted them all down and gave Dad a receipt. Sad and bare-headed, we walked home. Many Jews could be seen carrying their furs toward the Judenrat. Hundreds of soldiers with rifles cocked stood on the sidewalks and did nothing (as yet) but this sight, together with the constant announcements on the loudspeakers, made for a terrifying atmosphere.

After lunch, our parents sent Gizia and me to all the relatives to tell them what we had done. When we came to Big David's, they told us that they weren't going to obey the order since they already had authorizations in hand for Nicaraguan citizenship and by law they didn't have to give in their furs. We got to Grandma's house last, and she was very sorry about Mom's beautiful coats.

On the way back home, the situation in the street was completely different. Now the policemen were urging the Jews to run by hitting them with whips and sticks. People were falling down and the police were kicking them and screaming, "Schnell, schnell!" to make them get up and run. We heard the sound of shots, and many Jews were killed. It was a terrible pogrom, and it was the first time my sister or I had ever seen such a terrible thing. I held my sister's hand the whole time we were outside, but for some reason we were sure they wouldn't hurt us, even when we heard shots and screams coming from several houses that we passed. When we got home we saw that our parents had been worried. They told us that Germans had come to check on them and they had presented the receipt stating that they had given in their furs. This pogrom shocked us and everyone else in the ghetto. People talked about it everywhere we went and were greatly worried about what would be the end of it all.

11.2 – A Serious Discussion

Several days after "the day of the furs," all our relatives gathered in our home except for our grandparents and Aunt Fela. We were still in shock from the murders we had witnessed, and the purpose of the meeting was to figure out what we should do as a result. The adults sat around the big table and the children sat or stood in a second circle around them. There was a heavy atmosphere in the room; everyone was aware of the seriousness of the situation – even the children. After a while, Dad asked all the children to go to the other room to play (the weather wasn't good enough for us to go outside). Little David's daughter, Gina, and Big David's daughter, Genia, were already 20 years old and my father let them stay with the adults. The older teens, like Morris and Jurek, protested; they also wanted to stay. Big David stood up, and with one look he emptied the room in seconds. To this day I don't understand why we were so afraid of him...

But never fear, we made sure to hear everything. There was a door connecting the children's room and the guest room, and we opened it the barest crack. Ziggy and Morris stood behind it, taking turns listening. There was also a secret opening between the two rooms that was well hidden. We could both hear and see partway into the room from there, and Jurek and my sister positioned themselves there. The other older children made sure that the younger ones were silent, and we put Sarenka to bed.

Periodically, those who were eavesdropping came to tell us a snippet of news. At one point, Morris whispered an update of what was being suggested: "They want to take us to farmers in a village;" "Maybe we should all escape abroad;" and "Let's hide among the Christians." My sister whispered, "Mom doesn't agree to us being separated." Both Aunt Hela and Aunt Genia were already widows at this point, and Hela said, "I have only my daughter left, I will not be separated from her." Genia spoke of her plan to live in a small village as the widow of a Polish soldier who fell in the war. From all these "intelligence reports" I got the picture that the situation was frightening and dangerous, we have to escape no matter what, and the possibilities were: to get to another country, hide with a farmer, or run and live on false papers among the non-Jews[8].

11.3 – A Sad Game and the Last Movie

At the end of autumn, 1941, we played our last war game in "children's country." We bravely fought off an attack on our territory and then went on the offensive, throwing rocks, and shooting arrows and slingshots. In our final push to conquer "enemy territory," one of the girls on their side got hit in the head and started bleeding very badly. It was quite frightening, and we immediately stopped the game and took her to our home. She was very scared and started to lose consciousness. My mother quickly bandaged her head and we rushed her to the hospital, which was very close by. It was very small, only three stories, but it was well equipped. She was treated for several hours, getting a blood transfusion and having her head re-bandaged, but the wound was superficial and did not endanger her, and at the end we took her to her home.

This was to be the last game before the really cold weather set in, but due to events that occurred that winter, it was also the last game we ever had in our remarkable playground.

---

8   *On the end of 1941 and the beginning of 1942 there was no suspicion of the Nazis' intentions to annihilate the Jewish people. But there were rumors of the slaughter in the Ukraine, so almost all the Jews made attempts to leave the ghetto and to hide among the Christians.* (More on the subject of "Going into Hiding" see Chapter 24, side note 7)

In the last movie shown in Podgorski Square before the "winter break," there was a German news conference in which we saw the Propaganda Minister, Joseph Goebbels, and victory in the East was declared. They claimed that the Red Army had fallen apart and been decimated, that the Soviet Union had ceased to exist as a country, and only a few scattered remnants of the Red Army were continuing to fight.

That night, I asked my father what the truth was. I already understood that any victory of the Germans was bad for us; it had been a long time since I'd celebrated the capture of Paris with the German children... Dad explained that the movie was just propaganda and that the Germans had yet to capture Leningrad or Moscow.

The next day, I went for a walk outside the ghetto with Jezyk and two other friends. I treated them to cake and chocolate milk in a bakery. (Everything was much cheaper outside the ghetto.) After that we went to see a Polish hospital that the German Army had taken over. Many policemen, Gestapo agents and curious Poles stood around it. Ambulances were constantly arriving with wounded soldiers. In the evening, my father explained that this meant the Red Army was still fighting and the Germans were incurring many losses.

11.4 – Good News

In December, as usual by now when the weather grew ever colder, there wasn't enough coal for heat, very little gas was allowed through, and the ghetto had no electricity from 3PM-9PM every day. Suddenly, one day, Mr. Romek burst through our door: "The Japanese attacked America, America declared war on Japan, and a general draft was declared in the United States!"

Dad sat down with his friend, spread a map out on the table, and studied it in the light of a carbide lamp, which was as strong as an electric bulb. Mr. Romek claimed that according to Radio London, the Germans were stuck fast in the snow around Moscow and there were fewer battles, but there was a feeling that the Soviets were planning something.

Just a few days later, on a Sunday morning, Mr. Romek again made a sudden appearance, with more sensational news: "Hitler has declared war on the United States, and the Red Army yesterday went on a broad counter-offensive with dozens of divisions and thousands of tanks brought from their Eastern Front opposite Japan." Mr. Romek was very excited: "This is the first time since Hitler came to power that he has made a fatal mistake in his calculations," he said. When we heard his words, we all sat at the table, rejoicing as if the Messiah had just arrived. We didn't understand how far away our liberation really was. The next day, the whole ghetto was abuzz with the news from the front.

11.5 – The Ghetto Absorbs Refugees and Gets More Crowded

That same December, the Germans started destroying the Jewish villages in the district and expelling the people to Krakow's ghetto. Thousands of refugees arrived, and three to four families were packed into each apartment. We took in two families with a total of six people: A couple with two children, and a woman with a young girl. They got our children's room, and we moved into the guest room. At first, our "tenants" slept on the floor, but several days later they managed to get two triple-tier bunk beds. The man was a carpenter and he put the beds together. I also helped him find other old furniture. The two families were very young, in their twenties, and their children were 3-5 years old. Both families were extremely poor and we had to support them. My feeling was that my parents did so very willingly. We gave them money to buy food that was sold cheaply in exchange for ration stamps. The man would go around from house to house offering to do work for people, and would earn a few zloty a day. Several times a week he would work the night shift at one of the bakeries and earn a loaf of bread.

Mom always had a two pots cooking on her stove: one with soup and the other with potatoes and cabbage. Sometimes there were even a few pieces of meat. So our tenants would always get at least one warm meal a day and didn't go hungry. Mom also let them use our toilet and shower twice a day for about an hour, and the rest of the time they either used the chamber pots in their room or went to the outhouse in the yard. Both families gratefully and lovingly accepted these arrangements. The women were always going to Mom and asking her to let them help with the housework.

We gradually learned to live with our new tenants. Gizia liked playing with their young children, and my little sister enjoyed her new playmates. We children also basically took our young guests under our wing, even giving them some of our toys. These families were quite lucky, as most of the new refugees lived in unbelievably crowded conditions – up to 30 people per apartment. Some even lived in the ruins and in attics, while others couldn't find any kind of roof for their heads at all and lived on the streets.

After these refugees arrived in the ghetto, we saw the same kind of horrific scenes that have been shown of the Warsaw Ghetto: Starving people running around the streets dressed in rags, with many of them falling and simply dying; it was very doubtful if they got any kind of medical help at all. The Jewish mutual aid societies did not know how to deal with these miserable people, and gravediggers were kept busy collecting dead bodies in wagons.

These village Jews[9] were generally much more modest than the city-folk, used to living in their little towns and not leaving them too often. They were also mostly very religious, and their way of life hadn't changed essentially for hundreds of years. They could not

---

9   *About 1 million out of the 3.5 million Jews lived in the big cities. The rest lived in thousands of small towns and villages.* (More about the village Jews see Chapter 24, side note 8)

get used to city life, spoke Yiddish and barely understood Polish. However, the two specific families that we had taken in were educated and of a higher class; one of the mothers was a teacher.

Several weeks after the refugees' arrival, the Germans used the excuse of the overcrowding to order the expulsion of 2,000 Jews who had no work permits. Overnight, the Jewish Police invaded the ghetto and collected about that number of refugees, old and young alike, and herded them in the morning to the Plaszow train station. They gave them a little bread and water and pushed as many as they could into each of the boxcars. People who saw these poor Jews walking to their deportation said that the sight was the most horrific thing imaginable. The train went east for about 10 hours, until it reached the Lublin region. In some completely inhospitable place, they stopped the train, threw the Jews out and told them to go find a place to live.

A good number of these poor people died on the journey itself, and many of those who were left died from cold and hunger, or were robbed and then murdered by the farmers in the area. Only a few found refuge in villages or towns. A tiny number somehow managed to find their way back to our ghetto; it was from them that we got news of the tragedy that befell all the others. Although the mass annihilation of Jews had not yet begun, this terribly cruel expulsion did not bode well for the rest of the ghetto's inhabitants.

Fortunately, all our relatives, as well as our tenants, survived this expulsion. The winter grew colder, with subzero temperatures and light snow flurries, although it was also frequently sunny. Our studies at teachers' houses ceased due to the overcrowding, as mentioned above, though once or twice a day one would come to our home to teach my sister and me. Sometimes another child or two would join us.

11.6 – Snow Sports

Terrible tragedies are quickly forgotten. The expulsion "cleaned out" the streets of the poor refugees, and soon heavy snow covered every level space in the ghetto. It seemed as if the whole Krakow Ghetto turned into a winter wonderland, with crowds of children playing games in the snow from morning to night. My friends, sister and I usually went to Krzemionki Hill, to ski or speed down its sides on a sled. There was one particularly long ski run around 200 meters long, and many other routes that were shorter. These sports were a source of great joy for hundreds of kids and grownups alike. Weather permitting, my mother would go with us every day to have some fun. We had a grand sled, and we'd plunk Sarenka down on it and off we'd go to Krzemionki. Every few minutes there would be a small skiing accident, and we'd hear screams and laughter. Someone coming from the outside world would never have believed that he was in a Jewish ghetto – and this was going on after the mass annihilation had already begun. My friend Jezyk was an artist on skates, and I learned a lot from him.

It is worth noting that I don't remember a single time the Germans ever bothered us during our fun in the snow, even though anyone coming into the ghetto could see us. Sledding wasn't limited to Krzemionki Hill, either. All over the ghetto streets – especially the steep ones leading down from Renkavki Street – children were sliding along using all kinds of skis, skates and sleds, and the SS and Gestapo saw them when they came to work in the building of the Jewish Police.

Once, when I was sledding on Krzemionki with two friends, I was sitting in front and steering. Very close to the end of our run, there was a building that stuck out part-way into our route, so a hard right turn had to be made to get around it. That day, I lost control of the sled and crashed into the building, with my left leg taking the brunt of it. I was in extreme pain (though I never cried; I only screamed).

They carried me on the sled straight to the hospital near our house, and got my mother. They had already given me an injection and prepared me for an x-ray before she got there. When she came, I asked her to tell my father that I had been strong and hadn't cried... The x-ray and other tests showed that the leg wasn't broken; I'd only torn a few tendons. But I still had to stay at home for weeks with a cast on the leg, and the snow had started melting by the time I started hobbling around with a cane. These weeks of "house arrest" weren't boring, however, since many friends and relatives came to visit and indulge me. I also spent hours by the window looking at ships passing by on the Vistula River. I could even see what they were carrying and the faces and uniforms of the sailors, because I had my small pair of binoculars. I could always tell the difference between cargo ships, passenger ships, and fancy boats where parties were held.

The news from the Eastern front cheered me up, too. From Mr. Romek's conversations with my father, I learned about the rout of the Germans near Moscow, and their hundreds-of-kilometers-long retreat. They left behind the heavy equipment of dozens of divisions and tens of thousands of dead and captured soldiers. As Hitler had promised, Germans marched through Moscow – but they were all prisoners-of-war... Hitler fired General Guderian, one of his best generals, who had conquered both Poland and France for him.

11.7 – Giving Up Children for Adoption

The lovely spring weather in 1942 still couldn't overcome the pessimistic feelings, tension and fear that prevailed in the ghetto. Stubborn rumors persisted of the murder of Jews in eastern Poland and the occupied areas of the Soviet Union. Many Jews escaped the ghetto, including our tenant with the young daughter; she went to hide with Christians in the city. Aunt Hela did, in fact, leave with her redhead daughter, Eva, as she said she would, to live under borrowed identities in another town. Later, my favorite cousin, Jurek, who was a few years older than me, also went into hiding on a farm. Big David and his family moved outside the ghetto due to the foreign citizenship he had managed to obtain thanks to relatives in the United States.

Mom and Dad would often close the door to their bedroom to confer in whispers. We knew that they were weighing whether to give us up for adoption to Christians in the city or perhaps to farmers out in the country. I decided with my sister that we would only agree if they didn't separate us. Meanwhile, our other tenants decided to give their four-year-old girl to a Christian family, and I was witness to the most amazing and hallucinatory sight imaginable: This little girl sat and learned all the Catholic prayers and practiced her new identity with a seriousness and diligence that an adult would be hard-put to match. For hours, she studied the prayers and stories about Jesus and the Holy Mary that every Christian girl would ordinarily know. She came to us all the time, asking us to test her: "What's your name? Who are your parents? Who are your aunts, your grandparents?" And she would answer each question with almost religious devotion. It was simultaneously pathetic, funny, and moved one to tears. I can't explain how this little girl had internalized the crucial need to learn these facts by heart, how she raised no objections, and how she was convinced to leave her parents when the time came.

What happened when the Christian woman came to our house to collect this girl was most astonishing of all: My mother, our tenant and her daughter (now called "Cudna" [Beautiful]) sat at the table with this woman and some food was served. The little girl sat there without saying a word. At some point, the mother turned to her daughter, pointed to the Christian lady and said, "This person will now be your mother." The girl got up, went over to the lady, and said: "Now you are my mother, may Lord Jesus bless you." She crossed herself, hugged her new mother and returned to her seat. A little while later, the Christian woman got up and took the girl by the hand to go. The girl said to her mother, "Come and visit me and bring me a present, and may the Holy Mother protect you." And without a hug or any parting words, they left. My mother hugged the girl's mother and both of them started to cry. They went into their bedroom, where my father hugged the girl's father, who stood there with tears in his eyes. I didn't find this whole incident strange or special in the slightest when it occurred, yet it was engraved in my mind in every detail. Only many years later, when I had young children myself, did I remember it and understand the depth of the tragedy that had taken place that day.

11.8 – Surprising Guests

We celebrated Passover in 1942 in a very modest way, only inviting Grandma and Grandpa, Aunt Fela and her children, and Aunt Genia. We also invited our tenants for the *seder*, and it turned out that the father was religious. He knew how to sing all kinds of Jewish holiday songs, and how to tell the Passover stories to children. But it was a very sad *seder*, because even though for some reason nobody worried about Germans invading the ghetto, concern about our future hung like a dark cloud over our heads.

A few days after the holiday, we had some surprise guests: Fraulein Gerta, our erstwhile tenant from our Sarego apartment, and her boyfriend (or perhaps by now he was her husband). Dad had connections to them through his business outside the ghetto, and they had set up this visit with him in advance. He came home earlier than usual and waited at the ghetto gate to greet them. They came in a car with a driver, and he got in with them. We children waited for them on the corner of Wegierska Street, and when they came we ran behind them for a few dozen meters until the chauffeur parked the car near the ghetto wall next to our house. While he stayed behind in the car, we led our guests through the ruins to get to our building's back entrance. On the way, of course, we passed the people who lived in all kinds of alcoves in the half-destroyed houses. I saw from the look on our guests' faces that this sight had made a terrible impression on them, as did our new apartment.

This meeting wasn't a normal, happy one of having guests come over. Mom hugged Gerta without saying a word. They had brought little presents for the children, and cologne and sausages for Dad. They were in civilian clothes, but I noticed what I'd seen before – that both wore the Nazi party pin on their clothing. After just a little small talk, they came right to the point. I felt that they had already spoken with Dad before coming, and had arrived to speak with Mom and explain to her the seriousness of the situation. Gerta's friend was a major in some kind of Intelligence, and was about to be drafted into the Intelligence unit of the regular army. It could be assumed that they knew a lot about the annihilation of the Jews and what was to be expected. I understood from what they said that we had to escape from the ghetto. Dad obviously trusted them completely, and they spoke freely.

"The best solution is to get foreign citizenship," they said, "even of countries that are allied with the Germans, like Hungary, Bulgaria, Slovakia, Spain and Portugal. You could get it either through relatives who live there or by buying it from their diplomatic embassies via middlemen. The latter is extremely problematic because most of the papers they sell are fakes. It wouldn't be enough that the citizenship was given or approved by the embassy in Krakow, either. It has to be approved by the immigration authorities in the foreign country itself. And the German Foreign Office has ways to check on the authenticity of anyone's documents."

Fraulein Gerta said that they could help us check the authenticity of documents we got before we brought them to the German authorities. She added that we had to hurry, because her friend was going to the army in just a few more weeks. It was also possible that she'd be transferred out of Krakow. She explained that they could also help us get to whatever country gave us citizenship. In their opinion, hiding

with Christians or buying another identity were both very dangerous options – but still preferable to staying in the ghetto. They could
also help us move even if we picked either of the latter solutions.
They also thought that giving the children to Christians was a good
idea, and could help by checking if the adoption was known to the
Gestapo... They said that the Gestapo was collecting information on
all the Jews who were escaping the ghetto, though they weren't doing
anything about it... yet.

In the middle of the conversation, Mom told my sister and me to
take some food and drink to the driver in the car, and to stay outside
to play. We went unwillingly to perform this task, because we very
much wanted to stay and hear more. When we gave the driver this
"*mishloach manot*" (packages of goodies given to friends on the holiday of Purim), he was very surprised and happy. It turned out that he
knew Polish, so we stayed and talked to him.

After our guests left, our parents whispered together a lot but did
not say a word to us about any plans that may have been made.

11.9 – Food Smuggling in the Ghetto

It was clear that the food supply was shrinking in the ghetto. Prices
soared, and the amount one got from the ration stamps – which
wasn't much to begin with – kept getting smaller. Extra food had to
be bought on the free market, and inside the ghetto the prices were
much higher than on the other side of the wall. The main sources of
food in this market were Jews coming back from their jobs outside
the ghetto, Poles who would manage to get into the ghetto by using various excuses, and children who would sneak out and bring in
food. The Germans didn't fight this market, and only cracked down
on the smuggling of pork.

Some time after my leg healed, I met Maciek, our former gang
leader. This tall and powerful boy suggested that I join a group that
smuggled food into the ghetto. He wanted me to come with my sister,

and it seemed to me that he was more interested in her than he was in me... I met the group, though, and found out that the main obstacle in this smuggling "business" were the gangs of Polish kids who tried to rob us of our money. Therefore, everyone had to practice fighting, and primarily – how to pull knives on others quickly and cleanly.

I was no stranger to fights between children, but I didn't like using knives. I was afraid of them. However, it turned out that the aim was just to threaten others with them but not actually get to the point of stabbing and hurting people, because then the police could very well intervene and that wouldn't be to our advantage. My sister refused to join, but I came and brought my friend Jezyk as well. We mainly practiced how to draw out the knives fast, and if it came to a fight, how to scratch – but not actually hurt – the other. The most important thing was to make our opponents fear us. We all had to obtain at least three switchblades. Maciek was a typical Polish kid and didn't know any German; it could be that he wanted me in his group because I spoke German well.

When it came time to tell all to my parents, I was greatly surprised when they didn't exhibit much opposition and Dad gave me money for my first purchase. And that's how I became a professional smuggler... It was no problem at all to either leave or return to the ghetto. We'd go out one by one and meet at a prearranged spot. We didn't look any different than the groups of Polish children on the street. The goal was to get to one of the many markets not far from the ghetto and make our purchases there. We bought simple things, like potatoes and other vegetables, and some "extras," like sausages, sugar, butter and chicken. Each kid bought food for himself, but there was also a joint kitty that Maciek was in charge of. We carried the food in knapsacks and bags.

The first few times, nothing went wrong. Then one day, a gang of five Polish kids showed up (there were seven of us). We didn't try to escape or get away; we kept walking, right up to them. I was terribly afraid, but covered it up and nobody saw my fear. When only a few meters separated us, apparently their leader said, "We know you're Jews, give us money and we'll let you go." Maciek answered, "If you want money, you'll have to fight us for it, and we'll see who lays out whom." The Pole shot back, "We'll beat you guys with our pinkys." Maciek replied, "We'll let you use all your fingers, and only five of us will fight you." He turned to Jezyk and me and told us to stand on the side and not intervene. Then he turned to the Poles again and said, "No knives, no hitting the head or stomach, the winner is the one who gets the other guy down first." Jezyk and I got out of the way – and now I can dare reveal that I was very happy to be left out of that brawl.

It quickly became apparent that our group was united and well trained, and had gone through many similar situations before. Maciek gave the order: "Come on, let's go," and within three minutes, all the Polish kids were lying on their backs, with my friends on top of them. The Poles were in shock. One mumbled, "These Jew-boys, these Jew-boys." Maciek got up and told them, "You fought bravely and lost honorably. You wanted money and despite being defeated you'll get some – but you'll have to earn it." We gave them a list of things that we wanted, and told them they'd get one zloty for every 10 zloty worth of food they bought for us. In two days' time, we would meet again at a certain spot. "For today, though," Maciek continued, "you'll act as our bodyguards and we'll pay you two zloty each" (about the price of an ice-cream). We went with them to the market and bought what we needed. I got sugar, butter and sausage, as well as a tiny doll for Sarenka and a bar of chocolate for Gizia, which cost about 10 zloty. I also got perfume for my mother. We parted from our new "friends" and went back to the ghetto.

Through my experiences smuggling food I came to recognize the power and importance of money. I had almost always gotten whatever amount I wanted from my parents, though of course that wasn't much, due to the modest values they had inculcated in me. At some point during the summer of 1941 I started putting money into some savings accounts, and by spring of 1942 I had about 500 zloty. This was a large amount of money, even by adult standards. After joining the smugglers, I even went into business, meaning that I would sell in the ghetto some of what I brought in. I didn't smuggle simple foods, focusing instead on fancier items like butter and sausage, on which I could make a larger profit. I ran my business with two friends: my loyal Jezyk and another older, bigger boy. One had to work in a group, because even in the ghetto there was a danger of being robbed. I would contribute most of the funding for the business, but didn't do the actual selling. That we left to a middleman who also made a bit of money from these transactions. In the beginning, neither my parents nor my sister had any inkling of my business deals...

The guard around our ghetto was very lax, and we also knew of many passageways dug out under its walls. There were also many houses like ours, with parts of them actually outside the ghetto, which could be used to enter and leave. In general, we would go out one by one so as not to attract attention. Once, when we had finished our shopping along the Vistula and were about to scatter to return to the ghetto, we were stopped by two "black" Polish Policeman who guarded the ghetto. These were Poles who were hated even by their own countrymen and were considered traitors. They carried rifles, and we knew that they could shoot Jews without the need to justify it to anyone.

They demanded our money and all our high quality goods. We claimed that we had no money since we'd spent it all in the market. Suddenly, three young German soldiers appeared; I think they were either pilots or paratroopers. They looked like they were on leave and were very jolly. When they came upon us they asked what was going on. The policemen didn't know German, and I had a chance to put my language skills to good use. I did have the problem of what to tell them, and decided to simply tell the whole truth. I explained that we were Jews from the ghetto, the ghetto was starving, and we didn't have what to eat so we would buy food on the outside and then bring it in. I told them that the policemen wanted to rob us. They asked us if we were allowed to leave the ghetto, and I said that children were allowed, and that's why we were the ones bringing in the food.

All this time, the Polish policemen were looking at me angrily. The Germans talked among themselves, and after a short discussion they told the Poles to let us go. Since the Poles didn't understand them, the soldiers showed them what they wanted them to do with hand motions. At this point, another Polish policeman joined them, and a whole argument ensued using sign language. I became the translator and negotiator, and of course used my advantage wisely, saying really anything that came into my head. For example, when the police said they had orders to confiscate smuggled food, I "translated" that soldiers had no right to get involved with the job of the Polish police... It came to the point where the Germans started to threaten the Poles with their weapons, and while the Poles had rifles, the Germans had sub-machine guns. Finally, the Poles gave up and I thanked the Germans very politely. We quickly gathered up our packages and went on our way. The soldiers didn't leave until we had gotten far away. One of the policemen shouted after us that they would settle their account with us one day. After that, we were very careful not to bump into any Polish policemen...

11.10 – Terrible Rumors

May, 1942. The weather was again wonderful, with the smell of flowers in bloom and the sound of birds chirping. But there was no happiness in the ghetto – not even among the children. There was no getting away from the persistent rumors of Jews being murdered in the east. A story made the rounds about a Jew who had supposedly come to the ghetto and told of a small town in eastern Poland in which about a thousand Jews lived in relative quiet. There was no ghetto there and the Jews lived normally, among the Christians. And then, this past Passover, on the *seder* night, huge numbers of Gestapo, SS and other police forces came in, ordered all the Jews to gather in the town square, and held them there until morning. During the night they took about a hundred Jewish men into the nearby forest and forced them to dig long, deep trenches. In the morning, they marched the Jews to that spot, and in groups of about 50, they stood them at the edges of the trenches and opened fire, killing everyone – men, women and children.

According to the story, the person who had come to our ghetto was one of the men who had been ordered to dig the graves, and then had to cover them up again after the mass murder was complete. He found his wife and children among the dead, and then managed to escape, killing a German on the way. He dressed in the soldier's uniform and took all his documents, and in that way managed to procure a false identity. He decided to go from city to city and from town to town to tell others what he had seen, and to kill Germans. They said that he looked pretty crazy, coming all dressed up as an SS man.

Guests who came to our home could speak of nothing else. Not one person had met him themselves; they all said they'd heard it from someone else. People began suspecting that this was a Gestapo provocation, meant to frighten us. It wasn't known if this man was still in the ghetto. A rumor floated around that the Gestapo was looking for him. Finally, several people said that they had actually spoken to this man, and the story became more credible.

Many other stories of atrocities made the rounds of the ghetto at this time. In the middle of May, there was rumor of another expulsion from the ghetto. This time it wouldn't be "wysiedlenie," that is, telling the Jews to leave and find another place to live like they did in 1940, but "przesiedlenie": It would be a transfer to a place that the

Germans would make sure to prepare ahead of time.

My mother and older sister had both started jobs in the beginning of May. They worked in the Madritch factory, making German uniforms. My parents had inflated our ages by two or three years on our papers, so officially Gizia was already 15 and I was 12 or 13. Since she was very tall, with a little bit of makeup Gizia certainly looked her new age. But even with "alterations" I couldn't go out to work. Mom and Gizia got beautiful documents attesting to their status as workers in a factory vital to the German war effort. A big "W" was stamped in it, standing for "Wermacht," the regular army. It should be noted that in this factory, named for its owner, the Jews were treated fairly, with the manager making sure to bring his laborers two meals a day. The factory was located on the border of the ghetto. Since the "womenfolk" were now working, things changed at home, with our tenant running the household and taking care of my little sister.

Shortly after Passover, my grandfather died after a short illness. My mother and her relatives were given permission to have a funeral and take the body to be buried in a cemetery outside the ghetto walls. I didn't go; I don't know if they buried him alone or in a mass grave. Of his five children, only my mother and Aunt Fela accompanied him on his final journey. He died in his own bed, with his whole family at his side, and didn't have to go through the torture and suffering of a horrible death.

CHAPTER 12

Deportation, June 1942

Towards the end of May, the German authorities ordered all the Jews to come to the Jewish Mutual Aid offices in order to get permission to stay in the ghetto. There was a huge hall in this office building, with dozens of tables. Each one was manned by someone from the German Labor office and an SS man. A long line of people snaked around the room. One by one, Jews went to a free table, and the two Germans would decide on the spot if they would give him the cherished papers. Having documentation and proofs that one was vital to the German war effort was not necessarily enough to get the authorization. The sum of money one attached to the papers played a large role in the decision. If permission was granted, it included the entire family; at this stage they weren't separating close relatives. What was absurd was that if someone was refused at one table, he could go back to the line and try again at a different one.... However, after three days they simply stopped giving out the new certificates and ordered everyone who hadn't received permission to stay, to report to Zgody Square. From there they would be taken by train to a new place to live. It was announced that every person could take up to 20 kilograms of personal belongings on the train.

This time, the Germans spread the word that the Jews would be taken to new settlements they were establishing in the Ukraine, and that they would work there in farming and manufacturing. SS men,

Gestapo agents, and primarily Germans who presented themselves as railway workers, came into the ghetto and spoke of how they had seen the new settlements with their own eyes. There were hospitals, movie theaters, and wooden houses with wood-burning stoves, with a lot of brush around to burn. In short, conditions were good, and more than anything else there was a lot of good food, like milk and cheeses – things we hadn't seen in the ghetto for a very long time. They announced that families could travel together, that children and the aged were welcome. Professionals like carpenters, blacksmiths and in general anyone who worked with metal were greatly desired and would get improved living conditions.

To the best of my knowledge, before this deportation, the people tended to believe – or perhaps it's more correct to say that they wanted to believe – what the Germans said. Our tenant decided to go with his wife and son, though I remember my mother trying to convince them to try and get permission to stay.

About a week before the "Action", a German named Neumann came to visit us. It was in the evening, and I saw that my father had been expecting him. I don't know who he was, but Dad had had some kind of connection to him from almost the beginning of the Occupation and he had helped us all along very loyally. Dad would meet him at his business. To me, he seemed to be a very restrained man, speaking briefly and to the point, never chitchatting politely. Neumann brought my father special certificates allowing my grandmother, Aunt Fela and Little David's family to stay in the ghetto. Despite his not saying much, he did keep repeating and stressing one thing, which I remember very well: "Under no circumstances should you be tempted to go, and don't let anyone else in your family go, either." He gave no reason for what he said. Before he left, he explained to my father how he could be reached in case of emergency.

***

Personal Comment

In my few conversations about the Holocaust with my aunt, Gina Milgrom, she told me among other things that this German fellow, Neumann, indeed helped the family a lot, totally altruistically. Gina survived the war much like me, but since she was 17 when it began, she of course knew and understood everything that happened a lot better than I did. I feel a deep sense of having missed out in that I hadn't been smart enough to write my memoir together with her before she died.

***

According to German calculations, at least 6,000 Jews were supposed to report to Zgody Square on June first. However, only about 2,000 came. The Germans went wild and burned with rage, as this spoiled their plan. The trains that had been prepared left empty, and the local SS and Gestapo authority was strongly rebuked by High Command. The tension in the ghetto went sky-high that very night, as everyone knew the Germans weren't pleased. The next morning, the Germans brought in hundreds of reinforcements to the police and ordered a house-to-house search. Anyone who didn't have the proper papers would be brought to the square.

If the first deportation took place in comparable quiet, without violence on the part of the Germans, this second round brought in an SS unit that was extremely cruel and aggressive. Mercilessly, they beat people as they walked to the trains as well as in the square itself. Many were injured and killed. There was torture just for torture's sake, and they robbed the Jews as they went, so many were forced onto the trains without even the little they had been allowed to take.

From June 2nd and on, it was impossible to go outside without risking arrest and deportation, even if you had all the proper authorizations – and that's how the worst happened to us: Grandma, Aunt

Fela and her two young children, Little David and his wife, and Dad's sister Genia were caught and sent away. This apparently happened on the very first night of the second round of deportations. We only found out about it a day or two later. Mom shut herself up in her room and couldn't stop crying. Dad took a risk and left the ghetto to find help. I know that he managed to call Neumann, who came to the ghetto and met Dad. But the trains had already left and there was nothing anyone could do. My father was terribly affected; according to what he said to my mother, I understood that he blamed himself. Actually, as usually happened in such situations, both my parents started blaming themselves: Why did we leave Grandma and the aunts alone, why didn't we bring them into our house, why didn't we make sure that they hid? Aunt Genia had had everything ready and was about to leave for her hiding place on the Christian side... After this "Action", Dad changed greatly. He became introverted, distant and sad.

Out of all the relatives who had come to the ghetto, the only ones left at this point were Dad's cousins, Little David's children (Gina, who was 20, and the twins, Morris and Ziggy, who were 16). As close as we had been before, after their parents were taken, Dad treated them as if they were his own children and they were always over our house.

I, too, didn't leave the house almost at all during this second wave of deportations, so I didn't see myself what happened in the square. On the third day, I went with my sister just a few dozen meters away, to the small hospital nearby, and saw the most terrible thing happen: Two trucks came and they loaded all the patients inside. It was one of the most awful sights I had seen until then. Some of the patients were brought down on stretchers and literally thrown into the trucks. I asked Dad how it was possible that they were grabbing sick and crippled people from their beds to send them to work in the Ukraine?! It didn't take long for me to realize that the Germans were liars and that these deportations were taking people to their deaths.

When the "Deportion" was over, the Germans took their forces out of the ghetto and the tight guard was relaxed back to its usual state. We only saw pairs of Polish police patrolling from our window that overlooked the Vistula. Since our remaining tenants had been deported, we had our apartment to ourselves again, and we put everything back the way it used to be.

In fact, since almost half the inhabitants were now gone, everyone's living conditions improved. Most of those taken had been the poor refugees who had been brought to the ghetto in the beginning of the year. They had had nothing, and caring for them had strained the aid organizations to the breaking point. Now that they had been deported, one didn't see ragged people in the streets begging or dying from hunger anymore and there was enough aid to go around.

***

Side Note 9: Eye-Witness Account

As I was not an eye witness to this deportation, I would like to quote from Tadeusz Pankiewicz's book, A "Pharmacy in the Krakow Ghetto". (He witnessed all the deportations from his small business in Zgody Square.) All the following passages from his memoir are my free translations from the Polish edition: see Chapter 24, side note 9

***

The situation had seemingly gone back to normal. The Germans stopped coming in very often, and my parents and sister went to work every day. They hired a Jewish woman to come do the housework and take care of Sarenka. For all intents and purposes, I was completely free all day long. I played a lot with Sarenka, and she became extremely attached to me.

There was one fundamental change in the ghetto that affected me: Most of the friends of my parents, Gizia and I had were gone. Most of the kids with whom I smuggled food had been deported, although not Jezyk. My sister's best friend, Dora, whom she had known since childhood, had also been sent to the East. Gizia sobbed when she told me this. I had loved Dora dearly, and though I didn't cry myself, Gizia saw how much this news hurt me.

There was one main topic of conversation everywhere one went in the ghetto: What was happening to those who had been deported, what was the truth in those terrible rumors, what would be with us and what could be done in order to survive. Rumors abounded of people who had received letters from the deportees. "*Machers*" (people with influence) appeared who would send a letter with Germans who were ostensibly going to the place where the families had been deported, and bring a letter back from them – for a price.

But I had no doubt that the people were already dead. It was also clear to me that we had to find a way to try and save ourselves, and I even discussed this with my father. That was another big change: We started talking freely among ourselves about our situation; everyone spoke to everyone now.

12.1 – Parting from Sarenka

One evening after putting Sarenka to bed, our parents told us that they intended to give Sarenka to Uncle David, who had Nicaraguan citizenship and lived outside the ghetto. They would officially adopt her and register her as their daughter. Our parents swore us to secrecy about this plan.

My relationship with my older sister had changed a great deal since the "Action of Deportation". Until then we basically only played and learned together. Afterward, I started talking to her about "grownup" topics. I found out that she was well aware of the situation and understood it. She opposed giving Sarenka to Uncle David. She maintained that she wouldn't be able to survive without her, she'd die of longing. I related to the problem in a more practical way. I understood that she would be a lot safer at Uncle David's. Our parents also explained that it would be easier to carry out our survival plans without her.

And so, several weeks after the "Action", my cousin Genia, Uncle David's daughter, came to visit. She was 21 at the time. As a "foreigner" she didn't have to wear the Jewish star on her arm. We all sat down, and Genia told us how they were managing among the Christian population. After a while, she turned to Sarenka, told her that she'd bought her gifts, and invited her to the other room so they could open them together. Sarenka knew Genia and her family well, and we hadn't prepared her for her new identity, as most others did with their children. A short time later, Genia and Sarenka came back to the room, with Sarenka completely involved in her new things. Mom then took her on her knee, and told her in a matter of fact tone of voice, as if by the way, that she was going to go now with Aunt Genia and play in their house with her cousin Lusia. At this time, Lusia was about 15, and loved little children in general and Sarenka in particular. Sarenka was also very attached to her.

A few minutes later, Mom took Sarenka into their bedroom to dress her. This process took a long time and Genia started peeping at her watch. Dad then stepped into the bedroom, and several minutes later they all came out. Sarenka was dressed like a doll, happy and beaming. I looked at her, and then she ran to me, hugged me on my leg and asked if I'd come visit her. I was very sad that she was leaving and really wanted to cry, but of course I promised to come and bring her presents. After that, Gizia went over to her, picked her up and they hugged for a very long time. It wasn't a sad or dramatic scene, perhaps because Sarenka was happy, or maybe because we didn't really understand the significance of this parting. At this point, Mom brought out a little suitcase that she had packed and a number of bags.

The moment of parting came. Dad looked in Mom's direction; apparently she was supposed to give some kind of sign. He understood that she wasn't capable of doing it, so he said to Sarenka, "Now it's time to go play at Aunt Genia's house." To everyone's surprise, Sarenka accepted this willingly and quietly. We all left the house, and Dad started off first with Genia and Sarenka. The rest of us followed at a distance. They got to the main gate and went into Podgorski Square (Dad had a permanent permit allowing him to leave the ghetto). They walked over to where the carriages always waited, and Genia and Sarenka got into one and left. Dad returned to the ghetto.

I don't know how Uncle David managed to arrange the official adoption, but she joined his family perfectly legally and became a South American citizen. There was no need to hide her. Dad kept in close touch with Uncle David, who told him that Sarenka had adjusted very quickly to her new family, the two sisters (especially Lusia) were taking very good care of her, and she was very happy.

Although I saw my cousin Genia later on, as I shall explain, I never saw my little sister again. Uncle David's family lived in Krakow until 1944, when they were deported to Bergen Belsen in Germany. That camp was where the Germans collected all civilians with foreign passports. They lived there until the beginning of 1945. My knowledge of what happened to my sister and my uncle's family came from two families who were in Bergen Belsen with them and survived the war. They told me that several weeks before the war ended, the Germans took 50 families from the camp and murdered them – and my family was in this group. Just a few weeks before they would have been free, the Germans killed my sweet little sister, only seven years old; and my cousins Lusia (17) and Genia (23). I never managed to learn how they were killed or why specifically this group was killed (most of those holding foreign citizenship who were in Bergen Belsen survived). I try to imagine how my sister looked at age seven, how they killed her, if she cried, if she suffered, if there was someone to hug her as they murdered her... To this day I cannot imagine how they could kill my little seven-year-old sister, and another million and a half children. How could such a thing happen??

After Sarenka left, we didn't speak much about it, but this parting constantly lay on our hearts and at the tip of our tongues. I was left alone in the house with the nanny and became proficient in taking care of myself and the house. I was in charge of a lot of things, like shopping, making lunches for those going to work, and warming up the food for my mother's and sister's supper. The factory in which they worked was only a few minutes' walk from the house and they always returned exactly at 5:10. I would dress up as a funny-looking waiter, insist that they sit down, then serve them the meal. Dad would usually return later, and I would do the same for him. While he ate, I'd talk with him.

Following the June "Action", my parents changed tremendously. As said above, my father didn't really recover, continually blaming himself because many family members had been deported. However, after a few days of crying, my mother rallied – but not only that. Her whole character and behavior changed. She began wearing simple work clothes, almost never wore makeup, became very energetic, lost a lot of weight and started taking her place as head of the household. Until the deportation, my father had been the leader and God in the family, and everything was done as he wished. When he spoke, everyone was silent. Now, Mom took charge and Dad humbly accepted it.

My relationship with Dad had changed as well. More and more, he treated me as an equal in our conversations. But when I asked him why weren't doing anything to try and escape and hide, he would only say that he and Mom were working on it and would speak to us about it soon. Gizia also told me that they were examining the possibility of living under false identities in a town where the Germans had little control and the true power lay with the local Resistance, who'd execute anyone who collaborated with the enemy. Unlike others, we had no relatives in countries to which one could get a visa.

I drew escape routes on a map to Switzerland, Romania and Slovakia, marking them with a red pencil. I even calculated how much time it would take us if we went on foot, rode in a wagon, or in a car. I had many, similar fantasies. What is interesting is that there were people who actually fulfilled these kinds of fantasies and survived…

A short time after the "Action", the Germans reduced the ghetto's size by cutting off two of the three main streets – Limanowski and Renkavki – though some houses on the Vistula side of Limanowski were still left within the ghetto borders. Since the Germans blocked off the rest of the street, people in these buildings had to enter through the back yards, as we did in our building. One of the saddest results was that our wonderful playground, Krzemionki Hill, was cut off from the ghetto. Only our street, Juzefinska, a few small side streets, and Zgody Square were all that was left. However, we got no new boarders as a result of this, and until the ghetto was liquidated we had our whole apartment to ourselves.

There was one apartment on the ground floor in which two families lived. They shared a wall with the empty space that used to be the garage. What they did was make an opening to that empty space and put up another wall about ten meters in so that anyone looking into the former garage would just see the four walls of an empty (smaller) room. The entrance from their apartment to that secret room was hidden by a closet. We were silent partners in this hideout, buying food and other necessities for survival to store there. The room also had furniture, beds, kitchen things and – very importantly – ventilation. We could hide there in case of another "Action". (I have to say that I, too, knew of many hiding places among the ruined buildings in "children's country.") There was one other advantage to our building: It wasn't easy to get into it, since one had to climb over and around all those smelly and filthy semi-destroyed buildings to get in through the rear entrance. I don't have proof that this was why the SS in their sparkling and polished uniforms didn't reach us, but the fact is that out of all the searches and invasions of the ghetto, they only came to us twice.

For some reason, in the June "Action" the Germans did not deport children without their parents. They took whole families, and older adults without children, but didn't touch the orphanage, for example, which had over 100 children. As a result, many children were left in the ghetto. Since they didn't go to work, every day the streets were filled with children running around playing happily. However, after June the Germans clamped down outside the ghetto and it was dangerous to leave without the proper papers. They would arrest any Jew who didn't have permission to be on the Christian side – including children, who would then simply disappear. I therefore did not venture outside the ghetto walls again and saw no more movies… My smuggling days were over as well…

The Germans also started getting stricter with Poles who were found to be hiding Jews. They declared that hiding a Jew was punishable by death, and it was no idle threat. Meanwhile, the Jews were trying to escape in ever greater numbers, although the Germans tried to prevent it. Therefore, whenever they caught people in hiding or with false papers, they would first bring them to the ghetto jail, so the rest of the Jews would "see and be afraid." Then they would be executed…

A story made the rounds of a Jewish girl who had been caught while hiding with Christians. The Germans executed the Poles but returned the girl to the ghetto. This was supposed to be proof that the Germans don't kill children. Moreover, if they wanted to kill Jews, and the deportation was to death, why didn't they deport all the orphans in the orphanages? There were many stories like that, since the Jews kept searching for hope and comfort.

The card games began again in our home. Out of the original group, Mr. Rapaport had left thanks to an American visa, and Mr. Bernstein had been deported with his family. New people took their places: Dr. Karol and a couple whose name I have forgotten. As I had done before, I sat at my little table and eavesdropped on their conversations. I learned that our small forum was divided in their opinions regarding the deportees' fate. Most didn't believe that the Germans would dare kill thousands of Jews; after all, all the foreign embassies in Krakow knew of the deportation and surely were asking what had happened to those people. Letters, too, had been received by some… And on the first day of the deportation, the Jews had been provided with bread and water; if they were taking them to their deaths, why would they have given them food?

Another common question they kept returning to was: "So what do we do?" Mrs. Bronia, who spoke the most, poignantly said that she wouldn't part from her children. "I prefer to die hugging my children than die alone or continue living without them." Dr. Karol turned to her and spoke in a tone of voice that was both explanatory and exhortative: "But our problem is not how to die, it's how to save ourselves. It's much better not to stay in the hands of our enemies; any kind of escape plan is preferable to that." Then he added forcefully, "To escape, to hide among the *goyim*, to buy a false identity – those are the best solutions." With his usual pathos, Mr. Zuckerberg said, "Dear Bronia, the Germans will lose the war; their situation is getting worse by the day, and soon they will start thinking about the judgment day that will follow their defeat." The club also talked of prosaic things, of course, like the price of food, gossip about people they all knew, and fantasies of what they do after the war was over.

Several weeks after the June "Action", we started hearing stories of mass murders in gas chambers, of making soap and clothes out of Jewish skin. The card-players even joked about it, saying things like: "I wonder how soap made out of me would smell." I came to one conclusion from all these conversations: The Germans are going to kill us all and it was imperative that we escape, no matter what. I talked this over with my sister, who maintained as before that if our parents wanted to put us in hiding, "the two of us have to stay together." My father saw that I was very preoccupied by this issue but he tended not to talk to me on this subject, dismissing my attempts to speak about it by saying that he and Mom would take care of us. He didn't talk much at the card club, either. I remember just one time when he said something very clearly: "There are thousands of tiny villages from which the Jews have already been taken. The room that was made in those places is now filling up with Poles from other regions of Poland, so new faces won't arouse anyone's suspicions. There's a good chance of hiding in one of them if one buys a believable identity."

Meanwhile, my days were also filled with playing with new friends, those who loved to learn as I did. I still had two teachers coming to give me lessons: A math teacher who also taught me geography and engineering, and a chemistry teacher who also taught me physics. I had managed to get junior high school textbooks, and these are what I studied. I even found a boy and girl who would come learn with me. During one period, a writer and poet came to teach me. Among other things, I learned how to write a memoir and how to rhyme couplets. I liked this very much, and with my teacher's blessings I began a diary. (This was not the first nor last time I tried doing this, but unfortunately I could never manage to stick to it for long.)

One evening at dinner, as if by the way, Mom started talking to us about the possibility of hiding us with Christians. As she had told me privately, Gizia immediately said: "But only the two of us together." Mom looked into Dad's eyes, and then answered, "It's hard to find a hiding place for two children together, and it's also very dangerous." After a pause, she asked us, "Do you know what a monastery is?" She then explained that it is a kind of boarding school where they teach all kinds of children, including orphans. Girls and boys are separated, but there are monasteries where both are taught, so it might be possible for us to be in the same place – but we couldn't go as brother and sister. Unfortunately, this conversation between us and our parents was never continued.

In his next visit, Mr. Romek told us that the Americans had joined the British in bombing Germany, Berlin was constantly being hit, and there were inconclusive battles going on all the time on the Russian front, with heavy German casualties. The main military thrust of the Germans was being made with two armies, one toward the Caucasus and one to Stalingrad. In North Africa the Germans were advancing toward the Suez Canal, with the British gathering forces for a counter-attack. The Americans were bringing more and more men and material to Great Britain. But would all this bring about our salvation? In general, after the June "Action", people had lost hope that the Americans would come to our rescue...

The second half of October came, with wonderful weather, all the leaves turning gorgeous colors, and flights of birds going south. The ghetto had been quiet for four months. Children played everywhere, especially near the orphanage that used to be on Krakovsky Street near the Optima Factory but was moved to Juzefinska Street, close to our house. About 300 children were being taken care of there now by a staff of 20 nannies and teachers, and there were always hordes of children around the building. There was a lot of hope and happiness in the air.

I was enjoying my independence and freedom. The woman who worked for us at home loved me a lot and took very good care of me. I was in charge of house maintenance and was very proud of myself: If the electricity suddenly went out in one room, I brought in an electrician; if a faucet leaked or the pipes got blocked, I got the plumber; and I also learned how to take care of various little things myself. The electrician taught me how to switch fuses and I also thought to buy a few spares from him to have handy.

CHAPTER 13

Deportation to the Destruction, October 1942

Suddenly, rumors began spreading of another deportation. On October 26th, a rumor spread that something was going to happen over the next day or two. The next day, it became fact: As evening approached on October 27th, we saw through our windows that the "Sonderdienst" – the German police force of the Occupation – was taking up positions opposite our house on the promenade. That meant that there would be an "Action" the next day, but it wasn't clear what kind it would be. Dad came home already knowing that the Nazis would be carrying out a deportation. A tense night passed as we packed parcels, suitcases and backpacks of every kind. Our neighbors came over and told us that they were going to the hideout that had been prepared in the apartment of those who lived on the ground floor. We went downstairs and found them preparing to enter the hiding place: The neighbors from our floor with one son, my friend Voichek, and the two families on the ground floor that had three children, all older. They offered for us to hide with them. As mentioned above, we all shared it, so we returned home and Mom and Dad closeted themselves in the bedroom to discuss what to do. After a long time, they came out and told us that for now we'd pack and prepare for every eventuality, and see what would happen in the morning. My sister and I went to sleep. About 5AM we were awakened by the shouting on loudspeakers outside that everyone who worked outside the ghetto should present themselves at the main gate on Wegierska Street.

My parents decided that for the meanwhile they wouldn't go to work. We still had the option of joining the others in the secret room. There were also many hideouts that I knew of among all the ruins of the ghetto, but we hadn't prepared any of them. Dad went outside to check what was going on while we stayed at home, waiting for him. Mom was stressed to the breaking point, and Gizia and I said over and over that we wanted to hide.

It seemed like an eternity passed before Dad returned and said, "They're doing a 'selection' at the gate where the workers are, they're not letting everyone go out to their jobs even if he has all the necessary papers. The 'selection' is being done on the basis of how people look – anyone who looks sick, weak or old is not being let out."

There was complete confusion outside. The German factory owners had come to the ghetto and could intervene to help their workers. Many people were trying to take their children with them to work but the Germans weren't letting them. They were promising that families of those who work would be allowed to stay in the ghetto – but of course no-one believed them. Fathers and mothers were running around with their kids, being screamed at, being beaten, and crying. What to do? This was the first time that I saw Mom and Dad at a loss. Meanwhile, as usual in such situations, we didn't do anything and just waited at home for further developments. Around eight or nine o'clock, the loudspeakers instructed that all residents had to get to Juzefinska Street by 10:00 and then walk to Zgody Square. Only bags that could be carried by hand would be allowed. If anyone was found in the buildings after 10AM, they would be shot and killed.

Dad went downstairs to check if it would still be possible to join the others in the hiding place, but found the front door closed and locked, and when he tried the key he had, he couldn't open the door.

Ten o'clock passed, and I kept nagging that I wanted us to hide. My parents didn't bother trying to shut me up. About half past ten, we heard a lot of shooting, and they decided that we would go outside according to the instructions and we'd see what we could do from there.

We left the house – and discovered hell. We heard shooting all around us; all kinds of German soldiers were crowded on the sides of the street and wouldn't let us get onto the sidewalk. Right on the heels of the masses of Jews on the street stood the Polish, Latvian and Estonian police, along with the Schutzpolizei, urging the people onward with blows and pushing them toward Zgody Square. On both sides of the street were the factory managers, accompanied by SS men, who were looking for their workers and trying to get them released. Whoever got to the sidewalk was freed. But there was a row of SS men on each side who wouldn't let the factory owners release workers who had children with them. Sobbing, begging and shrieking, people tried pushing onto the sidewalk to find someone to free them, but they were screamed at and beaten back harshly. Dad found someone who would free him, but without the family. The SS man who accompanied the civilian who wanted to free Dad said that only Gestapo or SS officers from the administrative staff of the ghetto were allowed to release a worker along with his family.

Our parents decided that Mom would try to get released along with my sister. An agent passed from the Madritch factory where they both worked. The SS man who was with him was prepared to release my mother, but not Gizia; she looked like a young girl to him and her papers were of no interest. Of course, our parents weren't about to be released without us. Meanwhile, more and more people were joining the end of the line, while we were constantly retreating in relation to the crowd, so we found ourselves close to where people were being hit and pushed by the Polish and Lithuanian policemen. I mainly remember one Polish policeman who was constantly hitting people with a stick and screaming, "Naprzod Szumowina! Naprzod Cholera!" (Get on with you, you garbage, move on, you cholera.) Dad saw someone else on the sidewalk whom he knew and this person really made a great effort to release us, but without success. Suddenly, my parents remembered that Dad knew a Gestapo officer who worked for the ghetto administration. I can't remember his name; I think it was something like "Mayer."

Dad tried asking where this officer Mayer was. Someone told him that he was standing along with other officers about 100 meters from where we were, on the corner of Wegierska Street. At that moment of supreme confusion, Mom saved the situation, telling Dad, "Go get released and then find this Mayer."

Dad got released. Meanwhile, two to three hours had passed from the time we had left the house and entered this insanity. After Dad left, Mom held us tightly by the hand, all the while trying to delay our progress to the square. She was yelling all kinds of crazy things to every German she saw on the sidewalk, things like "We're here by mistake," "I'm from the Goering family," and "There's an order from Krueger (SS commander of Poland) to free us." One German in uniform – I don't think he was SS – told her to come over to him and clarify what she was screaming about. Her explanation didn't help. Everyone around us looked at Mom in amazement and wonder as she fought like a lioness for her cubs…

Meanwhile, long minutes passed since Dad had left, every moment of which was an eternity. We had already gotten to the corner of Targowa Street. We crossed the intersection and were quite close to Zgody Square when on the other end of it we saw how they were taking people out through the gate in groups and leading them to the trains. We got very close to the square; it was clear that if we entered the square, all would be lost. Mom intensified her screaming and wild behavior; it was a miracle that no SS man simply shot her. Maybe they thought that there was a chance that there was something to what she was yelling. It really looked like all was lost. And then, just like in every movie thriller, at the last second before we entered Zgody Square Dad suddenly appeared with that Mayer and two other uniformed soldiers. We saw that they were looking for us, and Mom started shouting in their direction. She even let our hands go to wave her arms about. They found us and after a discussion with the SS men who were guarding us, they took us out to the sidewalk and started walking us back home. We then found out that behind the crowds of Jews whom the policemen were pushing to the square, the whole area was free. People were walking around who had been released from the deportation and the Germans weren't doing anything to them. The Germans who released us accompanied us until this "liberated" area. (I assume that this Mayer was from the Gestapo, since the SS men had tried to argue with him by claiming that only an SS officer had the authority to release children.)

We learned later that Major Haase, who had overseen the deportation, was very pleased by the "Action". In contrast to June's deportation, by 4 PM that day about 4,000 Jews had been deported from the ghetto, just as the Nazis had planned. So as soon as they reached that number, they stopped taking Jews out of Zgody Square and let those who were left go home. All at once, the "Action" was over and by 6PM all the Germans had left the ghetto. Many people who had gone to work came back to find that their whole family had been deported. All over the ghetto, people were walking around crying, trying to find their loved ones.

This time, the Nazis didn't try to trick anyone or cover up their deeds. They didn't tell stories about transferring people to work in the East. It was clear that those who were put on the trains were going to their deaths, for the emphasis was on getting rid of as many of the children, the elderly, the sick, the crippled, and the least useful ones, as possible. The entire orphanage, with its 300 children and 20 staff, were taken to the trains. The old age home was emptied of its sick and terminal residents. And each and every person in the hospitals – patients and doctors alike – was deported. Many of the patients were even shot and killed inside the hospitals. As the Nazis had threatened, on that morning after 10:00, every person found in their homes instead of the street was shot and killed – and so 600 more Jews were murdered in addition to the 4,000 taken to the gas chambers in Belzec. The Germans didn't make a thorough search of the houses, however, so anyone who had a good hiding place was saved.

We made our way home in total silence, as far as I can remember. There was no sign that a search had been made of our apartment; apparently the Germans hadn't even reached our building. Dad went to check on our ground-floor neighbors. The door was still locked, so Dad stood there for long minutes banging on it and yelling. Suddenly, they opened the door and Dad went in. He told them that it was all over and that the Germans had gone. All the neighbors in that hiding place had been saved, and they started dancing and crying in joy. When I came down, I saw all of them dancing around Dad, hugging him as if he had been the one who had saved them.

We eventually said goodbye, and I went with Dad to find out what had happened to our relatives: Gina, Morris and Ziggy. It turned out that they had gone to work. We got to their house just after they'd returned, and they were still in shock. They were so happy that we were safe, they laughed and cried. Dad invited them to come to our house for dinner the next night. Then we went home and sat for many hours together, long into the night, going over what had happened to us, telling and retelling the story from each one's point of view. We alternately laughed and cried and hugged each other. Dad told me that tonight it was OK to cry and it's not a weakness. Late that night, he invited all our neighbors in and Mom took out all the food we had so we could celebrate the postponement of our death sentence. One of the neighbors stood on a chair and declared that from now on we'd live each day as if it was a whole year. Another said, "We won't let them bring us like cows to the slaughter," and everyone applauded.

Only several weeks later did Dad tell me that on the day of this "Action" my parents and Gizia could have gone to work but didn't do so because of me, since the Germans wouldn't have allowed me to go with them. The mistaken idea – completely based on emotion – that one had to make sure the family stayed intact, had been victorious. There is no doubt that the cold calculation should have been to leave me alone and hidden while they went to work, but go try to convince any parent to do such a thing… And yet, according to the statistics, 30% of all Jews who escaped or hid during the Holocaust were saved, in contrast to only 2% of those who "kept the family together" in the ghettos...

Several days after October's "Action", life in the ghetto started returning to normal. The woman who had worked for us had been deported, and Mom found a replacement. One of the two families on the ground floor had escaped the ghetto. In general, every day there were rumors of families who had run away. Most of my new friends were taken in the "Action", but my close friend Jezyk had escaped once again. He and his parents had been saved in a hiding place which was really well camouflaged that they had prepared beforehand.

Many of the survivors of this "Action" were the ones who had managed to hide. One can assume this fact didn't escape the Germans but for now no action was taken against anyone[10].

Almost every day the Nazis brought new Jews to the ghetto who had been caught outside. As always, the impression was that the Germans were purposely displaying those who were caught to warn the rest of us against escape. For example, they'd bring them to prison on foot along all of Juzefinska Street so that the whole ghetto

---

10   *Tadeusz Pankiewicz gave in his book a very touching and realistic description of the October deporting* .(See chapter 24, The "Action" of October 1942 According to Tadeusz Pankiewicz, side note 10)

could see them. (A few days later they would take these people to the Plaszow execution place to be murdered.) One assumes that their "show" deterred many, but the stream of escapees didn't stop. The feeling was that there was nothing to lose.

We still had a lot of money. Dad helped many friends, and even gave one family a large sum so they could pay for a hiding place in a tiny village. We heard that Aunt Hela and her daughter, Eva, were all right. Dad still managed to get money to them as well. Gina, Morris and Ziggy came over every night. It was sad for them to be alone in their apartment, and Mom appreciated Gina's presence. She was such a smart and brave young woman, and she understood the terrible pressure my parents were under.

The "Action" in October was different than the one in June. Back then, nobody imagined that "resettlement in the East" meant being murdered in death camps. The first day of the June "Action" had even gone relatively smoothly, with a large number of people going to the trains of their own free will. In contrast, this deportation was sudden, cruel, and accompanied by terrible slaughter. The Nazis' behavior was pitiless and wild. During the first deportation my family felt completely protected, as if it couldn't touch us. This time, we simply found ourselves being taken to the death camps and were only saved by a miracle. My father was shocked: He couldn't protect the family anymore.

CHAPTER 14

October 1942 – March 1943

Days passed, and then weeks. The Nazis spread rumors that there was nothing to worry about; there would be no more deportations. The ghetto calmed down, and the remaining children returned to playing in the streets and in Zgody Square, which had so recently had been a plaza of death. I think that in those last few months I matured a few years. My thinking became more mature; I understood very well what was happening. "We have been condemned to death and the only unknown is when the sentence will be carried out," was how I summed it up. In contrast to the thinking of the adults, I had no illusions about what was waiting for us. I started thinking about how I could save myself if my parents couldn't help me. The concept of "being strong" also continued to occupy me, and I asked myself if my father was still strong. I told myself not to let illusions and fear control me, and that I should always think of what I should do.

I would construct for myself an imaginary world in which I put myself into various situations and thought of things I could do to get out of them: Here I am escaping, hiding in all sorts of places, fighting those who want to catch me, making up all kinds of alibis for imaginary characters. My friends and I would frequently practice all kinds of fighting games that included hitting, biting and using knives. We would do battle with other kids and we'd always win. I learned to always attack, never hesitate, and never show even a drop of fear.

As already mentioned, I was a bit of a weakling as a young child, my nature being one who tried to avoid tangling with other kids, avoid being hit, acting the peacemaker. But when the war began, when Dad first told me that it was forbidden to show that one was afraid, and that we had to be strong, I tried changing myself to be more like that. At first I only acted the part of the brave one, looking at others straight in the eye – "There's no such thing as lowering one's gaze," Dad had said – and after a long time, I became that person. I learned not to let emotion and instinctive urges rule over me. I always felt that my natural fear was trying to control me but I would manage to suppress it. Eventually, I suddenly really started to not be afraid.

I reapplied myself with greater urgency to listening to my father's conversations with Mr. Romek as they continued discussing and analyzing the course of the war. "Now the Nazis are losing on all fronts," they said. "Just a few weeks after Hitler announced the capture of Stalingrad the whole German Sixth Army with its hundreds of thousands of soldiers found itself besieged in the city by the Red Army." And: "In Africa, the British army had a great victory, the German army retreated westward for about 1,000 kilometers; tens of thousands of Italian and German soldiers were captured, the Americans landed on the African continent in Morocco and are closing in on the German army from the west." "As a sign of the Allied victory in Africa, Churchill gave the order for all the church bells to ring in London..." "After all the defeats in the war against Japan, the American army has started to recover and taste victory." And lastly: "Radio BBC broadcast a communiqué regarding the annihilation of the Jews in Europe, but how are they planning to help us; what is America doing to save us?"

I kept on making plans of how I could escape to Switzerland, Sweden, Slovakia or Hungary, and started practicing what I would say if they caught me. Surely, I thought, they'd ask me for my name, where I lived, who's my father. Even before we entered the ghetto I had experimented with pretending to be a German child, but learned from that experience that it would be better to pretend to be a Polish kid and know how to tell airtight stories. I spoke excellent Polish, and knew all the slang of Polish street kids. They always mentioned Jesus' and the Holy Mother's names, and they would always cross themselves when they talked. I started practicing saying "Jezus Kristus, Matka Boska," and crossing myself, even doing this with my friends in the ghetto. I don't remember them commenting on this to me or saying that it looked strange. I would even do it all the time at home, until at one meal Mom jokingly commented, "Nasz Leosz chce byc katolikiem" (Our Leosz wants to be a Christian).

On November 14th, Official Order 96 of the GG (the region that included the Krakow Ghetto) was publicized, stating that the Jews would now be permitted to live in peace in the ghettos of this region. There would be no more deportations, and there would be amnesty for anyone who came out of hiding and went back to the ghetto. A number of Jews actually returned from their hiding places, with some of the "veterans" speaking of the great difficulties entailed in surviving outside. When they really were not arrested, an atmosphere of trust was created; people believed that now everything would be better. I was not won over, however. Nothing altered my deep and utter conviction that our verdict of death hadn't changed and wasn't going to change. My convictions were greatly reinforced by the October deportation. I wasn't afraid to die even though I didn't understand what that really meant, but I loved life and very much wanted to live...

Of course, it should go without saying that this was all another Nazi lie and trap. In January 1943, the ghetto was divided into two parts: Ghetto A and Ghetto B. I remember that they put up a fence with a gate on Juzefinska Street, before the left turn onto Targowa Street. According to the order, anyone without a job had to go live in

Ghetto B. However, to the best of my recall, until the last few weeks of the ghetto's existence, the gate to Ghetto B was usually open and one could go through it freely.

The last winter in the ghetto was very cold and sad. There were very few coal deliveries and the price was high. We warmed ourselves at a single stove in the guest room and only heated the bedrooms for a few hours in the afternoon. In addition, just as in the previous winter, there was no electricity for several hours each evening. Since the Krzemionki Hill and the winding roads that descended from Renkavki Street to Limanowski were cut off from the ghetto following the "Action" in June, there was nowhere to sled down and I made do with ice-skating on the flat roads and in Zgody Square. Gina would come with her brothers to visit Mom almost every day, and their friendship grew ever closer. Actually, many people would gather at our house in the evenings, neighbors from our building among them. Some of the members of the card club would come over even though they didn't play anymore; they only came to talk and exchange opinions.

The evening discussions among the adults always revolved around three subjects: How to survive the war, news of the war, and food. The few children who were there too, sat quietly and listened. I will note that I understood everything very clearly (I was already 10-11 years old). I would even discuss the same things with my friends.

On the subject of survival, most of the time was spent discussing and arguing over "what to do with the children." From here I learned – but didn't understand – how hard it was for parents to separate from their children. One woman stated that, "In any case, the children are in great danger; and if I give my children [to someone else to save] there's every chance that I'll never see them again." Another woman claimed, "But then you'll have a greater chance of saving their lives." But the other woman stood her ground, saying, "I don't know for sure how I'll save my children but every additional day with them is a world unto itself."

One day, a new woman showed up at our house, whose name I remember as "Pani Cukierka." In Polish, this name means something like "a little candy." She was a relatively elegant woman for the ghetto and she really looked like a Pole. She related that she had given her two young daughters to a Christian family that had specifically moved for this purpose to a small village where no Germans were stationed on a permanent basis, and where the Underground took care to kill all informers. That family already had a year-old son, and they moved there under the pretext that the father had found a job in the local sawmill. All their papers were arranged and they were registered in the municipality as a family with three children. Mrs. Cukierka herself was also planning to escape; she and her husband intended to hide separately[11]. Her husband would hide with a farmer and she would go live in a nearby village to live alone under an assumed name she had bought, and would sometimes be able to see her children from a distance.

Pani Cukierka had a lot of money, so she could allow herself this whole sophisticated escape. I really didn't understand why she told us all this, because my parents forbade us from ever speaking of Sarenka. In fact, since Sarenka had left our house, I never heard my parents even once refer to her in front of other people.

As mentioned above, the Jews in the ghetto who used to live in Krakow did not go hungry. In contrast, both the "old" refugees and the several hundred new ones that the Germans had recently sent in from small villages in the region suffered terribly from hunger and lacked the most basic things needed for survival. Since for all practical purposes, only refugees moved to Ghetto B, it was only the kindness of a few Jews that kept them from starving to death. In general, the tension and worry of the Jews in Ghetto A apparently didn't

---

11   *The best places to hide among the Christians outside the Ghetto were small villages and towns.* (More on this subject see Chapter 24, side note 11)

leave much room for concerning themselves over the poor refugees in Ghetto B. Certainly Gutter, the head of the Judenrat, was mainly concerned with how to please the Germans, and in contrast to his predecessor, he didn't try to provide any aid at all.

But Ghetto B was only to be a temporary holding area. According to subsequent German orders, all refugees were jailed in several selected houses and were not allowed to leave. Cut off from the more established ghetto, they spent several weeks there in what were subhuman conditions, any way you looked at it. Their suffering continued until they were all deported to their deaths in March 1943.

Even though people in Ghetto A didn't starve, however, there was a hunger for something of better quality and a more varied diet than potatoes, cabbage, beets and carrots. We had long forgotten what meat looked like, and it was impossible to come by real tea or coffee. You could buy substitutes, but one was worse than the next. Forget about white sugar – you could only buy a kind of brown sugar that tasted bitter and was no better than the nauseating saccharine. You could still get apples, but there was only a small supply and they were very expensive. One evening, my mother and Gina decided to make a presentation of the best dishes one could make out of these vegetables. Mom could even prepare various kinds of cake: Cabbage cake, carrot cake, or beet cake... There wasn't much awareness about the lack of vitamins and essential nutrients like proteins. However, in all the conversations about the lack of food, someone would always comment, "This should be our biggest worry."

Around February 1943, I heard for the first time about a Jewish Underground and armed resistance in the ghettos. I also heard about the revolt in the Warsaw Ghetto (the small one in January), about the Partisan movement in eastern Poland, and in the occupied part of the Soviet Union. At this stage, the thought of armed opposition to the Germans hadn't even entered my mind. After all, I saw the German war machine and couldn't imagine that we Jews could fight against it. I wasn't at all aware of the existence of an Underground in the Krakow Ghetto. So I had my first spark of a thought about local armed resistance to the Germans in March, which I will describe shortly. What I did think of all the time was passive resistance: Running away, hiding, actively resisting being caught. In the discussions about this at home, Dr. Karol explained that there was no place in the Krakow Ghetto for a Resistance because the ghetto was so small and transparent that even the slightest organization would immediately be revealed by the Gestapo with the aid of their Jewish collaborators who infested the ghetto. The Germans would then have a pretext to immediately kill us all.

The Germans now came out with an order to establish a day care center in Ghetto A so that children whose parents worked could spend their time productively. They had a grand opening, with the participation of the head of the Judenrat and Jewish Police chief, as well as a number of SS and Gestapo officers. The place was well stocked, the Judenrat drafted teachers and nannies, the children got good food and were very happy there[12].

But I saw this day care center as a Nazi deception and a trap; I had not a single doubt about it. Of course I didn't go to it, and nobody at home ever thought of sending me there. I would stay at home and play with those neighbors' children who also didn't go to the center. The streets were no longer full of children playing.

My good friend Jezyk disappeared from the ghetto. I then befriended a boy named Shimek who was around my age. Shimek's father was in the Jewish Police and was high up in the special department that collaborated with the Gestapo. He had a white ribbon on his cap and a fancier uniform. (Unfortunately, I can't remember

---

12   *There was a high-quality, wonderful Underground in the Krakow Ghetto which was mainly organized by the religious Zionist youth movement. But in the real time I did not know anything about it.* (More about the Jewish resistance in the Ghetto see Chapter 24, side note 12)

his family name and so cannot identify him via the literature on the Jewish Police.) Shimek lived nearby, in a building that was relatively very fancy, and his family had a big, beautiful apartment.

Shimek, like me, loved to learn and play with mechanical toys and building sets. Compared to me, Shimek had much fewer toys and books, and he would always ask that we take my toys to his house and play there. I did this willingly, since his mother was home and would make us wonderful things to eat – foods I hadn't seen for a long time in my house. Shimek would also ask me every time if I could leave my toys at his house. Shimek's father was friendly with my father, and the families would occasionally get together.

Over time, when it seemed as if there was no danger in going to the day care center, more and more children were sent there. I will also note that on the German side there was no attempt to force the parents to send their children there. I would sometimes go to the center to eat lunch; most of the time it was a meat meal with a candy at the end. Whenever I went, I was always prepared to run away if the Germans ever came close.

In the second half of February, persistent rumors spread about the imminent destruction of the ghetto. According to the rumors, all the workers and their families would be transferred to a labor camp built on the site of an ancient Jewish cemetery in Plaszow, a village close to Krakow. Many Jews from the ghetto worked on building the camp, and they claimed that conditions there were reasonable, the food there was better than what they got with their rations in the ghetto, and they didn't even have to pay for it. Some of them even lived there permanently. They said that they were building a big children's compound in several barracks that could hold about 500 children of all ages. According to the rumors, the Germans promised that everyone who would transfer to the camp could take his whole family with him, including the children. Another rumor circulated that someone had heard on an overseas channel on the radio that the annihilation of the Jews had ended, that the Germans wanted to preserve the Jewish work force, that the Germans wanted to keep the Jews as hostages for negotiations of a cease-fire. These rumors gave some people hope, but others kept escaping from the ghetto; they had no faith in the German promises.

Our parents didn't speak with us a lot about escaping, but I knew that they spoke and argued a lot about it between themselves. I remember only one time – several weeks before the ghetto was liquidated – when our parents started talking about their plans during supper. I don't remember the details of the conversation because I was hearing countless discussions on the subject everywhere I went, and they were all alike. Mention would be made of all kinds of '*machers*,' people who knew their way around and offered to get families out of the ghetto and into hiding places they knew of – all for a hefty price. But of course, we couldn't rely on them and leave our fate in their hands; that would almost be like committing suicide...

On this night, Mom began, "You don't have to worry, Dad and I are always thinking about how to take care of you and the whole family." She added something about the importance of preserving the family unit and that the worst was already behind us. Both said that if we went to Plaszow, I'd go with Dad and Mom would take Gizia with her. This was something new, since my sister had told me that our parents were planning to transfer her to a convent (I wasn't really sure what that was) and that I would be hidden with a farmer. As I was actually very scared of the idea of leaving the ghetto to hide, deep inside I was happy to hear that I would stay with my father.

I very much wanted to go with him to the camp, as I was very worried about him. He was very thin – his pants truly hung on him – and he looked tired all the time, as if he was cut off, disconnected. It's possible that he was ill with something.

To a certain extent, our roles even became reversed. I, a child of eleven, started worrying more about him than he did about me. On the other hand, my mother, who was about 30 when the war began, aged a lot – in the good sense of the word. She had completely stopped fussing over her outer appearance and put all her energy into the war for survival.

At the beginning of March, it was already clear that the liquidation of the ghetto was going to happen soon. My friend Shimek, the one whose father was a Jewish policeman, told me that he and his family would stay in the ghetto after it was liquidated. They'd help collect and sort all the possessions that would be left behind and then they'd go to America... He offered to take my toys and books, promising to keep them safe and return them to me after the war. So with my parents' consent, I gave him most of my things. I don't remember that it made me sad in any way. After the transfer of ownership, I would often go to his house to play with my toys.

A few days before the ghetto was liquidated, Mr. Romek paid a routine visit to my father. I remember the visit well because it was his last. The tension was very thick. As usual, Mr. Romek brought news "authorized by foreign sources": "The German and Italian army in North Africa, about 300,000 soldiers, is under siege and surrounded by the British and American armies. The German Army has no way of escaping and it's just a matter of days until it surrenders. This will be the biggest defeat for the Germans since Stalingrad; Africa will be free of Germans and Italians and the way will be open for an invasion of the European continent from the south."

Mr. Romek continued to lecture: "On the Eastern front, after the rout at Stalingrad, the German Army – which is spread out over thousands of kilometers – is being worn down in small battles, and the Red Army is getting stronger. *Panie Wimisner, niemcy wiedzo ze przychodzi godzina zaplaty za mordowanie zydow* – the Germans know that the time is coming when they're going to pay for the murder of the Jews." Mr. Romek sighed in satisfaction. "The Americans are preparing to invade Europe via France. In the meantime, German cities are being bombed night and day, and many hundreds of Germans are being killed every day."

Dad and Mr. Romek started talking about what the Jews in the rest of the world were doing, in America and the neutral countries, to prevent the mass murder of the Jews under German occupation. I listened closely but the only thing I remember of what they said was: They're doing very little.

This was also when Mr. Romek informed us that there were ghettos where Jews were fighting. He spoke of a small January revolt in the Warsaw Ghetto, where after a few days the Germans had retreated. There were only about 60,000 Jews left at this point, almost all of them young, working in various German factories in the ghetto. But they had planned to militarily oppose any attempt by the Germans to carry out any more deportation "Action"s.

This was a completely revolutionary idea to me, beyond my wildest dreams. Until that point, I had indeed thought that if I needed to escape someone who was trying to catch me, I could use a knife to stab him and run away. But I was completely unable to imagine using guns against the Germans.

In the last few weeks before the ghetto was liquidated, we talked a lot with Gina and her brothers about our fate. They had heard of the Resistance in the ghetto and the anti-German activities on the outside. The general opinion was that our goal was to survive the war and stay alive, that the attempt to fight the Germans wouldn't contribute much and would only give them an excuse to increase their murderous activities. They said that there was a good chance that in Plaszow they would let us continue living since we were doing "useful work."

About the children (and here they all looked at me), though, they said, perhaps there's a place to hide them outside the ghetto. Once, Dad commented, "You young ones will surely survive." At this time, it seems that our parents had decided once and for all that we would all go to the camp at Plaszow and abandon all other options. I come to this conclusion because during these weeks I heard no more arguments between Mom and Dad on the subject. It was a decision to choose the most comfortable, easy and worst solution. However, I was at peace with this decision, because I didn't want to be separated from my father and felt that if I left him he wouldn't survive.

A few days before the date the ghetto was to be liquidated, we starting preparing for it by packing all the things we'd take with us to the camp. According to the Germans, anything we could carry in our hands or on our backs would be permitted. Children were indeed being allowed, as workers who had already gone to live there had taken their whole families with them. There were even people who hadn't yet moved to Plaszow but had smuggled their children in, and those kids were now hiding in the camp.

(It should be noted that just a few days before the liquidation of the ghetto, the command staff of the Plaszow Camp was replaced; the old commandant had been considered a pleasant and fair man. The one who replaced him, Amon Goeth, was a completely different story, and I will have a lot to say about this further on. But even Amon Goeth seemed easy-going, polite and intelligent in the first few days, until the ghetto was liquidated. Only later on was he revealed in all his horrific cruelty.)

CHAPTER 15

The Liquidation of the Ghetto
and My Escape

Via my window in the early afternoon of March 12, 1943, I started seeing that the guard was being reinforced around the ghetto. It came in the form of extra Polish policemen in black uniforms who were the regular guards, with the addition of the Sonderdienst, the German police force of Occupied Poland. I was alone at home at the time. The cleaning woman hadn't come to work that day and my parents and Gizia were still at work outside the ghetto. There was no way to reach my parents. I went down to the street to see what was going on but it was deserted as people hadn't come home yet. So I went to my friend Shimek's house to see how he was taking care of my toys… On their door was a big notice in German that was signed by the Gestapo. It said: "Here lives the family of a Jewish policeman (with his name, position and number). This family is allowed to stay in the ghetto.[13]" I rang the bell and Shimek's mother opened the door. I saw that she was surprised at my arrival and was very embarrassed. She invited me in but said that they weren't allowed to have anyone

---

13   *There were about dozen Gestapo and SS officers who ruled the Ghetto. SS-Sturmbannfuhrer Haase was the highest ranking officer and the commander of the SS in the Krakow District. He organized and actively carried out all the "Action"s and murders in the Krakow Ghetto.* (More on the the the Nazis that operated in the Ghetto see Chapter 24, side note 13)

but family members in the house. As far as I can remember, I wasn't insulted or hurt; I accepted her words at face value, told them good-bye, reminded Shimek to take good care of my toys and books... and went home. My mother and sister returned from work and a tense wait ensued for Dad. He came back rather late and we all jumped on him... He, too, already knew that the next day we were going to go to Plaszow.

That evening there was a "procession" of friends and acquaintances who came over to hear the news and consult together. Everyone was worried, especially about the children. Dad left the house to see if he could find out other news from friends. Our ground-floor neighbors discussed whether there was any reason to hide, as they had done during the October deportation, but if they were liquidating the ghetto it would be of no use. On the other hand, they had also said in October that they were liquidating the ghetto and yet at the end, everyone who had hid was saved. Nobody really believed the German promise that everyone would be allowed to move to Plaszow, but since they had no choice they hoped that the rumors were correct.

Gina and her brothers came over late in the evening. For some reason they were in a good, optimistic mood. In their opinion, the Germans were going to ask for a cease-fire at any moment and there was no doubt that the first demand of the Allies would be to stop the murder of the Jews. Gina was 21, her two brother were 17; all three were young and of working age and they didn't have anything to worry about.

It was only when Gina asked, "What are you doing with Leosz?" during their tense and emotional conversation, and everyone looked at me, that it occurred to me that everyone's greatest worry was – me. Even though the Germans had announced through the Judenrat and Jewish Police that taking children to Plaszow was allowed, and even though the big children's compound that had been built there was supposed to be proof of that. Dad had arranged papers for me saying that I worked in a German factory that was vital to the war effort. The papers said I was 2-3 years older than I really was; I believe they said I was thirteen. I had only one problem: I was very small... I barely looked as if I were ten, and this was after a whole "overhaul" had been done on me. In contrast, my sister Gizia, whose false papers said she was already 15, actually looked the part after the make-up job she received.

15.1 – Failure of the Efforts to Smuggle Me from the Ghetto

I went to bed late that night. I think my parents barely slept at all. They were mainly worried about the rest of the packing and how to divide and hide money and other valuables. Several packets of bills had been sewn into various clothes of mine, and in addition, my parents gave me my own money. All in all, I had quite a respectable amount of cash for those days. I even had dollars and tiny bags of valuables – mostly diamonds and gold.

Truth be told, on the last night of the ghetto's existence, nobody slept (except for me and a few others...) People walked around, gathered together, tried to gather up a few more crumbs of information. But I fell asleep sitting up in the guest room and remained hung over the chair, as my sister told me later, until my parents put me to bed.

I slept soundly and woke up late the next morning. When I did, my mother came in to dress me. I objected, but she asked me to let her because this might be the last time for a while that she could do it... Somehow, I softened and let her go ahead. Then she asked me to give her a hug; I did so and told her that lately she had been strong and brave and therefore I love her and she should always remember to be strong... Mom hugged me again with eyes spilling over with tears as she struggled not to burst out crying – until my sister came into the room and said, perhaps mockingly, "Look, you've found time to hug and be indulged." When I was once again left alone in the room, I hid in various places in my clothes and backpack a number of small switchblade knives and two pocket-knives that had a lot of tiny implements in them. I also hid two small switchblades in the ends of my jacket sleeves, where I could quickly and easily slip them into my hands. I don't remember what I was thinking at that point, maybe about what I would do with the knives – or maybe I didn't think at all. Later that morning, I think around 10:00, Dad went out to the street to see what was happening. Even before he came back, we heard broken-off and unclear instructions being announced by the Jewish Police to go to Juzefinska Street by 3 PM and group ourselves according to workplace in order to leave for the Plaszow Camp. We were to leave our apartment doors open. Then they said something unintelligible about children.

After a long and nerve-wracking hour, Dad came home. Mom was very worried by that point and when he walked through the door she released all her stress by yelling, "You always leave us during the hard times!" And then she jumped into his arms and they hugged. Dad did not have good news. Many SS and black-uniformed police had entered the ghetto, screaming a lot and trying to sow fear. Many people were already standing in line at the gate, not taking care to arrange themselves according to where they worked, so we could go there together. But the bad news was that they weren't letting people take their children. SS men were searching for and pulling out children from the line of people who were leaving. As they did, they were saying that the children should be brought to the daycare center, that they would be brought the next day to Plaszow, "and in Plaszow we've already built a children's house that is big and furnished." The Germans were screaming this message themselves, without the aid of the Jewish Police.

We went down to the street around noon. Dad had a relatively large suitcase and a backpack, Mom had a small suitcase and a backpack, Gizia had a backpack and a bag and I, too, wore a backpack. We approached the end of the line waiting to get out, which was a few hundred meters from Wegierska Street. We immediately saw mothers and fathers with young children who were running around in despair after they had been taken out of the orderly lines at the exit. On both sides of the street stood SS men and the German police, who were constantly screaming that we should stand in rows of five. The SS and the Jewish police were passing between the rows, thrusting the children out and searching for very young children in suitcases and backpacks. Arguments were going on and blows were being rained on people, while others shouted and begged. I saw places where they dragged the children out and the parents stayed in line, and others where the second children were removed, the parents stepped out as well. When we arranged ourselves in a row, I noticed that people were following me with their eyes but they didn't say a thing and we started moving toward the exit.

While we were inching our way along, Amon Goeth passed by with his stick and his two dogs. This was the new commandant of the Plaszow Camp; he was tall and striking, dressed in a beautiful leather coat, with the rank of major in the SS. In one hand he held a sub-machine gun and in the second hand, a "pajch," a stick that had a piece of leather on it that was embedded with pieces of metal. This "pajch" caused tremendous pain and wounds when he struck people with it, but at the time he just stopped every few meters and said quietly and politely that the children should be brought to the daycare center, and they would be brought the next day to the camp. He also said that everyone could take their valuables to the camp – money, even foreign currency. If someone had hidden some at home or forgot to take something along, there was still time to go back and get it.

I stood in the center of our row, with Mom, Dad and Gizia crowded around to try and hide me. When the group of inspectors got to us, one of the Germans spotted me and called me to get out of line. Mom immediately intervened and said to the German very politely that I was 14 and worked for the German war effort. She tried to present my papers proving this, but he wasn't interested in them. He just spit out something to the effect that I was too small and told one of the Jewish policemen to take me. Mom wouldn't let go of my hand so she left the line with me and went to the sidewalk. My father and sister immediately followed.

After we got onto the sidewalk, I saw that not only children were being thrust out of line; anyone who looked old or ill was, too. The Germans weren't at all interested in work permits; they were doing a 'selection' according to looks alone. But I didn't see a single case of the Germans not allowing the parents to leave with their children. We went back to the end of the line to try our luck again.

Behind the lines of those leaving, along the entire length of Juzefinska Street up to the gate of Ghetto B, fathers and mothers were running around with their children, despair written on their faces. The Jewish Police and the Judenrat – apparently under orders from the Germans – were also running around, trying to convince them to put their children in the daycare center and leave for the camp. They kept repeating the promise that the children would be brought to Plaszow the next day. There was also the very sad sight of many young children running around alone and crying. Did their parents abandon them? Dad tried to talk to the police or the people of the Judenrat whom he knew, but I guess nothing came of it. It turned out that the Gestapo agent whom Dad knew and who had save us in the October "Action" was not in the ghetto.

This time when we joined the line, Dad settled with Mom that if they took me out of the row again, only Dad would go out with me and Mom would continue toward the exit with Gizia. Step by step we came closer to Wegierska Street, just a few dozen meters from the exit gate. The "child-pullers" passed by us several times, but either they didn't see me or they ignored me. On the other side of the gate we saw how groups were being formed to march to the Plaszow

Camp. Then an SS man approached us, accompanied by two Jewish policemen. The German actually looked like a nice person; he wore glasses and looked like an intellectual. He glanced in my direction and I tried giving the impression that I wasn't paying attention to him. I focused on my finger tips, but it didn't help. He yelled, "You, little one, come here." I tried ignoring him, but then the Jewish policeman caught me by the arm and pushed me out to the sidewalk. Dad immediately followed, and the German barked at us, "Bring the child to the daycare center and get back into line." Dad said something to him and the German went on. We stayed on the sidewalk until we saw Mom and Gizia leaving through the gate safely. Then we walked about 100 meters back to the end of the line, again.

On the way, we met friends and acquaintances, many of whom asked if we could possibly believe the Germans, maybe after all they actually would bring the children to Plaszow? To me, personally, the picture was crystal clear – and horrifying: We were in a death trap that would be hard to escape. It didn't even occur to me to believe the Germans and go to the daycare center, and we didn't bring up the possibility at all. The whole time we were walking, I was discussing with my father what we should do, saying there was no reason to try again, it could make things even more complicated for us, etc. After going back and forth on the subject, it seemed to us that the less bad option was to hide, and then after several days, when the ghetto would be calm, to find the chance to escape. Once we'd be clear of the ghetto, we could call Christian Polish or German friends to ask for help in hiding us. This was a very dangerous idea with a low chance of success, but the only practical choice.

At one point, we met the Jewish policeman who was Shimek's father. He was accompanied by a German and told Dad to stay where he was and he'd come back to us soon. About a half hour later, he returned and told Dad that he couldn't help us right now, but if we would hide in a certain apartment (he gave us the address) he'd come over late at night. Meanwhile, he'd try and think of a solution of some kind. However, he reminded us that he had a sister with two children and he had to first take care of her.

15.2 – Parting from My Father

We stood there for a few minutes, and then suddenly – almost instinctively – without thinking about it at all on a conscious level, I said, "You know what, Dad? It will be a lot easier for me to hide and run away alone than if you are with me." Dad answered something like, "You're crazy to think of such a thing, you know that?" But I remember that the moment I said it the idea grabbed me and I started to think of how I could convince my father. I told him that I knew many secret exits from the ghetto that we used during the period we smuggled food, that the openings were narrow and small so only children could get through, that outside the ghetto a lot of kids were always running around and they wouldn't pay attention to me. I kept repeating the claim that I wasn't scared, that I already had experience getting by outside the ghetto, that I knew places outside and would meet him at his job in a few days, that if we were together, even if we managed to escape the ghetto, we'd immediately get caught. At first, my father really didn't pay attention to me, and just mumbled something.

At the time I didn't understand how much Dad was suffering in the face of having to choose between two horrible possibilities. But no matter how awful the option of separating and leaving me alone seemed, how unethical and unacceptable, if one thought about it coldly and logically, it really was the less bad choice. But in "real time," I didn't see it as a great tragedy, or the hell that my father was going through because of it.

I don't remember the exact details of this dramatic scene, but at a certain point Dad started yelling at me not to drive him crazy, that he would decide what to do. I kept bringing up more reasons why I was right, including that Dad had to go to take care of Gizia and Mom, and help them… I explained how hard it would be for two of us to hide, escape and pretend to be Christians while we were together. I repeated that the escape routes were small and narrow, meant for kids, and Dad wouldn't fit.

Suddenly, Dad asked me, "And if you manage to get out of the ghetto, where would you go?" I felt that this question showed he had given in to me. We went into one of the nearby apartments that stood open. Dad asked me where I planned to hide, and I said that I'd go to one of the ruins in the area between our house, Limanowski Street and the alley of Podguze Square. I knew the ruins well, the passages between them and several exits from there to the other side of the ghetto wall that weren't obvious to the eye. (I will note here that since the front of our building faced the outside of the ghetto, there were several secret passageways leading from it, but the back of our house faced an open area opposite the Vistula promenade where there were many guards. Anyone who used that exit would be seen immediately.)

I didn't have an escape plan ready, but in order to convince Dad of how serious I was, I spoke fast and thought quickly while I was talking. I told Dad that I'd hide for several days, and once the Germans reduced the guard on the ghetto, I'd escape at night. Dad noted down the addresses of several acquaintances he had on the other side whom I could go to, and said that he'd find a way to warn them about me in advance. He also gave me two addresses of employees who'd worked for him before the war. Of course, he also gave me Uncle David's address (which I knew by heart already), but he warned me that I couldn't enter his house because they were constantly being followed by the Gestapo. I told Dad again that I could hide among the street kids. Dad also gave me the phone number of the German, Neumann. Finally, I gave Dad a long, long hug – without kissing – and he told me that he was relying on me and that I was strong and brave. These words from my father encouraged me to have the strength to survive, to have courage, and stand up to all the tests that were waiting for me. I was as happy as if I'd just won a medal for bravery... Now I couldn't disappoint my father; I had to save myself.

At this terrible and tragic moment, I was more worried for my father than I was for myself. Our conversation at an end, we went back to the sidewalk and Dad joined the line of people going to Plaszow. I saw myself as a soldier who had received the mission from his father to save himself, and I wouldn't let him down... I walked all along Juzefinska Street until the corner of Wegierska Street and went up to an apartment on the second floor which gave me a view all along Wegierska up to the main gate. I wanted to see Dad leaving the ghetto. A few minutes later I recognized him in the line and watched until he left through the gate. I searched through the two apartments on that floor for food; I found a little bread, red (not fully processed) sugar, and even a piece of salami. I packed it up in a satchel, along with a few rolls and even two apples that Mom had prepared for me earlier.

Before descending, I went once more to the window – and what did I see? Right next to the gate of the house, under the window, was none other than SS Obersturbanfuhrer Haase, the great murderer of the ghetto and commander of all the "Action"s. Right there below me was that elegant killer, with his whole staff and a few dogs. SS men and Jewish policemen kept coming up to him and getting orders, saluting and running off to obey them. There was no way to leave the house by the front door, because I would run right into them... I quietly crept down the stairs and left via the back yard. I passed through one back yard after the next, moving toward Targowa Street and Zgody Square. Finally I found a building with a clear passage to the street and went out carefully. I was in an area that was behind the line of people leaving the ghetto, very close to the gate to Ghetto B. I noticed that there was a small truck standing very near one of the houses, with its open back almost against its gate. The building was open, and I remembered that it was a storage place for Jewish property – mainly furniture, but also house wares, coats, bedding, etc. There were a number of such warehouses on both sides of the ghetto wall, which the Germans used to hold the contents of people's homes. Without thinking about it much, I sneaked into the building and entered the first apartment.

All the apartments were being used for storage. I heard the noise of furniture being moved, and voices talking in Polish and German. I hid under a bed and lay there quietly until the noises stopped and I heard the sound of the truck leaving. I found myself in a situation that I hadn't planned on, but the possibility of hiding in the mini-warehouse wasn't a bad idea. I'd told my father a completely different plan, but with the last light of day I made a tour of the place (I had a small flashlight that helped). It was like a department store in there, with all kinds of different things in each apartment. On some floors there were binders full of papers in which they apparently made lists of the contents.

On the top floor, I found an apartment with two windows that looked out on the street. One of its rooms was filled with coats. If the Germans came in, I decided, I'd hide in one of the closets in that room, behind the coats. The house also had an attic, from which one could go up to the roof. I went up there, and saw that I could jump over to the next roof, which had a big chimney. I decided that if they'd break into the house to search it, I'd go hide in that chimney (I knew there were rungs inside that I could stand on).

I saw that the street was empty below except for various figures here and there that were slipping away – and the Jewish police who were on patrol. The Germans had already left the ghetto. I decided that later I'd weigh whether to move to the hiding place I'd originally thought of. By now I was getting cold, and in the closet I found a splendid leather coat that had a thick lining. It was a short men's coat which reached my ankles… I also found a padded hat that went over my ears. One of the apartments had a room full of mirrors, so I looked at myself; how funny I looked! But since I was very tired I decided to go rest in an apartment that had lots of beds. I also found a thick blanket. I fell asleep – and woke up late the next morning from the sounds of screams and shots being fired outside. It was a beautiful day, with the sun high in the sky… Through the window I could see that Juzefinska Street was filling up with German police.

15.3 – Massacre on the Ghetto Streets

From the window, I watched as SS units entered the ghetto, led by their officers. They were armed as if for battle, carrying bayoneted rifles and sub-machine guns, with grenades hanging from their belts. I had never seen these SS before; they weren't from the permanent force that ran the ghetto. I could see both ends of Juzefinska Street from this window, depending on which side I stood, which gave me a good view of most of the ghetto.

I stood glued to the window the entire day, changing sides constantly. What I saw was a hell that was extremely hard to believe could even happen. In the morning, the Jewish Police ran around announcing through loudspeakers that everyone had to leave their houses immediately and walk to Zgody Square. If anyone would be caught inside, they'd be killed immediately. Slowly, slowly, people started coming out – whole families, women with children, and also children alone. The SS men would beat them with sticks and bayonets, driving them toward Targowa Street, which led to Zgody Square (I couldn't see the square itself from the window). They would shoot anyone who fell down. I also heard shots fired from the direction of the square. From the direction of Ghetto B I saw how the Jewish Police were directing groups of Jews toward the square. These were mainly the refugees who had been brought several weeks earlier from the tiny towns around Krakow. They looked awful; the men with unshaven beards and torn clothes, most of them barefoot. They walked as if hypnotized, as if they didn't understand what was happening to them, looking neither right nor left. They walked quietly. I noticed that they didn't speak to each other. Children held hands and didn't cry. It was a scene of ghosts from hell. It wasn't clear if they knew they were being led to their deaths or if they had no clue.

Later in the afternoon, there was much more shooting. Groups of SS and Jewish Police were going into houses to search. From time to time they'd bring out individuals or families, stand them on the sidewalk facing the street, and shoot them in the backs of their heads. When the people fell, they'd kick their bodies into the street. Blood flowed in the gutter along the sidewalk. They'd lay the young children down on the sidewalk, shoot them and kick them into the gutter. If children were being held by their mothers, they'd first shoot the children and then the mothers. It was obvious that these SS men were expert killers. They did their job mechanically, doing the same measured motions repeatedly, like a kind of game they'd practiced over and over: They'd either unholster their gun (or cock their sub-machine gun), go close to the victim, shoot, take two steps back, and put the gun back in the holster. Over and over again.

This ritual of sidewalk execution took place in a terrible silence; only the shots were heard. I didn't see people crying. They didn't beg for their lives, they didn't ask for mercy. I'd say that they didn't degrade themselves before the Nazis; they kept their self-respect. The executions were carried out by SS men in green or black uniforms – mainly by the officers. These were apparently special units who had been brought in specifically for this purpose.

The black-uniformed men (Ukrainians, Lithuanians, etc.) would mostly help stand the people on the edge of the sidewalks. The Jewish Police helped in the search of the homes. I have tried to remember what I felt when looking at this horror, if I cried, fainted, was in shock, or trembled from head to foot... As far as I can recall,

I simply didn't feel a thing, except when I saw how they were herding the children from Ghetto B to Zgody Square. That hurt, for some reason. Maybe I couldn't believe it was really happening, maybe I got used to it... After I escaped from the ghetto and I had time to think and review my memories, I thought of the murder of the children and the memory of what happened pained me.

A few hours later I saw them leading wagonloads of children from the big daycare center that they had just built a few weeks earlier. These were the kids whose parents had believed would be joining them in Plaszow... They were all dressed in their best, as if they were going on holiday. I recognized a number of them. These children were sent directly to the gas chambers in Auschwitz. Did they guess that they were being taken to their deaths? I mean, at some point they had to have understood; did they cry? Did they try to escape? Is it possible to describe putting hundreds of children into gas chambers in order to choke them to death? These questions haunt me now a lot more than they did back then, when it was actually happening...

Since the Germans didn't have enough trucks or trains to bring them all to Auschwitz, some of the children were shot and killed in Zgody Square. Late in the afternoon, burial squads of Jews started lining up the bodies on the sidewalks in front of the buildings. By evening, they started bringing carts to gather the bodies. I went up to the roof where I could see even more parts of the ghetto. By now the executions had stopped, but what pulled my attention were the hordes of Poles who were standing in various places outside the ghetto and watching what was going on inside. I saw people standing on Krzemionki Hill, on Renkavki Street, on roofs and balconies, and really anywhere with a good view of the ghetto. The Germans made no attempt to hide the massacre that was taking place. The wagons loaded with bodies of those murdered passed through kilometer after kilometer of city streets until they reached the old Jewish cemetery (in Plaszow, where the camp was), where they were buried in mass graves. Many bodies fell off the wagons on the way, and the Poles saw it all…

That night, I decided to try getting to my original hiding place, in the "children's country" of the ruins near our house. The ghetto streets were completely empty, but the guard was tight all the way around the walls. I decided to go though all the back yards of the buildings along Juzefinska Street until I got to the wall near the Vistula. Near the wall I'd cross the street to get to our building, and then I'd go to the hiding place. Crossing through the yards was easy, but just as I was about to cross the street near my house, I hesitated. It could be that I had taken fright over something I barely sensed. I waited several minutes, then retraced my steps to the storehouse. On the way, I stocked up on food by going into apartments and finding what people had left behind.

The next morning, on the third day of the "Action", just as on the previous day, German police units entered the ghetto, mainly the SS. This time, though, the Sonderdienst came in too, along with the Jewish Police who continued searching for Jews. The same scenes of execution repeated themselves, but they only caught a few people. I noticed that sometimes they would wait until they gathered a group of several together before executing them. They stopped searching by late afternoon, the carts gathered up the bodies and the German units left. At twilight, a truck was driven to the gate of the storehouse where I was hiding. A uniformed German policeman stood on the step of the driver's cabin. Then a man and woman dressed in civilian clothes came out of the truck (the man looked like he was Gestapo), along with two Jews and one who looked like a Pole. One of the Jews opened the gate and they all entered the building except for the German policeman, who waited outside near the truck. I saw all this from the room on the upper floor which I'd made into my "home." I was ready to slip into the coat closet, but after a short while they brought some furniture down to the truck, loaded it on and left.

I understood: They were just a German couple who had come to choose some furniture for themselves.

In the evening I went up to the roof. The ghetto was quiet but as far as I could see, the guard around it was still very tight. That night, I started thinking of a plan to escape via another truck that would come to take away furniture.

My fourth day in hiding was spent the same way – watching fewer Germans and fewer search parties, who found just a few families. Sometimes a long time would pass before they murdered them. Some of the Jews were taken to Zgody Square, so I couldn't see what they did to them. I spent the time on two tasks: Figuring out how to get into the next truck, and constructing my new identity. For the last two months I'd known that if I had to, I'd become a Polish kid, Christian to the core. I reviewed again all the Polish street slang, the incessant crossing of myself, uttering the words "Matka Boska" (Mother of God) with pathos, as well as constantly referring to "Jezus, Maria and Moj Boze." I imagined all sorts of scenarios, and practiced saying the short prayers (like Grace before meals) and stories about Jesus that Poles commonly told.

I knew many stories about Marshal Pilsudski, the hero of Poland who fought the Russians in World War I and had become the president of Poland in the Twenties and Thirties. Polish children all considered him "Good Grandpa Pilsudski," as when they were little they were weaned on stories of his courage and how he loved children. Many, many stories were written about him, and my legendary nanny, Zosia, would tell them to me over and over – to the extent that I felt I could talk about him as if I knew him personally. So I built my new identity around Pilsudski. My name would be Brzezyk Panczewsky, my father would be a soldier now fighting with the British against the Germans, and I "killed off" my mother in the beginning of the war from an air raid. I decided to say I was from an orphanage, but had run away. (I even made up a story of the town I'd come from, including my street's name and house number, which unfortunately I don't remember anymore.)

The "father" I adopted for myself was a hero who had fought bravely for Poland's independence. He had tons of medals, and the cherry on top was that he'd fought shoulder to shoulder with Pilsudski! I practiced these stories so many times that I began living and believing them. I even prepared a story in which Pilsudski was my godfather and had participated in my baptism ceremony...

I prepared for my escape very carefully: On the ground floor there was an apartment whose door was exactly opposite the entrance gate to the building. I made a tiny hole in the door so I could see the gate and know who was coming. As soon as the truck would be partially loaded, I'd jump in and hide; and I'd run away from the truck after it left the ghetto. The apartment also had a back door leading to a yard, which I could use if the Germans decided to enter when I was there.

After that fourth day, there were fewer and fewer German-led activities. I now saw Jewish Police and workers coming – apparently from Plaszow – to take furniture out of houses, load them on carts and take them to various storehouses in the ghetto. On the fifth day, a truck came to my building around noon, but there were many people around and I didn't have a chance to jump inside. That night, when I went up on the roof, I saw that the guard around the ghetto had decreased significantly. I decided that I'd wait two or three more days, and if I couldn't manage to get out by truck, I'd escape through one of the openings in the wall that I knew of.

15.4 – Escape from the Ghetto

In the late afternoon of the sixth day following the liquidation of the ghetto, a huge truck came to my building. I saw it approach from the top floor and speedily descended to the apartment I'd prepared with a peephole. I saw three Jews (identified by the ribbon around their arms) and one without a ribbon, and two Jewish policemen on the steps. I didn't see any Germans in uniform. They started bringing down all kinds of furniture to the truck, and at some point the Jewish policemen disappeared.

I sat there in great suspense. Every time the people went upstairs, I debated whether this was the moment to jump into the back of the truck. But I couldn't get up the courage; something glued me to my seat. I made a supreme effort to overcome my fear. Suddenly, I gathered up every shred of mental force and willpower that I had, opened the door and started walking silently toward the truck. I got into the back, which was filled about half-way, and clambered over furniture to get as close to the cab as possible. I found a comfortable spot where I couldn't see a thing but could hear talking and the noise of people loading the truck with more things. Since the truck had a canvas covering, I cut a few holes in it above the driver's cabin and in the sides so I could see out. That's when I found out that there was also a German soldier or policeman sitting next to the driver's seat. Finally, the truck started moving towards the ghetto gate. At the gate, the German got out and reported to the guard standing there. After making only a superficial search, the guard let us drive on, without the German escort.

CHAPTER 16

Using a False Identity Outside the Ghetto

And so it was that at age eleven, I left the inferno for the unknown. The truck left the ghetto, crossed the bridge that spanned the Vistula, and after a pretty long drive, we got to a poor section of town which had factories as well as run-down apartment houses. The first stop was apparently at some kind of storehouse where they took out some of the furniture, but I didn't have a chance to jump out. Luckily for me, it was already completely dark, because at some point we were also stopped for an inspection. Finally, we got to another warehouse, where they continued emptying the truck and there was enough room for me to get out. I wasn't able to make completely sure that there was no-one around the truck at the time, but the moment there was nobody in my field of vision and I didn't hear anyone, I gathered up my courage, hesitated, then got out of the truck. I walked away without looking back. For some reason I felt no fear; I just felt that I was free at last. When I had gone a short distance, I glanced behind me and saw no movement or sign that anyone was following me.

I kept walking in the dark. The sidewalk was broken up and dirty; in certain sections it simply disappeared and became a path between buildings. There was a single gaslight at one intersection. I saw ugly houses, half destroyed. I peeked into yards and saw wrecks of buildings, sheds and junk. In short, a poverty-stricken neighborhood. I started going into yards to look for a place to sleep. In one of them, I felt movement in one of the rooms that was half destroyed and didn't have a door.

A decently friendly voice called out, "Who's there?"

I answered in Polish, "Przyjaciel," which means "a friend." In Polish slang even used by the children, it meant, "I'm a friend and have only good intentions."

The voice from the room answered, "Come closer, don't be afraid." I came in and saw a typical lair of a homeless person.

"What are you looking for, my child?" asked the man. I answered that I had run away from an orphanage and was looking for a place to sleep. He invited me to sleep in his room.

After the loneliness of the last few days, I was very happy to be near another living being. I didn't see the man's face. He gave me a blanket and told me to lie down next to him. I told him that my father was a "pulkownik," a big fighter against the Germans, and added partially in pride and partially as a threat that I, too, knew how to fight...

He merely said, "Don't worry, you won't have to fight." I lay down beside him and was asleep in seconds.

Late the next morning, I woke up, but my neighbor was gone. So was the blanket I had lain on – and to my shock, so were my shoes. My satchel was partially open and my neighbor had searched through it and stolen a few hundred zloty. I was shaking with cold, anger and frustration. In addition to all these troubles, it was raining outside. I was lucky that he had only stolen a small part of my money, since it was hidden in many places. All together I had over 2,500 zloty. (A loaf of bread at the time cost three zloty, a bowl of soup, only half a zloty.) So I was really quite rich... I put a few hundred zloty in an inner pocket of my coat and a few dozen banknotes of lower denominations in my outer pocket. This was money to be whipped out quickly if necessary. I checked for the knife hidden in my glove. It was a small one with a little button that would release the blade, which would then stick out a few centimeters from the glove. I held this knife in my left hand, for two reasons: First, I was a lefty, so this was my stronger hand, and secondly, it was more common to hold a knife in one's right hand, so I would have the advantage of surprise... I decided to wait a bit until it stopped raining, and meanwhile kept a lookout on the street. It was pretty empty, with people or wagons passing by only infrequently. I saw farmers' wagons go by with produce to sell, and a few isolated children perhaps on their way to school.

The farmers' wagons gave me an idea: Surely they were on their way to some kind of market; maybe I could get there with them and buy food and shoes. The rain had stopped but the streets were wet and there was no reason to get my socks wet or even wrap them with rags or papers, so I just took them off and went barefoot. I noticed that some of the kids who passed by were also barefoot – as were the farmers' kids in the wagons – so I wouldn't stand out in any way. I did have one problem, though; I wasn't used to going barefoot... I went outside, and must have looked very strange with my splendid coat, big hat that covered most of my face – and bare feet. I waved at the farmers passing by. Suddenly, I saw a bigger wagon than most, hitched to two horses and loaded down with goods. In it were a farmer and his wife.

I signaled them to stop and yelled that I wanted to help them only in return for food, that I was an orphan, that my father was a "pulkownik," and that I knew math. It turned out that these farmers spoke in a slang I barely understood. The woman asked me straight out where I'd stolen my coat. I told her my father had given it to me and there were plenty more coats where that came from. The farmer signaled to me to jump aboard. On the way, we stopped in several places where the farmer would take out a bell, ring it, and announce what he had for sale. People came out of their houses and started looking through the merchandise and asking prices. The farmer told me beforehand what the prices were per piece, as he had no scale. A potato cost 10 gerush (one gerush was 1/100 of a zloty), a head of cabbage was 50 gerush, etc. Women asked me if I was the farmer's son. I suggested to the farmer that I do the talking, since I knew the city slang. I did a very good job and the farmer was very pleased. He didn't know multiplication, and if a woman took several apples he would add up one apple plus another apple, plus another apple... I told the buyers that a small apple cost 10 gerush and a big one cost 15, and the farmer was very happy with my great idea. He just wondered how he'd calculate the price. When he saw how I calculated it on the spot he was amazed and gratified and couldn't stop singing my praises to his wife. I absolutely loved the work and the praise and didn't realize the danger of sticking out so much in public.

At the end, we got to a pretty big market which was right in the middle of the city. I didn't see any Germans there but there were many Polish policemen. We parked the wagon and started selling. Merchants came who bought large quantities, as well as regular people who bought smaller amounts. People again asked if I was the farmer's son, and he would answer that I was a "pacholek," (a lowly helper). I mainly stuck out because of my coat, and I heard several barbed comments about it. After a while I decided to take it off, and a little after that a man came over and offered to buy it for 100 zloty, and he'd give me another coat in exchange as well. I told him that I also wanted shoes, and he asked the farmer for permission to take me with him. To anyone willing to listen, I proclaimed that I had run away from an orphanage and that my father was a "pulkownik," who fought with the British against the Germans. I would also repeat that my dad had told me that "Pan Jesus" and "Matka Boska" loved me and would protect me. I can see it now in my mind's eye, how the man who wanted to buy my coat was walking quickly, with long steps, with me half walking and half running barefoot, declaiming my mantras about my warrior father...

We got to a big market stall that sold used clothes. I chose a simple coat that was well padded, had many pockets and reached down over my knees. I had a problem with shoes, though, because he didn't have any for children. At the end I chose high shoes that were more like half boots, with really long laces, that were two to three sizes too large for me. (Most of the shoes there were 10 sizes bigger...) I think I actually took a pair of women's shoes. But wearing shoes that were too big was not a strange thing; most children did. I returned to "my" farmer to continue working, but noticed suddenly that I was drawing too much attention to myself and decided to get out of there as soon as I could.

While I was getting my coat and shoes, someone had brought the farmer a scale so he could sell by weight. He had a lot of trouble figuring out what to charge, but I decided not to get involved this time, so as not to call even more attention to myself. Suddenly, the farmer's wife turned to me and asked if I'd like to come with them to their village. They had two pretty daughters, they'd give me food, and I could stay with them and work until the end of the harvest season. I didn't quite understand what they meant but said very politely that I would like to stay a bit longer in the city and if they would come again, we'd see. They told me when they'd return and we parted without them giving me any of the food they'd promised me.

16.1 – I Buy a Friend

I went off and bought a few rolls, cheese and two apples. Many children were in the market, some alone or in groups and some with their parents. I sat down in a corner to eat. A boy a little older than I passed by, riveting his eyes on my food. I called out to him and asked if he was hungry and would like to eat. I saw that he was very hungry, and that he had kind eyes. I invited him to sit next to me and gave him part of my meal. I felt that I had bought a friend. His name was Jasiek. When I saw that he was still hungry, I got up with him and bought the two of us a big bowl of cabbage. I asked him if he'd like us to be friends. I told him the story of my father being a great soldier, that I knew how to use knives and could protect him. I saw that the boy felt attached to me and trusted me. He told me that his father had also been a soldier, but he'd been killed in the war. He lived with his mother and little sister, didn't like going to school, and belonged to a very secret gang which he couldn't tell me about.

I was already pretty experienced in how to gain people's trust. One of the things I had learned was that children loved being flattered. I told Jasiek about my father and about how he had fought side by side with Pilsudski. Jasiek knew a lot about this legendary figure and admired him, so his reaction was, "Co ty mowisz," which meant, "What do you know?!" I answered that I bet his father was also a big hero and if he ever met my dad for sure they'd be blood brothers.

Like all other Polish kids, Jasiek crossed himself often and would say "Jezus Maria, Matka Boska." Whenever he did that, I'd cross myself too and say, "May their memory be blessed." This was completely natural behavior for me by now and I didn't even have to think about it. Jasiek told me my hat looked really funny, and I looked at it again. He was right, but it wasn't only funny, it was dangerous for me because it made me stand out in a crowd. Almost all kids wore a typical Polish cap on their heads, so we found another stall where I bought a used cap that made me look like all the other kids running around the streets.

As evening came Jasiek asked me if I would like to meet his mother. I almost yelled, "Sure!" but restrained myself and answered politely in the affirmative. We went to his house. He lived in a poor, neglected neighborhood in a 1 1/2 room apartment. His sister, who was about four years old, immediately reminded me of my sister, though she looked completely different. She was a typical Polish Christian, blonde, blue-eyed, with an upturned nose. Despite the neglected surroundings, the apartment was clean and neat inside. Jasiek's mother was a downtrodden lady who worked as a cleaning woman in various places. There were pictures of her husband on the walls. Jasiek told his mother my story and I noticed that she kept peeking at me admiringly. We sat down to eat supper. On the way I had had the presence of mind to buy all sorts of foods to bring with me. I told his mother that I'd saved some money that my father had left me. I didn't want her to think that she'd have to support me.

As it got later, I told Jasiek's mother that I was going to go find a place to sleep[14]. The woman looked around and suddenly said that maybe I could stay over. I started saying that the apartment was small and I didn't want to be a bother. After trying to convince her, I "acceded" to her invitation. (Of course, the whole time I'd been worried that they'd suddenly give in and let me go...) I said that I'd stay on condition that I pay for my board and for breakfast. I claimed that my father had taught me that it was forbidden to take things for free... To the best of my memory, we agreed that I'd pay 4 or 5 zloty per night. I got to wash up and change my underclothes for the first time in a week. The woman told me to leave my things and she'd wash them for me, as well as my other clothes. I was afraid they'd see that I was a Jew. I knew that as a Jew I had something different and my father had warned me about this, that I shouldn't get undressed in front of strangers. If someone did see and ask, though, he told me to say that when I was four I'd had an operation for some kind of disease whose name I didn't remember.

I slept on the floor on a single blanket, which felt like a royal bed to me. Earlier in the evening I had successfully managed to befriend Jasiek's sister. However, this caused me a problem when I bathed, because she very much wanted to watch how I did it... When I woke up

---

14   *Because the mass killing of polish Chrstian men, hundreds of thousands – if not millions – of Polish children were orphaned, So the phenomenon of orphaned street kids was a common one. on the street I was in a good company.* (More about the orphaned street kids see Chapter 24, side note 14)

in the morning, I was suddenly afraid that I'd talked in my sleep. To check on this, I told Jasiek that I'd heard voices in the middle of the night. I wanted to see the family's reactions. His mother relieved me by saying that surely I'd been dreaming because nobody had spoken during the night.

In order to capture the little girl's heart, I offered to take her with us to play for a while, and then we'd bring her to the family that took care of her during the day. The girl, Mirka, was very happy. She became attached to me because I gave her the feeling that I cared about her, and I really did play with her. In addition, it was a beautiful day, and I bought her an ice cream and a ball. We played with her in the playground and then brought her to her nanny. I suggested to Jasiek that we go to the market and try to earn some money. He agreed, but warned me not to say that I was homeless because kids like that were grabbed and taken to orphanages.

I noticed that besides the Polish police, there were many agents and Gestapo in the market. I quickly modified my behavior and the way I spoke in order to look and sound more like a typical Polish boy. For example, a Polish boy would never walk in a straight line; he'd always jump about and swing around. In short, he sort of danced as he walked. Many kids would also hum a song or whistle as they walked.

For a few hours we helped two farmers sell their merchandise and each of us earned a few zloty along with a bit of food. Jasiek got a job helping ladies carry their packages, and I then found in one of the stalls where their regular worker hadn't come in. I earned a few more zloty that way.

I spent the next several days in this routine of working and playing in the market. One evening when we got home, a woman was there whom I didn't know. We sat down to eat and during the conversation I found out that this woman had also lost her husband in the war but she was well off, working as a top assistant in the municipality – and that the real reason for her visit was to check me out. She had a big apartment, and two daughters who were slightly older than me who went to school. She was prepared to adopt me on a trial basis, she said, and if I got along with her daughters I could live with her. She added that later she'd arrange to be my guardian, that I could stay with her until the war was over and meanwhile I could go to school. She also added, perhaps humorously, "The girls and I need a man in the house." What man – that made me laugh.

Her offer looked fantastic, since my whole goal was to find a hiding place and save my life. But with the sharpened sense of a wild animal running for its life, I felt the danger inherent in the generous offer. Having no choice, however, I went to visit them. It had been over two weeks since I'd seen a normal home, with a room that had books and toys. I'd missed it so much...

The two daughters were very sweet and friendly to me, telling me that they'd always wanted a younger brother. They were older – and much taller – than me. Since I was pretending to be an only child, I was very careful not to mention that I had a sister their age... I slept at their house for several nights. The girls treated me like their doll; they very much wanted to bathe me in the tub. I told them that the priest in my orphanage had taught us that we were not allowed to get undressed in front of other people, and that it was certainly a sin to do so in front of girls... I also had another problem with them: They kissed me all the time, which I didn't much like...

The most embarrassing thing was when the older girl came to me and asked if I'd like for her to show me her "pee-pee" and if I would show her mine. At this stage of life, I still didn't know the sexual role of the penis and just saw it as the way to pass urine. But I knew that it was not acceptable to show it off. Since I had had two sisters and we were open in our family, I had seen my mother bathe, so it was no attraction to me to see a girl's private parts. However, so as not to hurt her feelings I said that of course I would like to see it. She came closer, got undressed, and asked me if her "pee-pee" was pretty. I said yes, and that she was in general a very pretty girl... From this incident, I understood that if I went to live with them I wouldn't be able to hide my private parts from them for long. Since that would be too dangerous, I decided to duck out of the "match." Luckily, they were going on some kind of vacation for ten days (possibly due to Easter), and they went off to relatives in a different city.

So I continued living with Jasiek, paying rent and bringing back all kinds of food every day so I wouldn't be a financial burden on his single mother. Meanwhile, I was a rich boy, what with the money and valuables sewn into my clothing in the ghetto and the money earned from the temporary jobs I picked up.

16.2 – I am Accepted into the "Top Secret Gang"

Jasiek told me one day that he'd spoken with the two leaders of his "secret gang" and that they were ready to give me the entrance test to join them. I met them in a hideout – an apartment in a half-wrecked building which was both their meeting place and a place for anyone to sleep if need be. It turned out that the leaders were boys 14-16 years old. They came to the meeting decked out in sharp suits, smelling of cologne – and the truth was, they looked pretty funny to me. They'd already heard my story from Jasiek, and asked me what I could do. I told them that I knew how to use knives and knew math. They asked me to show them what I could do with a knife, and to try and stab one of them.

I had to put on an impressive show: I slipped the knife out of my left glove, with my right hand I drew out a pocket knife from my pants, and made a move to stab with both of them at once. They were very impressed, but said that because of my size I wasn't worth much as a fighter. If I wanted to be accepted into the gang I'd have to swear to secrecy and obey every order. My nickname would be "Malutki," which meant "Little One." But usually they jokingly called me "General Pilsudski" or "Maly Pilsudski." I suggested to one of the leaders that I could also train his soldiers in using knives... Regarding my obligation to follow every order, though, I told them that there were things I couldn't do, like kill, steal, lie or even hurt someone badly. I would only scratch with my knives, not stab someone in the body. I reminded them that these were things that Jesus and Holy Mary forbid, as taught to me by the priest in the orphanage. We agreed that I'd only break my rules in special situations. I went through the swearing-in ceremony. They told me that I wouldn't know the commanders' real names, only their nicknames, which were something like Tiger and Leopard. They told me that among other things, their gang worked as messengers, delivering packages to certain places – apparently merchandise from the black market. I would get two zloty for every package as well as a tip from the one who received the delivery.

I found out that the commanders got five zloty for every package, and charged three zloty for protecting me and bribing the police. They paid the Polish police who worked in the area so they wouldn't bother us or search the packages. If a Polish cop stopped us we had to say that it was a delivery from the Leopard... From now on, they would take half of what I earned in any job I took, even those they didn't get for me; in exchange, they would protect me.

After consulting with each other, they told me that I could have higher paying jobs once I proved myself with the simple deliveries. Jasiek told me afterward that these "jobs" were stealing from stores, breaking in and stealing from warehouses, grabbing handbags and pickpocketing. In addition, there was work in selling food to Jews that they'd bring to the places the Jews worked. Another money-earner was catching Jews. If we gave over a Jew to a policeman or bring one into the station, we'd get 150 zloty. They had a whole theory of how to identify a Jew, and they'd usually demand 200 zloty from one in exchange for not bringing him in to the police. I knew how dangerous it would be to belong to this gang; there would always be the danger that they'd expose me and then I'd be a huge source of income for them.. But I actually looked at the danger and gamble as a challenge – and I loved it.

I very much wanted to tell my parents that I was alive and had been saved. I thought that maybe I could join the group that sold food to Jews where they worked, but the danger in that was that one of the Jews could recognize me and turn me in. At the end, I gave up on the idea.

During the first two weeks of my stay with Jasiek, I had avoided going to church, but the third week I finally had no choice and that Sunday morning, I went off with Jasiek's family. It was a small neighborhood church. After Mass, we went to accept the holy wafer, and when it was my turn the priest blessed me warmly. It turned out that he already knew about me. Jasiek pointed out one man and told me he was a Gestapo informer, and I shouldn't tell him that my father was a "pulkownik" in the Polish army in England...

Meanwhile, the woman with the two daughters returned. Some man that she had "hunted down" some place came back with them, and the woman never again mentioned her offer to adopt me. However, she did invite Jasiek and me to play with her daughters. She was amazed by my knowledge of math and geography and that I'd read many books. Once she commented, "What an excellent education they provide in these orphanages..."

16.3 – A Priest's Exhortation

One day, as I was playing outside with some members of the gang, a man suddenly passed by who kept looking at us in a suspicious way, as if he was searching for someone. I suddenly felt him give me a piercing look, as if he was taking a picture of me. I started suspecting that he was a Gestapo agent who was trying to find Jews, and felt that I was in danger of being exposed. Almost instinctively, I pointed at him and yelled out, "He's a Jew, grab him!" In seconds, about ten kids were all over him, felling him to the sidewalk. But while fighting us off, he managed to draw out his whistle and blast it. A couple of minutes later, two Polish policemen arrived. We yelled that we'd caught a Jew and they took him to the station. The Leopard went along with them together with another kid so they could collect their reward for having caught a Jew.

According to their custom, I would get half the reward since I'd found the Jew. But when the Leopard came back he gave me only 50 zloty. He explained that he'd only gotten 100 zloty since that Jew worked for the Gestapo... I became a little famous for having caught a Jew, but I didn't feel good about it. It's true that when I screamed out "Jew!" I was sure that he worked for the Gestapo, but what if I'd been wrong? Maybe I would have really turned in a Jew. My new fame was another disadvantage, because it was very important for me not to be prominent in any way.

About two weeks after this incident, I visited the church. After Mass, the priest called me over and said he wanted to speak to me. He took me to a private room within the church, and his assistant brought me some cake. It was one of the tastiest cakes I have ever eaten in my life... After a short talk and exhortation on the importance of doing good deeds, he told me that Holy Mary, mother of God, wasn't happy about turning Jews over to the Germans. I crossed myself at the mention of the Holy Mother's name and protested almost instinctively: "But he was a Jewish agent of the Gestapo!" I almost added that if he had been just a Jew I wouldn't have turned him in, but kept quiet. I don't know how the priest understood my protest; at the time I didn't understand what danger I'd put myself in by saying that. But suddenly I felt very close to the priest – after all, he opposed handing Jews in! He even exhorted me not to do it! I was very close to jumping on his neck and confessing my whole story, but I managed to restrain myself and keep quiet. How absurd it was that a priest was preaching to me that it wasn't nice to betray Jews...

After that, I would often think about the priest and about how I could possibly be helped by him in the future if there was trouble, because he was a good man. I even thought to ask him to find me a place to hide in a monastery, but I didn't go through with these ideas. (After the war, I thought a lot about how much I would like to go back and meet that priest and tell him what had happened to me and how much he had encouraged me. While writing this and bringing up memories, I think of Jasiek, his little sister and his mother, of the woman with two daughters who wanted to adopt me.... I would have liked to tell her daughter why I didn't want to show her my private parts, and meet the gang and tell them – especially the Leopard – how I'd tricked them, and meet the stall owners in the market and ask them if they hadn't suspected that I was a Jew...)

Weeks passed in my "theater of the absurd" in which I played the part of the "pulkownik's" son, participating in the gang's activities, sometimes making deliveries for two zloty and a tip... Sometimes, these deliveries were to German families, and I have to say that they gave the best tips. Sometimes I'd sleep in the gang's hideout and act as a guard. I was well known in the farmers' market and the merchants would hire me happily because of my knowledge of math. Meanwhile, I missed my family more and more, I felt lonelier and lonelier, and my fear of being exposed grew all the time.

After much deliberation, I decided to put an end to this situation. The first thing I decided to try was to find Big David's family, my uncle with Nicaraguan citizenship who had adopted my little sister, Sarenka. Suddenly, I was overwhelmed with the desire to meet and hug her after not seeing her for almost a year. Uncle David's house was near the intersection of Gertruda and Starowislna Streets, but my father had warned me not to go there because the Gestapo was watching him. I decided to try locating someone from his family and passing on the message that I needed help.

After much thought, I reached the conclusion that going to Uncle

David's neighborhood by myself would be very dangerous, since it was in the center of town and was crawling with all kinds of police-men and Gestapo agents. I decided to take along some company. I told Jasiek and one of the other kids in the gang (who looked very Aryan) that I had a secret mission and wanted them to come with me as guards. I told them I had to meet someone who'd give me money for some work I'd done for him, and since it was a very important mission I'd pay each of them five zloty.

They were very happy about this mission – perhaps because of all the mystery involved. Near the intersection where the house stood was a big electric tram station. Under the assumption that my uncle's family used the station, I decided to keep a lookout there and try and identify one of my relatives. I didn't see anyone on the first day, but not long after we got to the station on the second day, I spotted my cousin Genia getting off and walking towards her house. I tamped down my emotions, followed her and quietly called out her name. She gave me a glance, and didn't recognize me at first. I said, "I'm Leosz!" and she was shocked. "Is it really you?" she asked me in con-fusion. I immediately fired questions at her: How's Dad, Mom, Gizia, Sarenka. She said everyone was fine. I told her to give me money right away, as my friends were watching us. She took out her wallet and emptied it into my hand (it was a few dozen zloty). Then I said in what was almost a tone of command: "Find me a hiding place!"

Genia sank into thought for several minutes. At the end, she told me to come back to this exact place in five days at a certain time. By then they would have found for me some kind of arrangement. We should only glance at each other upon meeting, and then I should follow her. I would only go over to her when she took her hand-kerchief from her bag and put it to her nose while looking in my direction. I went back to my friends and gave them five zloty each, as promised. We then went into a bakery and I bought them each a piece of cake of his choice and a cup of soda. They were very happy;

they'd participated in a secret mission, gotten money and even cake. I swore them to secrecy upon Jesus' and Mary's names.

16.4 – My Apartment Hideout, and the Righteous Among the Nations

Five days later, I returned to meet my cousin in the designated spot, still accompanied by my guards. I took along my satchel, which contained my worldly goods. I hid my money in various places; I thought I still had most of it but I hadn't counted and didn't know exactly how much there was. I told my escorts that it could be that this time I'd be going away for a while, but I didn't know for how long. I swore them to secrecy again, because they could spoil the whole mission for me. I gave them 10 zloty each and promised that when I came back they'd continue being my partners and would get a lot more money in the future.

We got to the area, but kept walking around as none of us had a watch so I could only approximate the time. I was terribly tense and felt as if we'd been there forever. Suddenly, I saw Genia walking on Starowislna Street. Without thinking, I took more money out of my pocket, gave it to the two kids, crossed myself, told them that Jesus should protect them, made some motions to get Genia's attention and – though I wasn't sure she'd seen me – started following her.

Several meters on, she turned her head and I saw that she had noticed me. I kept following her in that dancing walk typical of Polish kids, crossing myself occasionally and whistling – especially when I passed a priest or a monk. I played the part of a mischievous, good Christian boy very well. I followed my cousin out from the center of town, and since I was concentrating hard on what I was doing, I didn't pay attention to what neighborhood we were in, but it was quite far out. On a certain street I saw a young couple with a baby carriage. Genia stopped next to them for a moment and said something, then walked on a bit – and took out her handkerchief. When I came up to her she told me to join the couple with the carriage.

When I got to them, the woman took me by the hand and told me to put my hands on the carriage and steer it. The couple walked on either side of me. Suddenly, the woman took a sailor's shirt and hat out of her bag and put them on me. It was a very common thing for children to wear. While we were walking the baby started to cry. The woman told me to calm him and say, "Quiet, Pusi, I'll play with you at home." She told me to sing a well-known Polish lullaby to him. After a few minutes I started communicating with the baby very naturally. We got to a certain building, but since I was completely focused on the child and on this whole strange and even hallucinatory situation in general, I didn't notice what street or even house number it was. We went up to the third (uppermost) floor and entered the apartment where the woman's parents lived. They were an older couple (maybe in their late forties). These people were to hide me in their home for several months. They had a son who looked about twenty, apparently single, who didn't live with them. Their daughter – who had brought me – was called Mika. Mika had another son who was a year or two younger than me. I never met him though, because whenever he visited I hid in my room since they couldn't rely on him to keep my secret.

I had never seen this couple before in my life, and I never asked them why they had decided to hide me. I have no idea if they were paid to do so or if they did it out of altruism and courage. It is important to note that the penalty for hiding a Jew was death.

My strange entrance to the house was a play that had been well planned in advance. The reason for it was a woman who lived on the ground floor who was rumored to be a Gestapo informer and would always nose around her neighbors' business. That's why I was dressed as Mika's son before we went in; all the neighbors were used to seeing him come visit his grandparents dressed in a sailor suit.

A little while after bringing me in, Mika and her family left and

Mrs. Maria led me to a small room that she had prepared for me. It was at the very end of the hall, far from the door to the house and the living room. There was also a door in it that led to the parents' bedroom. It was usually used as a guestroom for the family and grandchildren when they came to visit Grandma and Grandpa. The room also had a big closet that held mainly coats, but also a full set of clothes and underwear for me. They had prepared well for my arrival.

Mrs. Maria immediately took pains to get me settled in and set down the rules of the house. The first thing she did was put me in a warm tub and tell me that in order to remove all the dirt, I had to lie in the tub for at least two hours... She decided to throw out my old clothes, and it took some doing to stop her so I could remove all my personal things first. The first thing I did, of course, was to get out all my money. I found that I had about 2,200 zloty, some foreign currency and some packets of jewelry. When I took out all my knives, Mrs. Maria started crossing herself...I told her that they were only to play with and to use against the Germans. When she saw the money, she told me in astonishment, "Pan jest bardzo bogaty," which meant, "The master is very rich; my husband has to work many months to make so much money."

The bath felt absolutely wonderful. I then got dressed in the new clothes, and finally, after so many long weeks of abnormal sleep, I went to bed like a prince. I woke up the next day at noon, and after eating a bit I started thinking of how I could keep myself occupied. It was clear to me that I couldn't leave the house or meet friends; for all intents and purposes, I was under house arrest. I asked Mrs. Maria to buy me a few books whose names I remembered by heart. I also asked her to get me several notebooks and writing implements – colored pencils, a fountain pen – and construction sets. I asked her not to take money from my uncle for these personal things; I'd pay her out of my own pocket. Luckily, books, toys and things to write with were all quite cheap. Books didn't cost more than five zloty apiece, so for 150 zloty I bought almost twenty of them, besides everything else I wanted.

At a later stage, I asked them to bring me a catalogue of reading books and school books for grades four through six. (The Germans had closed all the academic high schools and only let technical schools exist, so there were no academic textbooks for high school.)

They called the owner of the house "Jacek," but I don't know if that was his real name, either. He was a very simple and modest man. He almost never talked, and ignored me almost completely. He worked very hard and would return very late at night. Neither his wife nor his daughter, Mika, worked. Mika's husband, Frank, was the only one who worked in some kind of "intellectual" job. He was a serious and learned fellow with whom I could have serious conversations. Mika's brother's name was Kuba. He was an adorable guy, with a great sense of humor. He was always joking around and he'd play all sorts of games with me, like chess and checkers. He'd also help me with my construction sets. The whole family would usually get together on Sundays for lunch, and the children would also come over some-times during the week for a visit.

I spent several long months in my "five star hiding place." I should note that not once during this period did I ever feel threatened or live in fear. I felt that these people weren't worried either, despite the threat that at any moment I could be discovered – which would cause a horrific tragedy for this family. They planned what to claim in case I was discovered: Our cover story was based on my old one. They'd say that that's all they knew about me; that they'd found me on the streets and decided to adopt me. As I said above, there were about a million orphans in Poland at the time, and it was accepted practice to even adopt older children. They called me Brzerzyk, using my "regu-lar" alias, or "Malutki," which had been my name in the gang.

After our very first family meal, we had a "practice raid" to drill what we'd do if the Germans came to search the house. Our street was a very quiet one; very few cars passed by, so if one stopped near the building we'd hear it right away. We could also see from the windows whoever came into the building. It was apparently not by chance that they chose the top floor for my hideout, as the building also had a big attic which was used for storage, a workshop and a place to hang laundry. Our little exercise had me escape to the attic in case of a raid, to either hide there or go up onto the roof and go from one roof to the next to another house where I'd hide until the danger had passed. This was the only time we ever practiced this – and it was my great fortune that I never had to use this plan. If the Germans had made a serious raid it probably wouldn't have helped anyway since they would have closed off the roofs in such a case.

In just a few days, I was all set in my hiding place and settled into a new routine. Most of the time I stayed in my room and studied, read and wrote. I decided to write a diary (as I had many times before). I wrote imaginary letters to Mom, Dad, President Roosevelt, the Chief of Staff of the Soviet Army... I also wrote critiques and reports about the books I read. When I needed more books, Mrs. Maria registered me in the library in her grandson's name and every few days she'd exchange my books, two or three at a time. The librarian was very curious to meet the boy who read so voraciously...

I asked that Mrs. Maria buy me all kinds of simple exercise gadgets like weights, a chin-up bar and a mat so I could do floor exercises. I gave myself all kinds of assignments, like doing a hundred crunches. I learned how to do a split, how to get up from a supine position by throwing my legs over my head. One day, Kuba brought me a punching bag and I started practicing like crazy how to box. I decided then and there that when I grew up I'd be a boxer...

The baby, Pusi, was almost a year old and started trying to walk. He became very attached to me, and whenever his mother brought him during the week, the first thing he did was come look for me. I loved to play with him, since I didn't have many friends. I requested that they use my money to buy him toys and every time he came I'd surprise him with a new one. I spent hours with him, which made both us and his parents very happy.

Once in a while, Mika would bring her older son to the Sunday lunch. When that happened, I spent the whole time hiding in my room. Mika and I developed a very strong emotional bond, despite – or maybe because – she had a son close to my age. She loved me and would say all the time that her older son needed a brother like me. She was younger than my mother and it was possible that she filled that role for me. I loved it very much when she hugged and kissed me. It made a bit of my loneliness disappear. For some reason, though I spent almost the whole day with Mrs. Maria, we never developed that kind of love between us. Our relationship was good, but cool. I was careful to be very disciplined and made every effort not to anger her or become an additional burden to her. I would always offer to help her in the kitchen and to clean the house, wash dishes and cook...

My happiest hours were during the Sunday lunches, when everyone in the family would come after church. I'd have long conversations with Frank, Mika's husband. The first chance I had, I asked him what was happening in the various fronts, since it was a long time since I'd been up to date. The war was the topic most on my mind and I was very happy to hear the news that the Germans were retreating on all fronts: In North Africa they had surrendered completely – and these were the elite of the German army. Sicily had been captured and the Americans were planning to invade via Italy. In the Soviet Union, fierce battles continued with no side victorious and the Germans suffering terrible losses. German cities were being bombed; Berlin was bombed almost every day. Each day, thousands of Germans were being killed. Even the Germans no longer believed in victory. Was there a chance for a cease-fire? It was hard to believe that Hitler would agree to give up all that he had conquered; there was no choice but to destroy Germany to its foundations. I found out that the Polish army had participated in the battles of North Africa and Sicily, while the Polish air force joined in the bombing of Germany. Sometimes on the BBC they would recite the names of Polish officers and soldiers who had received medals.

Since the Sunday lunches were always a time to report on and discuss the war situation, several weeks later, I was informed of the German defeat in Kursk. The Germans had had about 150 divisions – about a million soldiers – and they attacked the "bulge" of Kursk. After three weeks of fighting, they'd lost over 100,000 men and it was a total rout. During their retreat, they had to leave behind most of their heavy armor while trying to evacuate around 200,000 wounded. At the same time, the Americans and British invaded Italy, Mussolini fell and Italy stopped fighting the Allied forces. I also began hearing an undercurrent of worry among the Poles over the possibility that the Soviet Union would conquer Poland.

From time to time I'd get regards from my family. I knew that my father had an excellent job in a laboratory outside the Plaszow Camp, checking textiles used for uniforms and military equipment. They valued his work highly and so he enjoyed special conditions. Because he worked outside Plaszow, he could bring extra food to the family. My mother and sister continued working for the Madritch factory that made uniforms and other military items. It had been moved to the industrial zone that was within the Plaszow fence. They were considered professional and zealous workers and were thought of highly. As I mentioned before, the owner and manager was apparently a fair man who even took care of his workers in the camp. He'd bring them extra food he paid for himself, so they didn't only depend on the rations they got in Plaszow and they weren't too hungry. (According to the law and official procedure, the Jews were considered workers who belonged the SS. The factory owner would pay the SS a certain sum for every Jew and the SS was responsible for the workers' food. It should be noted that there were other factory owners who also supplied their employees with extra food, such as the famous Oskar Schindler.) Uncle David told my Polish family (who told me) how overjoyed my parents and sister were when they were told after long weeks of uncertainty that I had actually managed to escape from the ghetto. They also told me that my parents had always believed that I'd manage to do so.

At some point I decided to check exactly what "treasures" my father had given me. I found out that I had about USD150 in $1, $5 and $10 notes; a packet with two rings with stones in them that I assume were diamonds; and another which held tiny gold bars that weighed perhaps 20 grams each. I suddenly had the idea to give one of the rings to Mika as a gift, as I was well aware of the danger this Polish family was in for having taken me in and I appreciated it very much. The very next Sunday at lunch, I presented the ring to her. The whole family was very surprised, and of course at first Mika refused to accept it. I made up a story about how my mother had given the ring to me before we had said goodbye and had told me to give it to the person who helped me after I ran away from the ghetto. The story made everyone quite emotional; Mika had tears in her eyes and gave a very long hug. I also made a second gesture: In a few days the Christians would be celebrating one of their holidays, so I gave Maria 100 zloty and requested that she buy a goose or turkey and other special treats for the holiday meal. And what a meal it was, when we shared in it on the day! I was the star of the celebration.

That meal was also memorable because everyone talked around the table – even Grandpa Jacek. It turned out that even though he was uneducated, he was a very smart and measured man. From the conversation of the younger people, I found out that they lived in constant fear and insecurity, and not necessarily because of me. They were always in danger of being taken for forced labor in Germany, being arrested on suspicion of being a member of the Resistance, of spreading news from the BBC, etc. It should be noted that the Poles also had very few rights, and if one was even remotely suspected of breaking the "German State Security Law" a Polish citizen could be executed or sent to a concentration camp. Practically speaking, any Pole who didn't collaborate with the authorities was automatically suspect.

There were always stories at the Sunday meal of people who had been snatched and disappeared. And once, Frank told me about the big Warsaw Ghetto revolt that began in April 1943 and lasted about a month. Everyone discussed *that* subject with great admiration and surprise – and with only one tiny anti-Semitic comment: "You see that Jews also know how to fight." They also touched on the question of why the Jews didn't revolt in Krakow. The differences in the conditions in our ghetto were mentioned: It was such a small area, the houses were small, and the Gestapo had a strong hold on everything due to the informers. In fact, Krakow did have an armed Underground (mainly teens of the Bnei Akiva [Religious Zionist] movement), but they were only active against the Germans outside the ghetto and didn't take credit for what they did so as to prevent revenge attacks against the ghetto. In this context, they emphasized that the Polish Resistance also fought the Germans outside populated areas for the same reason. I was very excited about the Warsaw Ghetto Uprising and was very proud that we Jews were fighting.

Occasionally, guests would come to visit – mainly Maria's friends or neighbors. I would then spend the whole time in my room in absolute silence. Sometimes the visits lasted for hours… I was also shut in my room whenever Maria left the house and I was alone. Despite having things to do all the time and I concentrated hard on doing them, these hours of being locked in were difficult ones. In an emergency, if someone came into the house or there was a surprise search when I couldn't get up to the attic, I had a primitive hiding place in a coat closet. They built a small shelf about half a meter up that ran across the width of the closet, and moved the closet about 30 centimeters from the wall. I'd have to go in, lock the closet door from the inside, and climb up to the shelf behind the coats. My body stuck out of the closet in the back but it was hidden on both sides. There was also a curtain hanging down behind the coats that acted as an extra layer hiding me from view if anyone moved the coats aside.

On several occasions, the family would ask me how I managed to escape the ghetto and survive the weeks before I got to them. For some reason, I was very closed-mouthed about my story. On the other hand, I was very interested in what they knew of the German activities against the Jews, of the liquidation of the ghetto and the massacre that took place there in broad daylight. I found out that they knew about everything. The thing that had shaken them the most was the carting of the bodies through the Krakow streets, and the rumors of children's bodies falling out of the wagons.

My hosts also knew of the death camps and gas chambers. They spoke a lot about the atrocities against the Polish population. (This would be the place to mention that despite the seemingly normal lives of the Poles there was still an unending campaign to murder Polish intellectuals and those suspected of being in the Resistance. University professors, high school teachers, newspaper columnists, radio hosts and writers were all targets. Auschwitz had originally been established to murder this entire echelon of society, and by the end of the war almost three million Christian Poles had died.)

I was very curious about what this family's motives were for taking on the terrible risk of hiding me. I had no actual knowledge. I didn't know if they were paid, and if so, how much; whether they just got back the expenses of my upkeep or whether they were paid well for the serious risk they took. I never saw any behavior that would make me think they were greedy people. But I also never heard them express any love for the Jewish people or say things to indicate they were humanistic and idealistic Poles who saw their act as being something moral or noble. When they talked freely they used many routine anti-Semitic expressions and didn't feel there was anything wrong with them. For example, they'd threaten a child that if he didn't eat, a Jew with a beard would come and eat him... And when I showed them my treasures, Maria commented, "No matter what the situation, the Jews always have a lot of money."

Except for Frank, Mika's husband, they weren't learned people. I think they barely finished grade school. Yet they were simple and good people. I imagine the argument that might have ensued when they made the decision to hide me. I asked myself many times and wondered: What would I have done in their place? Would I have been ready to take a huge chance for a moral and noble cause? The easy answer to that was that such a decision could only be made in "real time," when it's not a theoretical question. I had already risked my life to save or help others, but would I have been ready to risk family and children? I think that my answer would be: Maybe!... But *they* did it.

I loved their son, Kubek. His happy and mischievous mood reminded me very much of my young uncle, Mom's brother, who shared his name (Kubek being a diminutive of Kuba). He would tell a lot of jokes, including ones about Jews. One of them went like this: A Christian enters a Jew's store and buys some things. The Jew says it costs 50 zloty. Suddenly the Christian whips out a beard from his pocket and sticks it on himself, so the Jew says it's only 40 zloty. Kubek didn't register at all that he was essentially saying something anti-Semitic.

My money started to dwindle; when I had about a thousand zloty left (still considered a very respectable sum in those days) I remembered that my father had told me that if I needed more money I could sell some of my hidden treasures. So the next chance I had, when

I was alone with Kubek, I brought out one $10 bill and a gold bar and asked him to sell them for me. He wasn't surprised by the question and I felt that he wasn't a stranger to such dealings. He told me he didn't know how much they were worth. I simply answered that whatever he got for them, 20% would be for him, and 20% for presents for the family. I hoped that I'd get between 100-200 zloty. Kubek asked me, "What is a percent?" I explained, giving him a thorough math lesson in percentages. But at the end I just told him the easiest way to do it would be to divide what he got into 5 equal parts, and take one part for himself, one part to buy things for the others, and give three to me.

Kubek, by the way, accepted very good-naturedly that I knew math better than he did, and he would often ask me afterward to teach him more – sometimes even a few times a week. This I did very willingly and with great enthusiasm. I was really quite proud of being his teacher. Later on in life, when I did a lot of teaching, which I usually really loved to do, I always remembered Kubek as my one of first teaching experience.

Kubek's mother was very happy that he was learning with me. She saw nothing unusual in it, and would mumble, "It's great that you're learning; too bad you didn't listen to your teachers in school." Kubek told me that he worked for the Germans in a small airport – I don't remember if he was a car or plane mechanic – and he had papers stating that he was vital to the war effort. This protected him from being taken to Germany for forced labor. His salary was less than 10 zloty per day and a bowl of soup. But he made a lot of money on the black market.

To my great surprise, a week later Kubek told me he had sold my treasures for some 800 zloty, several times more than I'd thought I'd get. We agreed on the gifts he'd buy, and the very next Sunday I gave out what he'd bought: little Pusik got a train, Maria and Mika got several kinds of simple jewelry, perfume and socks, and the men got ties, shirts and cigars. He also bought meat, which Maria made into a delicious roast that we all enjoyed tremendously. It was a happy meal, and I enjoyed all the praises they heaped on me for my generosity. This was the high point of my happiness in this hiding place.

After that, things deteriorated. I suddenly started feeling that the family was getting a little irritated with me, and sensed a certain withdrawal. I had no idea what had happened, and on my part I just tried with all my might to be nice and behave myself. But apparently things had gone beyond my control. They didn't say anything to me, but I felt they weren't comfortable with me, and maybe something had happened to give them a reason to be frightened.

The peak of this crisis came straight out of my nightmares... All these last months I had been playing the part of a big hero. But the truth was that inside I was full of fears. I pretended to be happy but all I wanted to really do was hug my mother and burst out crying. Maybe during the day I did feel happy sometimes, but it all fell apart in my dreams. I had two kinds of dreams. In the good kind I relived the good and happy times with my family. In the bad ones, I was running away, hiding, people were trying to kill me and I was fighting them off. In one of them I actually stabbed an SS man who was walking toward me with a raised gun and a smile wreathing his face. After I stabbed him he stopped smiling and said, "I'll tell your father what you did." I yelled back at him: "My father would let me!"

Whenever I woke up from a good dream I'd try to go back to sleep so I could continue it. With the nightmares, I'd wake up suddenly, sometimes with a yell, and be happy that I was now awake. One night I woke up from a nightmare and saw Maria standing over me trying to calm me down. My yell or yells (I don't know if this was the first time they'd heard me scream) apparently added to their concerns. After this incident, I felt their discomfort with me even more strongly, even though they still didn't say anything outright.

A few days later, Maria had a guest over and as usual I was staying silent in my room. Suddenly, she called me to come out, introduced me to her friend and told me that this was a childhood friend of hers and I didn't have to worry about her. Then, in the ensuing conversation, she commented offhandedly that I would be leaving them soon... I understood. It was a huge shock for me, but I didn't say a word.

Several days after that, Mika came to visit and she and Maria explained that while it had been very pleasant hosting me, their friends and neighbors had noticed a difference and were asking questions. Their main problem was with Mika's older boy, who was constantly asking why he hadn't been able to sleep over at Grandma's house for months, and why his parents weren't taking him there on Sundays. They told me that my uncle had found me another hiding place, and I'd be leaving them in a few days. They also said that it was possible that later they'd transfer me to a monastery, where I could even play outside. I don't remember that this "official notice" of my move caused me to feel hurt, insulted or afraid, despite my having gotten used to the place and attached to the people, besides being quite comfortable.

When the time came, our parting was quite emotional. Only Maria and Kubek were home. They had bought me a new satchel, and Maria had sewn my treasures back into the coat lining, while the money was spread out in secret pockets in my pants and shirt. I also took along one pocket knife and one switchblade.

CHAPTER 17

The Route to Family Reunification Runs through Hell

Kubek began explaining how I was going to get to my new hiding place: I had to leave the house alone, turn right, and at the corner I was to turn left. There I would meet my cousin Genia, and after we would make eye contact I would follow her. When she stopped at a store window or a kiosk and took out a handkerchief, I should go up to her and she'd tell me what to do. Meanwhile, Kubek would follow me in case something went wrong and I needed help.

It was rainy and cold outside. I met Genia as planned and started following a few dozen meters behind her. After a while, I got very tired, while Genia for some reason speeded up. There was no way I could ask her to slow down. Because I was so tired, I forgot about walking in a carefree manner, whistling and looking people cheekily directly into their eyes. It could be that the way I walked betrayed tension and lack of confidence, and was therefore suspicious. There weren't too many people on the street, but suddenly I saw two young men walking toward me. They weren't dressed in any special way, but a couple of minutes after they passed me they obviously doubled back, because I felt one of them catch me by the hand and tell me to come with them. Apparently they were either Polish secret police who worked for the Gestapo or simply criminals who would catch people they suspected in order to get a reward. I started screaming that I hadn't done anything wrong, I didn't steal anything, that "Holy Maria will punish you, I am the son of a Pulkownik!" One of them said in Polish in a threatening tone, "Shut up!" So I did...

We came to a station of the "black" Polish police. I also saw there German police from the Schutzpolizei, in green uniforms. There, they registered me – and while I was waiting for my turn it might have been possible to escape since no one was watching me in particular. However, for some reason I didn't try it. The one who registered me only asked some basic formal questions which I answered fluently, without any hesitation.

When I was then interrogated, I claimed that I had only reached Krakow two days earlier. I gave them the name of the orphanage in a tiny town in Eastern Europe from which I'd escaped. I remembered to put on the show of crossing myself and mumbling "Jezus, Maria, Matka Boska." I had no inkling what they suspected me of. They put me in a cell with several other children and teens. There were several holding cells there for boys and one for girls. Most of them were older than me. We introduced ourselves and they immediately asked why I was arrested. I told them my cover story very convincingly, and didn't see anyone who doubted it. Most of the lads had been arrested either for putting up announcements made by the Resistance, thievery, vandalism or simple vagrancy. We got very little food to eat and everyone there was very hungry. We constantly spoke about food.

I was interrogated twice in all. They kept asking me the same questions over and over and writing down my answers. According to what was being asked, I understood that they were mainly trying to figure out if I was a courier for the Resistance or was involved in putting up their posters. At the second interrogation I got hit a few times, because I acted quite impudently. Instead of answering a question, I'd yell that I was hungry, that I hadn't stolen anything, that I'd had a proper education, and that he could ask the priest at my orphanage. Suddenly, the investigator gave me a few ringing slaps, and told me to just answer his questions.

Towards the end of the interrogation, I told him that I had money and asked if he could please buy me some food. I took out 30 zloty from my pocket. To my extreme surprise, when he was finished, he called over one of the policemen and told him to go buy the food. I managed to tell him that I would give part of it to the other children. He brought me 20 rolls (they cost 1/2 a zloty each), some cheese and a few apples. I gave each boy in the cell two rolls and a piece of the cheese (I was left with four rolls). I asked all of them to get up and say Grace over the bread, then ate my rolls and the rest of the cheese feeling like a king. To this day I remember that feast of rolls as one of the best meals I ever ate in my life...

After we ate this, I told the kids that since I didn't have enough apples, each one would get a half and I'd get a whole one for myself. So in the merit of a few bits of food, I became God and king to eight Christian boys. But I didn't get to rule for very long; two days after this a policeman came and informed me that I was to get ready because I was being transferred somewhere else. I parted with some emotion from my new friends. It's interesting how people connect and make friends so quickly when in very difficult situations; I saw this happen in the future as well.

The policeman who took me was a nice guy who treated me well. He put handcuffs on my wrists and also handcuffed me to him. This was the first time that they had handcuffed me. I have to admit that this entertained me a bit... I asked him what his name was and if he had children. He answered that it was forbidden for him to talk to me at all. I tried to promise him that if he'd take off the handcuffs I'd swear in the name of the Holy Mother that I wouldn't run away. He didn't take them off, but he did talk to me. I repeated the stories of my Pulkownik father and how he fought with Pilsudski; I also asked him why they had arrested me, but he refused to tell me. Still, he encouraged me with the promise that surely they would free me soon.

We crossed half the city together until we got to the command post of the Gestapo in the 'Montelupich,' which was also the central prison. This was a huge, gray and frightening building, full of German soldiers with drawn sub-machine guns. When I got there I understood where I was; perhaps I had seen the name of the street, or maybe the nice policeman with me told me. I knew about this place even in the ghetto; everyone knew that if someone got arrested they would get sent to Montelupich. I even remember the ditty they would chant in the ghetto, it went something like this: Montelupich, Montelupich, dla modrych i dla gupich" (Montelupich, Montelupich. for those who are smart and those who are obtuse).

Immediately upon registration, I was interrogated by two men. One of them was a Pole (according to his accent), while the second barely knew Polish and needed the first one to translate for him. I declaimed my mantra so well that it sounded very good, believable and convincing – to me. I answered their questions immediately, even the surprising ones. They asked me why I had come specifically to Krakow, had someone given me something to pass on to someone else... I already had a story ready as to why I'd come to Krakow, saying that the priest in the orphanage had told us of "Kosciul Mariacki," the Church of the Holy Mary – and when I said this, I piously crossed myself.

As usual, I tried talking a lot. When the interrogator asked me, "So who would give you the posters to give out?" Instead of answering, I said, "Take me to see the church, I promise not to run away." This time, I got two slaps and a threat to put me in a cell with rats and snakes. So I protested, "Ale prosze pana, nie wiem co to jest plakat" (But sir, I don't know what you're talking about, what are these posters?) So they'd ask me again, "So why did you come to Krakow, who sent you? Who sent you? If you don't tell us the truth we'll send you to an orphanage for criminal children - 'dom poprawczy.'" In Polish children's tales, this was the most frightening thing, a kind of correction facility for children, where they'd "correct" children by starving them, beating them and giving them freezing showers. At the end, the interrogator said that it would be worth my while telling the truth – I'd get a reward. And so I understood that they hadn't believed me...

I was then taken to the basement. Apparently there were several floors of jail cells, with long and threatening corridors. They put me in a cell with about 10 people. Conditions were better there than in the first jail in that every person had a bed with a mattress and two blankets. As they were arranged in triple tier bunk beds around the sides of the cell, I happily climbed to the top of one of them. In a corner of the cell there was a bucket in which one could go to the bathroom, as well as a water faucet. In the middle of the room was a table and a few chairs. It was stifling in the cell, it stank terribly, and there was no ventilation. All of the detainees were young men and two teens, all of whom were extremely hungry. Twice a day we got some very thin soup that contained rotten vegetables, and each morning we got two slices of bread. There was no way to get more food. I think that the Gestapo deliberately used starvation as a means of pressuring the prisoners.

Naturally, most of the conversation revolved around food. There was a whole discussion about how one should eat the morning bread: Eat a tiny bit right away, or maybe eat it with the soup. One prisoner had the theory that it was best to save at least half of it and eat that right before going to sleep... Among all the stories about food, I told mine about the rolls in the previous jail and it became an instant hit. They asked me how I'd eaten the rolls, if I'd put the cheese into the roll or eaten it separately, taking a bite first from the roll and then from the cheese...From this a whole discussion developed about rolls. Each one had something to say about various rolls, how to eat them, what to spread on them. It turned out that one of the prisoner's uncles had a bakery and he talked for hours about how one bakes various kinds of rolls... As I also learned later in the German concentration camps, when people are hungry almost the only subject that interests them is food. Hunger is a terrible torture, and it certainly breaks people. It was also a tool used during interrogation. Meanwhile, for those who smoked – and most of the adults in my cell did – the lack of cigarettes was just as hard as the hunger.

I spent about ten days in this cell, which wasn't enough time to get to know many people. In general, they kept very quiet about their identity, what they did, and why they were in jail. But I still managed to learn that two of them were quite young, 15 years old, and they were suspected of being connected to the Polish Resistance. They would return from being interrogated with signs of having been beaten, and dripping blood. Common tortures in this jail were: freezing baths, being hung by the hands, and being whipped on a bare back or backside. It was vital to the Gestapo to get information from them, so they also constantly tried to entice them by having a table full of food in the interrogation room, with the promise that if they talked, they'd eat.

I managed to get friendly with two of my cell-mates: A Pole named Wojek, or Wojchek, and a second, older man whose name I can't remember. I'll call him "the assimilator." Wojczek's nickname was Wojcz, and he was a member of the Resistance. They had caught him with a radio and incriminating documents, and he wasn't denying it. He didn't give his comrades away during interrogations and would be happy to die for his country. I would say Grace with Wojcz over every quarter slice of bread that we'd eat. I asked him if was possible to escape from this place, and he explained that sometimes there was a chance to do so, but it was very dangerous. My friendship with Wojcz continued until he was taken to the firing squad and executed.

The "assimilator" was around 30 years old. He told me that he was a Christian, married to a Polish woman of German extraction. After the defeat of Poland, she was considered a "Volksdeutsche," and received German citizenship. As a result, the Gestapo had investigated his antecedents very carefully and found out that his grandfather had been a Jew who had converted to Christianity. He hadn't known a thing about it and neither had his wife; otherwise, she would never have requested German citizenship. They had a six-year-old daughter who was with his wife and her parents. The Germans had demanded that she divorce him, and then she and her daughter would get all their rights as Germans, but she refused. He had already been in jail for several months, and the Gestapo was demanding that he write her to say that he wanted the divorce. If he did so, they'd get their rights and he'd be taken to a labor camp as a Jew.

The Germans were very frightened of getting ill and were careful about hygiene. Every few days they would take us in small groups to the shower. After we washed, they would spray us with some kind of substance. Of course the water was cold, but at least there was soap.

17.1 – From the Firing Squad to Meeting My Father

After ten days in jail, the Gestapo called for me, Wojcz, the "assimilator" and another two men. They also took people out of other cells, loading about 20 of us into a truck covered with a tarpaulin. It was a mixed group of young Poles accused of working for the Resistance and families of Jews with their children. One of the men from my cell was actually reunited with his wife and two children on the truck. Some of the Poles were handcuffed and chained together in pairs. Some SS men were also in the back, pointed their sub-machine guns at us.

We started off. A kind of command car with a machine gun on it followed the truck. It was a scary sight. I held the lapel of Wojcz's jacket and it was hard for me to control my fear. I asked Wojcz if they were going to kill us, and if there would be a chance to escape. Then I asked him if it hurt to get shot. Wojcz comforted me, saying that it didn't hurt, and you go to sleep right afterwards. He didn't think there would be a chance to escape but said that we should behave with honor, and not beg for anything from the Germans or show them any fear. The Germans would pay for everything they'd done...

After a long ride, the truck stopped. As I found out later, we were in the Plaszow Camp. We were brought to the headquarters of the Jewish Police. There were many SS officers and Jewish policemen in the building. Outside, about 20 policemen in black uniforms stood neatly in rows (apparently they were Ukrainians). They took us into a big room that was used as a holding pen. We were guarded here by the Jewish Police. We asked for something to eat and everyone got a piece of bread. There were about five children of various ages who had been on the truck, and as far as I remember none of them cried. I think that most of the people knew that we had been sentenced to death. After a while they called for the "assimilator," another man, and the family with two children. I found out later that they let them go into the camp. I even met the "assimilator" again – just once – and it was a very emotional meeting. I introduced him to my father and he heaped praises on me for my behavior under difficult conditions, and I was very proud of myself.

I waited a long time in that room until they ordered me (and others) to come with them. A group of Jewish policemen surrounded us, and they were ringed by black-uniformed men with rifles. Both leading and following this group were SS and Gestapo men with drawn sub-machine guns. I had always thought that in such a situation I should try to escape, but something delayed me. I held Wojcz by the hand and told him, "Let's try to escape." He answered that now was impossible, maybe later. The whole way to the execution it didn't occur to me that they would kill me. I wondered why everyone was so quiet. I noticed that even the Germans were quiet; could it be that it wasn't pleasant for them to kill women and children? I always wondered why people being taken to their deaths don't try to do something – after all, what do they have to lose? I felt that all of us – including myself – were being controlled by some kind of overwhelming sense of peacefulness and apathy.

Suddenly I told Wojcz, "You know that I'm a Jew." I think he answered, "Yes, I know." All of this occurred as if we were in a cloud or a dream. It could be that I told him that I wanted to die as a Jew, and he said, "You'll die as a hero..." Suddenly, I asked him, "Are you sure it won't hurt?" I don't remember the rest of the conversation. I was suddenly overwhelmed with a great wave of love and closeness to Wojcz and I was happy that we were dying together. I remembered the stories Aunt Rozia had told me about Heaven, but since I was there as a Jew then I had to die as one. All sorts of crazy thoughts ran through my head. The entire journey from the Jewish Police building to the execution site was only a few minutes long. We stopped next to a small shack, where they divided the group into two. One of the groups entered the shack. I remember that the children were very quiet. One of the fathers held his son in his arms. It's possible that the Germans had given the children tranquilizers.

I was in the first group, and we continued walking until we got to the bottom of a small hill. Here they told us to take off our coats and put them on the side. I didn't take mine off, and when a Jewish policeman reiterated the order, I said that I was cold. At least I had rebelled a little bit... I dimly remember that I had the passing thought that I should try to escape now since there was nothing to lose, but in actual fact I didn't do it. The Jewish policemen arranged us in a row with our faces to the hill and for long minutes we stood there and nothing happened. Then everything went blank, and I remembered nothing more.

When I suddenly regained consciousness, I found myself lying next to a big trench. I opened my eyes to see more people lying around me, some with blood on their faces. Several people were running around stripping the bodies. (I learned later that these were the members of the camp's burial squad.) I lay there for a few minutes with my eyes shut half-way, and figured out what the situation was: I was alive, not in Heaven, lying next to a group of people who had been killed, and I had to get out of there. I looked at those who were running around. They were dragging one body after another to a place where there were two Germans, on standing and one sitting on a chair. The prisoners would strip the body and conduct a search. I waited for a moment when I thought the Germans were focused on their work, got up and walked away. I didn't turn my head, I just walked toward a row of sheds that I saw in front of me. It doesn't seem reasonable to me that they didn't see me; perhaps they just ignored me and let me go.

I started walking around the sheds. I saw figures who looked slightly strange, some dressed in the striped uniforms of concentration camps. I started asking for my father,and one of them pointed to a certain shed and said that my father lived there. In this way, a few months after saying goodbye to my father, I was brought to an execution site that was less than 100 meters away from where my father lived. Doesn't that seem impossible, like other things in my story?? Even I have a hard time believing that all this happened to me, and this is the reason I have not told this story very often until now. But this is what happened, to the best of my memory, and I have evidence and testimonies that support it...

I entered the shed. The first person I met was the "blockaltester," the block commander in charge of the barrack. It turned out that he knew my father well. Even before I asked about my father, though, I said that I was hungry, and asked if I could have a little something to eat. He looked at me, and apparently saw the blood on me. He took me to his room and gave me some soup that he heated up on the spot (he had a coal-burning stove there). Sometimes when we talk now of gourmet restaurants, I have the urge to mention this soup... I also asked for a piece of bread – if possible, a big one. I think that he looked at me a bit bemusedly and commented, "One can tell you haven't eaten in a while." I told him that they had brought me from Montelupich, but didn't tell him the details. After a little while, he told me to climb onto one of the beds, to the third tier, and hide under the blankets. When my father returned from work, he would call me out. He also bandaged my leg, which had been hit by a bullet. I also had wounds on my face and temple, apparently from having fallen down and being dragged. He didn't treat my hand, which had been seriously hurt. (It got taken care of later.) I did as he said, and I think that I was asleep before my head even hit the mattress.

I have no idea how long I slept. I suddenly heard my name echoing in my sleep. I heard a lot of noise, and my name being called again. I turned around, and saw many, many people crowding between the rows of beds and looking up in my direction. Among them was my father – a little thin, but definitely my father... Was I dreaming? What could I do so that the dream wouldn't disappear? I decided that the best way to prevent that would be to jump down. In seconds, I was in my father's arms, and both of us started to cry. We completely forgot that we had to be strong and it was forbidden to cry... Around us stood many young men looking at this wondrous sight, some of them crying themselves, some just wiping away their tears. Suddenly, someone brought me a piece of Swiss chocolate. "What's this?" I thought. "Have I gone to Heaven? Where is God's throne?" While this was going on, the block commander, who really was friendly with my father, managed to get the message to my mother. But we only got to see her the next day.

For hours upon hours, into the wee hours of the morning, I had to repeat everything that happened to me in the ghetto after everyone had gone to Plaszow. How I'd hid, how I'd escaped, what I did on the outside. Many of the people had children who'd been left in the ghetto, some who had even hid with their mothers – and these men had no idea what had happened to them. I had the brains not to say too much about the horrific scenes I had witnessed. I said nothing about how they had taken all the children from the orphanage. They asked me a million questions about what I'd seen and who I'd met. By my presence, I perhaps gave hope to some that their loved ones would also suddenly pop up from somewhere...

I slept all night in my father's arms, and for a change I slept happily, with no nightmares. The next morning, Dad went out to roll call and work, and I stayed in the shed, hiding most of the time in the bed on the top tier. There were three people in charge of the shed: the blockaltester and two others. They spent the day cleaning and neatening the block. The Germans in charge of the camp didn't walk around it much. Mostly it was the Jewish Police who patrolled. If a German did walk near, I was immediately warned and would jump into my hiding place.

CHAPTER 18

Plaszow 8/1943 - 8/1944

That night, when everyone had come back from work, the block commander brought me a doctor who examined my injuries and bandaged them. Dad returned from work with a lot of food. We ate a light meal and left part of the food to bring to Mom and eat as a family together. Later in the evening, we walked to my mother's barrack in the women's camp.

My mother wasn't the only one who knew about my sudden appearance in the camp. A few hundred women were waiting for me when we got to the shed. Supper was forgotten as I leaped into Mom's arms. Although she was crying, this time I did not, but I hugged her tight and stroked her hair while Gizia hugged me from behind. The women all stood around us, some of them crying as well. Then, just as the night before, I had to repeat my entire story of the last days of the ghetto and what was happening outside, in Krakow. I had to answer hundreds of questions, many of them from women who had left their children or relatives in the ghetto and wanted to know if I had seen them. Typical questions were: Had I met or seen a girl with a braid in a pink coat, or a boy with striped pants and the kind of hat that protected his ears... These mothers – just like the fathers in the men's block – always hoped that their children would be saved by some miracle, and I was a symbol of this shred of hope.

Finally, the women let us have the time to reunite as a family.

Although we really didn't have privacy, sitting on two beds (a kind woman lent us hers) in the middle of the room, we spent hours over the next two days together. I told them all the details of what I had undergone during these last months alone, and found out that Mom and Dad had been told that I'd been caught, but nothing else. I also adhered to my father's request not to tell my mother and sister about being taken out for execution. I just told them that they had brought me to the camp and released me, and said that my injuries were from having fallen down, nothing more. Then my parents brought me up to date on their lives. They still got word about Sarenka, and she was doing well at Uncle David's family. Dad no longer worked in his business but in some German business that dealt with examining textiles, and (as mentioned above) his work conditions were relatively good. He could even buy extra food on the outside and bring it into the camp. Mom and Gizia had continued working in the same factory making uniforms and cloth items for the German army. They said their conditions were good, too, as the factory owner, Madritch, brought food to the factory in addition to what was given them in the camp. So all in all, they weren't hungry, though I noticed that my mother had gotten quite thin. However, she looked great, and Gizia was both taller and prettier. Both looked healthy and in good spirits as well. They also showered me with compliments about how I'd grown (which wasn't true…) and that I was already beginning to be a young man. Dad, however, worried me greatly. He was thin, pale, and looked tired.

For the next two weeks, when everyone went out to work I stayed in the block with the blockaltester and his two helpers. Of course, I helped them clean the barrack; I didn't have to hide all the time. I was especially interested in the corner that the blockaltester used as his office. He had to do all the office work but had no aides to assist him. Since filling out forms, copying names, making out reports about transferring people, or about who was sick or had died, was all good fun for me, I volunteered to help. I did it all very enthusiastically and even read all the orders, procedures and regulations with great interest. In fact, I think I was the only one in the whole camp who read and took them seriously...

Plaszow[15] was divided into three parts: the blocks where the prisoners lived, the industrial zone, and the area where the German commandants and administrative staff lived. The latter had a row of houses for the officers and barracks for the soldiers and Ukrainian guards (I call them Ukrainian because they were the majority, but there were also Russians, Lithuanians, etc.). There were also horse barns, a garage, and other service buildings

In the prisoners' compound, the women's camp was on the lower parts of a hill and the men's compound was on the flat ground beneath. A barbed wire fence ran between them, but there was a breach in it, and the official gate always stood open, so it was easy to get from one to the next. There was no guard kept there, either.

18.1 – Taken for Execution - Reprise

The headquarters of the Jewish Police stood at the edge of the men's compound. Behind it was the big yard used for roll call, and a few hundred meters beyond that was the area where the Germans had their headquarters. Our block was right behind the Jewish Police building. It stood a few dozen meters closer to the roll call area than the rest of the line of blocks. When I lay down on the third tier of beds where I hid, I could see both the Jewish Police building and the yard from the narrow windows of the block. One day, something

---

15   *Plaszow was defined as a labor camp and was administered by the region's SS commander. It differed organizationally from the concentration camps in the Third Reich. The Commandant of Plashow named Goeth was Vienna-born and an educated man – as well as a psychopath, sadist and cold-blooded killer.* (More about Plashow and its Commandant Amon Goeth see Chapter 24, side note 16)

happened that I will never forget: I saw a group of about 20 people surrounded by many policemen being brought to the Jewish Police headquarters, followed by some SS officers. Some time later, the group came out and started walking – if anything, surrounded by even more police of various kinds. They passed a few dozen meters away from me, and I clearly saw families with children dressed in their holiday best, but with despair written on their frozen faces. I found out later that they were Jews who had been hiding under false identities among the Poles, and had been caught. I would assume they knew that they were being led to their death. This sight, of the march of these families, with their children, to their execution, so close to where I sat, was one of the most difficult and emotional experiences of my life. It was much more difficult for me to see this than having marched down this same road myself several days earlier...I started crying very hard, but put my hand over my mouth so that no-one would hear me.

The group was being taken to the same place I had been brought. Now I didn't think, "Why aren't these people trying to resist and escape?" I saw them placed in front of the same hill where I had been. This time, they were ordered to undress down to their underwear. Then they shot them all. After they fell, the SS officers went among them and shot them with their handguns. They were the first to leave, followed by the guards and soldiers. All the murdered people's clothing was piled in a small truck, and the Jewish burial squad started taking the bodies in wheelbarrows to a burial place that I couldn't see.

I didn't tell anyone what I had seen. It had been a terrible shock, and it caused more anger and a greater desire for revenge than anything I'd seen or experienced until then. I was furious that I had allowed myself to be taken for execution, and that I had looked on without doing a thing while others had been shot to death. It was unbelievable to me that I had just seen an identical execution to that which I had (almost) experienced myself so recently.

This is one of the reasons that I didn't talk about it much in later years. In addition, while writing down my memories, I always try finding evidence to help prove my story... for example, I have the scars from being shot. I've tried finding a map of the camp[16] as it was in the second half of 1943 so I can locate the execution site, the exact site of the police headquarters, and the prisoner blocks, so I can prove that there really was a block where I said it was, where one could see what I say I saw.

In this case, I have yet to be successful, as a short time after my arrival they changed the execution site to somewhere else, so later maps were of no use to me. About ten days after my arrival, Dad managed to register me as a regular prisoner, so I was a formal member of the Plaszow Camp and could have a job. I went to work in a factory that produced furniture and other utensils made of wood and metal for the army. It was in the industrial zone that was situated right next to the prisoners' compound.

Among the Ukrainian guards, my father had a "friend," a Russian from Kharkhov who was a former officer of the Red Army and had been taken prisoner. In the camp he held the rank of master sergeant. He was an educated man who knew both Polish and German as well as Russian, and they would have very open conversations, sometimes joined by other prisoners. He claimed that he had volunteered to serve on the German side because it was either that or die as a prisoner of war. However, even though he had sworn to serve

---

16   *The Jews in the ghetto who helped build Plaszow convinced many that the camp was a safer place for their children so many were smuggled in. But the special children's houses that had been built in Plashow stood empty; not trusting the Germans, the Jews preferred to hide their children.* (More about the Children's Compound in Plashow Camp see Chapter 24, side note 17)

Hitler even unto death, he didn't believe in National Socialism – or in communism, either, for that matter. He was very worried about his fate, because any way the war ended it would be bad for him. He wondered how he could escape and change identities; he even said he wanted to have a Jewish identity... It should be noted that this was after the Germans had been badly defeated in Kursk, the Italians had switched sides. No one, including the SS, believed anymore in German victory.

Interestingly, it was not only the Jews in Plaszow who hated the commandant, Goeth. The whole German staff that ran the camp hated him, too – mainly because of his extremely strict methods of discipline and because he didn't share any of the loot he took from the prisoners. An example of the latter was when the ghetto was liquidated. Goeth encouraged the Jews to bring to Plaszow all their valuables. A few weeks after their arrival, he then ordered that everyone bring him these valuables, on pain of death. But he shared none of it with his underlings... (In 1944, his staff officers actually sent an official report on his corruption to the Judge Advocate General's office of the SS. That September, Goeth was arrested and interrogated extensively. They found dozens of crates full of jewelry and gold looted from the Jewish prisoners – some of which he had even sent home to Vienna – and tens of thousands of dollars. He managed to escape the SS prison, but was arrested by the Americans in the end. As mentioned above, he was tried in a Polish court, convicted and sentenced to death.)

18.1 – Routine Life in Plaszow

Life in camp became routine. Every morning would start off with roll call, and then each of us went to their place of work. In the evenings, I would sometimes go with my father to visit my mother and sister, and we'd eat dinner as a family. Sometimes we'd even have luxuries like a piece of cheese or sausage, an apple, or cucumbers. Our get-togethers would be even more joyous when Gina, Dad's cousin, would join us. I remember that she was always optimistic and would lift the whole family's spirits. For some reason, I don't remember ever seeing her twin brothers, Ziggy and Morris, in Plaszow. I suppose they were transferred to one of the secondary labor camps that were established near other factories in the Krakow region.

There were two reasons why we – and the other prisoners – didn't starve to death within weeks, considering that our official rations were 500 calories a day (1/8 of a loaf of bread and a cup of soup). One was that the factory owners supplied their slave labor with a meal of sorts, and the other was the prisoners' ability to smuggle in food from the outside. In this, one always ran the danger that Amon Goeth would decide to choose to search your specific group for contraband, and then a large part of the group would pay with their lives. But Dad was lucky and was never caught, though he smuggled food in almost every day. So although my stomach was never full, the hunger wasn't fatal.

Despite the difficult conditions, Mom was always in good spirits, for the simple reason that the whole family had survived and there was hope that the end of the war was coming, with the defeat of the Nazis. In fact, all the conversations in camp revolved around two subjects: food, and the progress in the war. Everyone was a general and a strategist; people would greet each other by saying things like, "Another thousand planes over Berlin," and "The Russians killed another 10,000 Germans and took 20,000 prisoners."

The factory where I worked was run by a Waffen SS master sergeant. He had been in combat and then wounded, and had many decorations to prove his courage, including the Iron Cross. However, he had no professional knowledge of the business, and for all practical purposes the factory was managed by a few Jews and a German civilian who knew woodworking very well. I was the youngest worker – the only child there, really – so they treated me well and I felt good. At a certain point I told one of the managers that I knew math well, and was also very good at reading and writing. There was a great need for writing in the office (after all, the Germans invented paperwork…), and one day the German director, the retired soldier, called me in. "Let's see what you know," he said, and told me to write up some accounts, calculate amounts and set up all sorts of tables. He hated to touch any of this kind of work, and it seemed to me that he also didn't really know it. I did it all diligently and enthusiastically, feeling as if I was on top of the world. Everyone was happy with my work, and that became my new job. This also entitled me to a "raise" – extra food.

I'd like to explain the significance of this extra food: At lunch they would bring in a huge pot of soup, and certain workers were tasked with doling it out by using a cup-like ladle. There were often harsh arguments near the distribution point, as someone would complain that they hadn't dipped the ladle in deep enough, so he'd gotten only liquid. Another would complain that when they poured the soup into his plate, part of it spilled out. Most of the time the soldier-director stood near the pot and whoever complained would get only half a ladle's worth as a punishment. As one of the office workers, though, I would get my portion of a ladle *and a half* along with the rest of the managers and office staff. Moreover, for us they dipped the ladle all the way to the bottom, so it came out full of actual content.

One of the factory workers was a young man who was tall and of large dimensions. He suffered terribly from hunger and would always whisper to the ones giving out the soup, "Dip the ladle in deep, dip it deep." Once, the German director overheard him and ordered that he be given the usual punishment of only half a ladle. I pitied him so much that after I finished half my portion I gave him the rest. He was so happy he almost cried, and he promised, "Boy, I'll remember this for the rest of my life. After the war, I'll buy you a motorcycle."

Goeth once came to visit the factory with some officers who were guests of his. He was very polite and friendly; apparently he was in a good mood. At the end of the tour he entered the office and sat down to check over the paperwork. He sat there for a long time, politely asking questions and demonstrating his knowledge of the business in front of his guests. He paid no attention to me... I never saw it myself, but heard from others how at other times Goeth had burst into factories with dogs, and hit and killed people.

In the beginning of the winter, I suddenly got quite ill, running a high temperature and suffering from tremendous headaches. I went to the clinic, where they suspected meningitis and brought me to the camp's hospital. The diagnosis was correct, and I spent almost a week in bed until I got well. This was a proper hospital that had all the equipment and medicines it should for treating the Jewish prisoners. Its various departments were spread through several sheds, and the Jewish doctors who staffed it were among the best in Krakow. I emphasize this point because in the concentration camps I was in later on they had some sort of clinics but they were for the exclusive use of the German administration and Jewish prisoners got no medical treatment whatsoever.

Dr. Biberstein, who was the director of the Infectious Diseases Hospital in the ghetto, wrote in his memoir that Amon Goeth was a hypochondriac of the first order, which is why he allowed the hospital to be built. He wanted to prevent the spread of infectious diseases because he was afraid of catching them... The Plaszow hospital was run by a Dr. Gross. He took an interest in me and came to visit me with other doctors. Dr. Gross had a son about my age, whom I met by chance a few days before the war ended. Both he and his father survived the war.

18.2 – Liquidation of Jewish Police; Loss of my Toys...
Toward the end of December 1943, due to the huge orders the factory had received, we worked overtime, until very late in the evening.

Now, the execution site had been moved several weeks earlier from near the prisoner barracks to a hill in the industrial area. The prisoners called this area "Hujowa Gurka" (Hujar's Hill, after Goeth's murderous assistant). They would also burn the bodies there, mainly using leftover pieces of wood from our factory. The burial workers would usually come with wagons to collect the wood. The practice was to put a layer of wood into a pit, roll the bodies down, put more wood down, pour gasoline and set it all on fire. One evening, they informed us that we had to bring the wood to them. About ten of us loaded some wagons with leftover wood and chips, and brought it to the site, accompanied by Jewish Police, Ukrainian guards and two SS.

It was already dark by the time we got to Hujowa Gurka. It was lit up by car headlights or special floodlights, and surrounded by many, many soldiers, Ukrainians, police and SS[17]. They didn't let us in, so we left the wood a few dozen meters from the pit. I looked where it was lit, though, and couldn't believe my eyes: The entire detachment of the special Jewish Police force from the ghetto stood there, along with their families.

These were the people who had stayed behind to help the Nazis wipe out the last Jews who tried hiding in the ghetto, and then had the job of collecting and sorting all the possessions that had been left behind. I also saw Spira, the infamous head of the Jewish Police, with his children, grandchildren and extended family. Then I saw my friend Shimek, to whom I'd given most of my books and toys. All of them were dressed in their best, with beautiful luggage by their sides. It was clear that they were all going to be executed.

---

17 *The Gestapo and the SS promised that all the special units of the Jewish policemen that collaborated with the Nazis in the Ghetto would receive citizenship in a South American country. Of course the Nazis did not keep this promise and the prize of collaborating in killing Jews was death on "Hujowa Gurka"* (More on the Role of Jewish Police in the Ghetto's Liquidation see Chapter 24, side note 18)

Many SS officers were walking among them and I saw the Jews trying to talk to them. And I remember what I was thinking at that terrible moment: If they kill them, all my toys and books will be lost forever.... A child is still a child.... I didn't witness their murder because we immediately returned to the factory, but we heard the shots and saw the smoke that testified to the liquidation of this heretofore privileged group of Jews.

18.3- unpleasant meeting with Commandant Goeth

A short time before the execution of the Jewish Police, I had a personal meeting with Amon Goeth. I was working that day with an older man. We were sitting and putting together folding tables when we suddenly saw one of Goeth's cars approaching. He got out a few meters away, along with one of his assistants, whose name was Hujar. This SS man was infamous for murdering many people on Goeth's orders. Goeth together with Hujar was very bad news...

I will preface a description of the event that follows with a camp "legend": There was a very big, fenced-in lot in the industrial zone that Goeth and his guests used when riding horses. One could see this riding area from almost any spot in the industrial zone. Now, Goeth had several mistresses, but one of them would sometimes come visit for several days at a time. When she came, Goeth wouldn't kill people; he'd go riding with her instead, We would always know when she came because we'd see them riding in the lot. And when she was there with him, it seemed that there would be no danger of Goeth coming and surprising us. However, unfortunately for us, it seems he never heard of this "rule"... When Goeth and Hujar reached us, we jumped to attention. The man I was with reported what we were doing.

He asked many questions, like what time we had started working on this project, asked his assistant for a notebook, paged through it for a long time, then noted something down. He then asked several more questions, said, "You're wasting time and doing very bad work," took out a gun and shot my partner from behind, right in his head. The man collapsed, and Goeth turned to me. Until that moment he had ignored me, but now he simply told me to return to the factory. I went, thinking the whole time that he was going to also shoot me from behind, but he didn't. While I was going back, the factory managers came running, apparently because they'd heard the shot. I entered the factory, reported what happened, and went to my desk in the office. However, I did not tell my family this story.

At the end of December they transferred me to work in a printing shop. I have no idea why they did this, and I was very unhappy about it because I'd had it good in the wood factory. The printing shop was a large and important business, called "Drukarnia" in Polish. Many Germans worked there, both in uniform and in civilian clothes. The Jewish workers included many graphic artists and illustrators.

Although they often used me as a messenger boy (which gave me the chance to visit other factories), my main job was to be a typesetter. I did this using a big machine that looked like a printing press. I would get typed or handwritten pages, and copy them by using the machine, which would arrange the letters in a mold. When I'd finish a page I would take out the mold, print it using a manual printing machine, compare the printed page to the original and fix the mistakes. Another person would also proofread it, to ensure accuracy, but I was highly praised for my work.

There were many different departments in this business, each one doing different, specialized things. The Jewish prisoner who had accepted me for my position told me that I was forbidden to talk about what the work was about, and I was never to enter any place that had a sign saying "Authorized personnel only." The only ones who went in there constantly were Gestapo and Intelligence agents and other special units. (Luckily, because it was considered a highly important and secret production plant, all the workers were fed better.)

But I knew what was going on. This was where the Germans would prepare and print secret documents, such as counterfeit passports of neutral or enemy countries. I once even saw a false American passport... They also printed false announcements that supposedly came from the various Resistance groups in Poland. For example, one was supposedly from the main Underground, A.K., that was under the command of the Polish government in exile in London. It called upon Poles to join the fight against the Bolsheviks, mentioned the mass murder of Polish army officers by the Soviet Army (which was true), and claimed that a Bolshevik Occupation would be worse than the Nazi one. They also printed out posters in Czech, Serbian, and English. I was told that we were considered a very high quality plant for these kinds of things... I also heard (but never saw) that the Resistance also used this printing house, to make counterfeit documents for Jews hiding among the Christians: travel documents, visas, train tickets, etc.

There were many highly talented Jews working here, who had good, original ideas for how to get things done. This fact gave these workers hope that because they were so vital to the war effort, perhaps they would be allowed to survive. I heard that before Plaszow was liquidated, the whole enterprise was transferred along with its workers to some place in northern Germany. Since I was only there for a short time, I didn't get to know anyone well, but after the war, I never met any survivors of this factory.

In the beginning of 1944, a small pamphlet was distributed among the prisoners that included a notice that the camp was changing from a labor camp to a concentration camp. There were many rules about how a concentration camp was to be administered. For example, it said that only Hitler or someone authorized by him had the authority to sentence someone to death, and that the commandant would have to get permission to carry out a whipping as punishment. There was even a detailed description of how food was to be distributed. I read this pamphlet several times, and to a certain extent did not believe what I was seeing – the Germans publishing rules and regulations regarding the treatment of Jews! After all, until now they would do whatever they wanted.

I remember that this switchover did not arouse much interest. Apparently people didn't treat it very seriously. My father also dismissed it derisively and didn't bother reading the booklet. I may have been the only one who related to it earnestly... In practice there actually were several changes made in the camp: Dozens of German staff came to run the place, as did several German doctors (one of whom became director of the hospital), and female SS arrived, whose jobs included running the children's houses. But the most significant change that was felt immediately was that Amon Goeth actually stopped killing people, except in isolated cases. For example, one of Dad's best friends escaped. Before the camp's status changed, they would have shot at least a good part of their particular group, and certainly my father would have been one of them since he was the man's friend. But now, they did nothing.

As per my usual practice, I tried finding evidence of this change of status, but could not find corroboration for this switch to being a concentration camp for a very long time. I asked some survivors of the camp about this event but they didn't remember anything about it. I came very close to excluding this piece from the book. Finally, I found confirmation in the testimony of that translator, Pemper, in Goeth's trial. He went into great detail about how in headquarters they received dozens of folders with hundreds of rules on how to run a concentration camp, down to the tiniest detail. According to Pemper, Amon Goeth could make neither heads nor tails of this vast thicket of regulations. He also said that Goeth had many ways of getting around them – which wasn't so hard, considering that he had nobody above him in the camp.

18.4 – I Find a Friend – A German Soldier

In February 1944, I was sent to a new job in a brush-making factory. The reason for my transfer was that a high ranking Intelligence officer connected to the plant complained about seeing a child there, as in his opinion one couldn't trust children not to chatter. My new employer made every kind of brush imaginable, from toothbrushes to brushes that cleaned tanks. As in the other places, I got jobs suitable for a child, as well as courier duties. A young German first sergeant or master sergeant was in charge. He was disabled in both legs but would limp along using a cane. He also had a lot of shrapnel all over his body, and had many decorations attesting to his bravery, including the Iron Cross. Just as the soldier who "ran" the wood factory, he had no interest in the business either, and just like there, it was managed by a few Jewish prisoners and an elderly German "meister."

I don't remember the soldier's name. I would call him "my friend," and he would call me "impudent boy." We became very good friends. He would sometimes buy me a candy from his canteen, and I always got the hearty part of the soup in my plate. Here I also worked in the office, doing bookkeeping, counting supplies, etc. The soldier told me he had gone into the army at age 17, and had fought in Africa as well as Russia. He had an older brother in an elite combat unit (the paratroopers), and the family always worried about him. He also had another two siblings. Uncles and cousins of his had been killed in the army or in bombings. He told me that it was much better in Krakow than in Germany. He talked a lot about the war in Russia, the terrible conditions and the difficulties. He loved to talk and I loved to listen. He admired Hitler but wasn't a member of the Nazi party because he believed it was corrupt and that all the SS who were in the camp were army deserters. This man had never been aware of the Jewish "problem" and the annihilation; where he lived in Germany there hadn't been any Jews and the first time he met any was in Plaszow.

The female SS officers who came when Plaszow became a

concentration camp started off by being very tough in the women's compound. They tried to forbid the entry of men, and in general made life difficult for the prisoners. This went on until they were all paid off. I don't remember exactly when that occurred, but after that they started being nice... I continued going there with my father for occasional meals with Mom, Gizia and Gina, who aside from being our optimistic cousin was also our medical adviser. She was considered knowledgeable simply because before the war she had been planning to learn medicine... These get-togethers were so pleasant! I'd tell all sorts of funny stories about what went on in my factory, as well as all the war news I gleaned from "my" soldier, like the bombings in Germany. We were also optimistic about my little sister, as we'd been told that Uncle David's whole family had been transferred to some place from which they would seemingly be going to America. Meanwhile, the report was that Sarenka had grown a lot, and was prettier and sweeter than ever.

There were two incidents that happened to me in Plaszow that for some reason were engraved in my memory as being particularly emotional and terrible. The first was connected to one of the rabbis of the Krakow Ghetto, a young man who was a close friend of the family. He had a wife and five young children and we loved them all dearly. I think that my father supported him financially. This rabbi survived all the "Action"s in the ghetto with his family intact by hiding in a very sophisticated hideout in the basement of his building. They had enough food there to stay for weeks, and on the day the ghetto was liquidated the wife and children concealed themselves there. The rabbi went to Plaszow, intending to find a way to get them out when everything calmed down. However, about a week later, the wife momentarily left the hideout just as a search was being made of the building. They caught her and the children and murdered everyone right on the sidewalk.

Once – before I knew of this tragedy – when we were visiting the women, my parents told me that the rabbi wanted to see me. When he came in, we hugged for a long time. He was very thin and had aged considerably, and I barely recognized him. After he asked about what had happened to me, I asked him where his wife and children were. He told me they were in Heaven. It took me several seconds to understand what he'd meant, and then I jumped into his arms and started sobbing and wailing loudly. It was only the second time in years that I let my feelings out in front of other people (the first being when I saw my father for the first time in Plaszow). I completely forgot that it was forbidden to cry and that one had to be strong... I screamed, "No, no, it's simply not possible, I'll kill all the Germans, I won't let a single one of them live, *where was your God*?!" Many women in the barrack gathered around us and it took many long minutes until they managed to calm me down. After witnessing the murder of Jews for days in the ghetto, after having experienced my own execution, it was unexpectedly this news of the execution of the rabbi's family that appalled me more than anything else.

The second incident also took place in my mother's barrack. A young woman of about 18 lived there, who was having a romance with one of the officers in charge of the camp. Everyone knew about it; he came openly to the barrack to get her. He gave gifts to her and her whole family, including her younger brother, who was about my age and often came to visit his sister. I saw him all the time when I was with my mother. Commandant Goeth heard about the affair, and ordered the officer to personally kill this girl and her family. One evening, three Jewish policemen appeared and told the girl to come with them. She apparently understood that something bad was going to happen, so she kissed and hugged her brother for a long time. After she left he started crying and screaming; the women tried unsuccessfully to quiet him. Then an hour later, the same policemen came back to get him. He ran to hide, and they spent a long time searching for him. When they found him, he started sobbing and screaming, "I want to live, I'm not ready to die!" He wouldn't walk, and the policemen dragged him, shrieking all the way. The sight of this boy being dragged and crying "I want to live!" left everyone aghast. Mom hugged me and cried, as did most of the women there, a majority of whom had already lost their children.

The officer did as ordered, executing the entire family. The story went that he only did it after getting himself drunk. But he got his revenge, as several months later he was among the group mentioned above, who informed the SS legal authorities about Goeth's corruption, which eventually led to his arrest.

Spring 1944, The magic words were survival and hope. Another day that passed in peace, another day closer to freedom. Conversations were either about food, or the front. Names flew of towns and cities in Russia and Italy that had been liberated, news was whispered of two million American soldiers who had gone to England, of tens of thousands of planes being prepared for the invasion of Europe, of planes bombing Germany around the clock. All this gave people the strength to hope. At this stage, many escaped Plaszow, including two more from Dad's group. There was no collective punishment, as the commandant only had permission to execute the runaway himself – but for that he needed to be caught... Indeed, several Jews who were caught either in the act or after they'd escaped, were hung. I rejoiced over each successful escape, for each one was another person who could inform the world what was happening to us.

CHAPTER 19

Children's "Action" in Plaszow - May 1944

According to Pemper's testimony, there were about 280 children in the children's houses at this time. It was already over a year since the ghetto had been liquidated, and nothing bad had ever happened to them. All the prisoners shared the parents' anxiety about their offspring; in essence they became everyone's children. They were a source of both worry and hope. After every parental visit, the talk of the day in the barracks would be how the kids were doing. For those parents whose children had been taken away from them at one stage or another, the good conditions here gave them a shred of hope that maybe wherever their children were, they were also being taken care of.

One beautiful day in May, apparently on a Sunday, all the prisoners were ordered to the yard for roll call. The Germans announced that it was a "health roll call," to determine how well every worker was, which would lead to each one getting a job that was appropriate to his level of health. Several stations were set up, with German doctors and SS officers at each one. The prisoners were divided into groups and marched, naked, in front of the doctors, who gave each one a cursory check and a notation was made next to his number and name. In principle, it was a selection like the infamous ones done in Auschwitz, except here the people weren't sent directly to the gas chambers. Here, they got a reprieve of a week.

Exactly seven days later, we were again ordered to roll call in the yard. This time, it was surrounded by a large number of police that reinforced our regular guard. Jewish policemen and SS started going through the rows, pulling out people from a prepared list. For the most part, they were people who were older, or who looked thin, or sick – and children like me, meaning those who were with the adults and who worked, but were small and looked young.

At the time, I was registered as being fourteen, but I was really only eleven and looked even younger. However, a twelve year old was already considered a legitimate worker, so I really should have been counted as an adult. Unfortunately, I didn't look it. At first, they put a whole group of children together in one part of the yard, but there were other groups as well. I was very surprised by the great force of Jewish police, SS men and women and Ukrainians that was guarding a pretty small number of children. I was also surprised to meet several children whom I'd known in the ghetto but whom I had never met in the camp. I was mainly overjoyed to see my great friend, Jezyk, again. We hugged, and these words just flew out of my mouth: "Jezyk, what are we going to do?" After all, this was Jezyk, the talented, brave boy who had taught me so much and smuggled food with me into the ghetto. Almost on the same breath, we both whispered, "We have to escape." After a while they started leading our group somewhere under tight guard. I told Jezyk that if they would take us in the direction of "Hujowa Gurka" we had to try to run away. But they took us toward the women's compound, then to the hill behind it, where the children's houses were located.

They brought us into the children's compound; it was my very first time there. The whole area was surrounded by dozens upon dozens of weapon-bearing personnel of all types, as if they were guarding the most dangerous of criminals. Inside, I met the three-to-ten-year-olds, who were with their Jewish nannies and teachers, as well as a number of female SS staff. We could walk freely around the barracks (there were several buildings) and the playground outside. It astonished me to see how neat the rooms were, and how nice the bedrooms, classrooms, dining rooms and playrooms looked. It was really a beautiful nursery and school. The SS staff treated us very well, giving us sandwiches, candy and drinks. Outside they played happy, pretty music. They were really trying to create a happy, calm atmosphere. And the little ones really were happy. They played, of course not understanding what was going on. Meanwhile, the older kids, and mainly the ones who had just come from the roll call, understood the situation very well, and where it could be leading.

I started whispering to Jezyk and another, older boy. We gazed down toward the women's section and saw a number of trucks partially covered with canvas near the gate that bordered the men's section. There were a lot of German guards around the trucks, and we immediately understood the exercise: They were going to take us and load us onto the trucks. We agreed that when we would be a few dozen meters before the gate, near the row of women's barracks, we would run towards them and try to hide somewhere. We decided to pass along this plan to other big kids, but only when we had already started walking, so that the Germans wouldn't hear of it.

It had always been clear to me that the whole children's compound with its good conditions was a honey trap, and just like the daycare center in the ghetto, its inhabitants would be killed sooner or later. And so it was no surprise that while we waited there, the Jewish Police told us that we were being transferred to another camp with even better conditions, where we would be able to call our parents, and eventually be taken to America...

They gave out bags with food and candy, and during the ensuing confusion of collecting all the children, we spread word of our plan to the older children. Jezyk, the third boy and I lined up in the rightmost column closest to the barracks. The way the little ones were so well-dressed, happy and looked cared-for really stood out in my eyes.

The nannies, teachers, SS women and some of the Jewish policemen were holding the children's hands, while we were surrounded by so many SS men with their weapons drawn. Incongruously, the happy music kept coming from the loudspeakers. It was a surrealistic scene that was simply unbelievable: This was how the Nazis were taking hundreds of pre-school and grade school children to their deaths[18].

As we neared the women's barracks, I looked into Jezyk's eyes and we yelled together, "Uciekac!" (Escape) and I started to run between the second and third row of sheds. I ran with all my might, as only one can when one knows his life depends on it. I didn't look back, but heard yelling and the sound of many feet pounding the ground. There were no shots, however. I ran down past the first barrack, then down the length of the second barrack. At first I thought to hide in that second one, but for some reason I didn't enter it. When I got to the end, I saw that between the second and the third sheds there was a door leaning on the wall of one of them at an angle. I jumped under the door and rolled into as tight a ball as I could.

I hid under that door for several hours. Dozens of Germans passed by me looking for the children who had run away. Once they even stood next to me and talked to each other. They also used dogs in the search. So why didn't they find me?? I don't remember that this question occupied my mind; I already believed that I could always escape...

After few hours finally, I heard the women returning and understood that the "Action" was over. As a "professional "Action" survivor" I learned an important thing: Usually after an "Action" was over,

---

18   *Once more, I found the most important source regarding this "Children Action" to be Pemper's account during Goeth's trial. In all Nazi war crime trials, the defendants argued that they just obeyed orders to kill. It turns out that in this case the initiative to kill all the children belonged solely to Amon Goeth.* (More about the "Children Action" in Plashow of May 1944 see Chaptet 24, side note 19)

the Germans would leave and the people were released. Whoever they hadn't managed to trap at that time would be left for the next "Action" and they wouldn't try looking for him again. So I left my hiding place and entered my mother's barrack, which was nearby.

When I came in, there was a complete uproar. Many women practically fell on me with a torrent of questions – including those who had children in the nursery or had an older child taken from the morning's roll call, like me. Everyone wanted to know if I had perhaps seen her child. I don't know if the women knew about the children who had managed to escape and hide. I assume I was one of the first that came out of hiding. It took me a long time to get to my mother, as I had to tell my story numerous times. When I finally reached Mom and Gizia, I was completely worn out. I only remember that I lay for a long time in a hug with both of them, while dozens of women surrounded us, watching. I assume I also told them of the day I'd had.

For the next several nights, I stayed in my mother's barrack and hid, until my father finally came to visit us. I won't go into detail describing our reunion; he had been with me when they had forced me from the roll call yard and I could only imagine his feelings and worry.

I finally returned to my father's barrack, where I was given a tumultuous greeting once again, and had to repeat the story of my escape. The noise upon my arrival wasn't to my benefit, as the Germans had informants in every barrack and there was no doubt they knew that I had survived. However, a week passed and nothing happened. No attempt was made to track down the escapees. The Germans publicized all sorts of false rumors about those who had been taken away – especially about the children. Some letters even arrived from them. Of course, I knew what had happened to them: death in the gas chambers. And I was right. According to Pemper's testimony in Goeth's trial, this consignment of children went directly to the gas chambers in Auschwitz, with no other selection being made.

After going back to the men's barracks, I returned to work. I don't know how this worked out officially, since according to their lists I was already in the World to Come. But as I said, they didn't look for those who escaped deportation, and I assume that the head of my block registered me as being present. This was duly noted where it had to be, and the deed was done. However, it was obvious that they knew that I had escaped, since I hadn't changed my name or number.

Back to work at the factory I was given a hero's welcome, as if I'd come from a battle. I had to repeat my whole adventure again. Several days later, the German soldier came over to me in the office and told me that he was happy I'd come back and that I should take care of myself. It should be noted that there were several dozen disabled soldiers serving as directors of factories in the industrial zone, and it was well known that there was great tension between them and the SS. They considered the SS to be shirkers of their army duty and they saw the extensive corruption among them – especially among the officers. The commandant tried to make a rule forbidding the soldiers from wearing their army decorations in the camp because it made it obvious that the SS men hadn't participated in the fighting. However, the issue was decided in favor of the soldiers.

My main job now at the office was to be a messenger boy; I even had papers saying that I was the mouthpiece, as it were, of the director himself. As part of my job I would come regularly to the camp's headquarters. There, I met an army officer who walked with crutches, who was sort of the commander of all the soldiers in the camp. I also got to know disabled soldiers who worked in other factories around.

19.1 – On the Run Again

News of the Allied landing in Normandy flew around Plaszow in the beginning of June, 1944. Everyone was extremely excited, thinking that freedom was on its way. That was also the month that I got another chance to run for my life, hide and escape.

One bright morning, a rumor spread that they were going to hunt down those who had escaped or hid in last month's children's "Action". My senses went on alert. In the shop there was always a lookout to warn of the approach of any unwanted guest. Suddenly, they warned that two Jewish policemen were coming. I told my colleagues in the office that I was going to hide, jumped into a stack of packages of raw materials and concealed myself. I could actually watch what was going on pretty comfortably from there.

The two policemen entered, and a short time later, they left. I stayed in my hiding place. About a half hour later, two different policemen showed up. They spoke to one of the managers, who had greeted them at the entrance, came into the office, and left a few minutes later, accompanied by the German director. I didn't know for sure, but guessed that they were looking for me. The whole business knew I was hiding. Another hour passed, and this time the Jewish policemen who came were with an SS man. This time, my friend the soldier greeted them at the door himself. I noticed that the SS man and the soldier talked for several minutes before entering the office. Then the soldier-director came over to the stack and told me that I had no choice but to go with the policemen. I remember clearly that I was calm and didn't panic.

I walked with him to the SS man, and it seemed that my friend looked at him with derision. The soldier carried a sub-machine gun and the SS man only had a pistol, while the soldier's military decorations contrasted sharply with the blank uniform of the SS. After talking again with the German director, the SS man gave the Nazi salute and left the business. I immediately recognized one of the Jewish policemen in the room. It was Finkelstein, the deputy commander of the Jewish Police, who was famous for his cruelty. He caught me by the hand and started alternately yelling at me and "comforting" me: "You are causing us a lot of trouble, we're very angry with you, you have nothing to fear, they're going to take you to America." I can't remember exactly what I answered but I was very impudent, saying something to the effect of "Don't tell me stories, you know they're going to kill me." He answered forcefully, "What are you talking about, what nonsense, you have nothing to fear." But the whole time he held me fast by the hand. We stayed in the office for several more long minutes. When we left, he had me by the hand and the second policeman was on top of me on the other side. We went straight to the Jewish Police headquarters and entered the big, luxurious office of the police commander himself – Hilowitz. Three SS officers were sitting on couches there talking to him as well as among themselves.

When I came in, Hilowitz got up, came over, and gave me two such hard slaps on the face that my head almost flew off. My mind blurred, but I didn't faint. Within the fog of pain, I heard him say: "Don't be afraid, nothing will happen to you and we will release you." They sat me down in a room next door for a long time, with two policemen guarding me. I heard a lively conversation going on in German in Hilowitz's office and saw many people going in and out. My guards refused to talk to me. Suddenly, I saw the officers leave, and a couple of minutes later, Hilowitz came into my room, and with no explanation, simply told me I was free to go back to my barrack.

I did so, and the blockaltester apparently knew all about me and treated me very well. When I told him I was very hungry and wanted to eat, he gave me a plate of soup and a piece of bread. When I had finished that, he filled my plate again. I told him everything that had happened while I ate. I asked him to inform my mother that I was all right, then went to my bed and fell asleep in seconds. Dad woke me up late that evening; he already knew my story. We didn't make a big deal of this incident. We got to see my mother two days later, but she had gotten the word that I was okay – even before Dad did.

It seems that the day's activity succeeded in hunting down most of those who had been on the list in May's "Action" but who had managed to escape. I couldn't find out if Jezyk or any of the others who ran that day managed to get away this time or not. But I did find out later why I was released this time – and it was for a very prosaic reason, indeed: The Germans had set aside two trucks to take to Auschwitz those who had escaped the previous "Action". It was coordinated with another transport that had come to Auschwitz from Hungary. The trucks had to get to the gas chambers by a certain hour and couldn't wait for me in Plaszow. Since I was late, they left without me. That's what I missed out on because I was late... Was there a deliberate delay after I was taken from my hiding place in the office where I worked? Perhaps that "terrible" Finkelstein knew that the trucks wouldn't wait and purposely delayed us in the office to give me a chance of being saved? Perhaps Hilowitz had instructed Finkelstein to delay my arrival[19]. Maybe, maybe, maybe... The conclusion from all this: You don't always lose out when you're late...

There was a great deal of excitement when I came back to work. Everyone had been witness to the whole drama of the search for me, and they had all seen how I had been taken from the office. From this time on, I was adopted by the whole company and got a bigger portion of soup at lunch even when the German director wasn't there. One of the Jewish managers told me that the German director had known that I was hiding from the very beginning, and when the

19   *The Jewish Police force in Plaszow was established even before the Krakow Ghetto was liquidated. Some of the men came from the ghetto. Hilowitz was appointed its head, with Finkelstein his deputy. in September 1944, Hilowitz and all his senior staff – along with their families – were executed on the order of Amon Goeth. (More about Hilowitz and the Jewish Police in Plashow see Chapter 24, side note 20*

policemen had come the first two times he would not hand me over. It was only the third time, when the SS man came and threatened to bring a detachment of police who would make a thorough search of the factory, and that a complaint would be brought against him, that he felt he had no choice and turned me in.

A short time after my second escape, I got a chance to talk to the German director, and thanked him for all his efforts on my behalf. I hugged him and told him he was my very good friend. Several days after that, he told me that his soldier brother had been badly injured, had almost been captured, and had received another medal for courage in addition to the Iron Cross he already had.

This matched the news we were getting that July. We heard that the Red Army had begun an attack along the entire front, captured Minsk and all Byelorussia, had several deep flanking maneuvers against the German army, destroyed some 60 divisions and took hundreds of thousands of Germans prisoner. All the Baltic countries were liberated, eastern Prussia was cut off from the rest of Germany, and the Soviet army reached the Vistula as well as the outskirts of Warsaw. Unfortunately, with tragic results, the Allied forces stopped its attack in our direction and concentrated its forces in capturing Romania and the Balkan countries. It was clear to all that Germany's defeat was imminent. This was all the prisoners talked about, and there was a very uplifting atmosphere everywhere.

Meanwhile, my favorite times at work were when I was sent somewhere with a message. I had a special pack that I could wear either on my back or hold in my hand. It was also tied to my hand and I was not allowed to disconnect it from my person. I would often go around the industrial zone, which was quite large. There were dozens of factories, some of whom were in an independent area that had a fence to separate it from Plaszow and its own entrance gate. On one of my "runs," I had to go to the headquarters' office of the officer in charge of all the Wehrmacht soldiers in the camp. When I met him, I found out that he already knew about me and how I'd hid in the print shop when they looked for me. He greeted me very nicely, asking how I was and hinting that he was happy that I had been saved from the deportation.

It should be noted that executions continued to take place this whole time in Hujowa Gurka, and even came more frequently. But it was mainly Christian Poles, people from the Resistance and suspects of various political offenses who were being killed now. In many cases, those being taken to their deaths sang the Polish anthem... At this stage they were still continuing to burn the bodies, and from the hill a thick smoke always rose in the air and spread the odor of the burning bodies throughout the camp. I noticed that just like the Jews, the Christians going to their execution did not try to resist or run away, even when they knew there was nothing to lose. I know of only one case when those being taken to be killed rebelled at a certain point and started running away. According to the rumors, they were all caught.

CHAPTER 20

From Plaszow to Mauthausen

A new rumor began making the rounds: that the Germans were going to evacuate the camp and transfer all the prisoners to a concentration camp in Germany. Everywhere in camp people were speaking of the possibility of escaping before the evacuation took place. The hope was that it would be enough to find a hideout for only a few weeks and the Soviets would arrive – and indeed, a great many prisoners ran away.

I don't know if we were warned of the evacuation ahead of time, but the whole family, including Gina, spent the evening before in Mom's barrack. We all had the feeling that it would be our last chance to be together. I think that all the families in the camp spent that last night together and the Germans didn't do anything about it. Everyone thought that the Germans really were transferring us so we could work for them and not in order to kill us.

In the morning, all the prisoners stood in the roll call area with bags and backpacks. Families stood together without Germans interfering. It was known that the women would be sent separately to different places and families would be split up once again. My mother was very emotional and cried; apparently she understood and felt that this parting could be our very last. My sister just hugged our mother and didn't speak. Dad looked somewhat apathetic and distant, while I, in all my 12-year-old worldliness, behaved arrogantly towards Mom, not caring at all about how she was feeling. With her maternal instinct, Mom understood the terrible situation we were in very well, and she was miserable and completely helpless. She needed encouragement and words of hope and love, and being the great sophisticate I could not read the situation and started to yell at her and exhort her that she has to be strong, that it was forbidden to cry, and all kinds of other things that were completely inappropriate. All my life, I've had pangs of conscience off and on about my behavior back then... What I wouldn't give for a chance to meet my mother just once more, to hug her and ask for her forgiveness. From women who were with my mother and sister in one of the labor camps around Auschwitz, I heard that both of them held out well, were considered strong and also helped others. Perhaps in her tears she had internalized my demand that she be strong... But this was the last time I ever saw my mother or Gizia.

After several long hours in the yard with our families, the order came to stand according to barrack again. After another roll call we started marching toward the train station, with the men and women going to different trains on different tracks. (All the women were taken to Auschwitz, where most of them passed the selection and were spread around the satellite camps to perform slave labor.)

20.1 – Trip to a German Concentration Camp

Hundreds of SS men stood in two rows about 200 meters before the train station. We were pushed between these rows (they were a few dozen meters apart) and as we walked they started raining blows on us with sticks and whips, screaming, "Schnell, schnell!" I was hit a few times on my head and back but was more worried about the blows my father received, as the people who fell or fainted were shot in the head. In this way they made us run to the boxcars, and many people lost their bags as a result. Dad and I were only left with the packs that had been strapped to our backs. All the boxcars were sealed except for one narrow window and a door in the middle, which stood open. Near the door, Jewish policemen and SS men stood and shoved us in. It was a hot August day, and the heat in these cars was stifling and unbearable. I held up just fine, but worried the whole time about my father.

It worked out that everyone along the walls of the car could sit and the rest had to stand. Later on, they brought in a kind of toilet – a big bucket with a wooden cover that had a hole in it. They also gave us a container of water and a few bags of bread. We were kept at the station for quite a while, and these were the hardest hours of the trip; it was really hell. I supported and encouraged my father the whole time. About an hour after we had entered the car, I managed to get a place near the side and Dad got to sit down. The situation improved enormously when the train started moving and some wind entered. It got easier to breathe and became the slightest bit cooler.

Meanwhile, a young man took charge of the boxcar. He got a few other people to help him organize the situation. This included taking all the people who had either fainted or died and putting them on one side of the car. The dead were put in a pile so they took up less space. They also arranged people in groups of five, where two sat and three stood, in turn.

It took several hours for us to get to Auschwitz, but apparently we didn't enter the camp itself; we stayed instead on the tracks, possibly near the town. At this point, they separated a bunch of cars, sending them to Auschwitz while we continued westward after a delay of several hours. The choice of who stayed and who went was completely accidental, since nobody knew who was in each car.

The next part of our trip would take three days. After traveling through the night, the train stopped near some open field and they opened the doors and let us out. We were immediately surrounded by dozens of soldiers or police (in green uniforms) with machine guns. I didn't notice what kind of police or soldiers they were, but they were comparatively relaxed. They didn't scream or beat anyone; their officers just constantly walked around the cars and gave orders. We were allowed to take care of the necessities, stretch our legs, and empty our chamber pots. There were also places where we could get water to wash them out as well as refill our water tank for drinking. All the bodies were taken out of the train and put somewhere, so there was more room in the cars. I noticed that there were about twenty boxcars in all for the prisoners and two cars for the German guards.

They did the same thing for the next two days, stopping the train once or twice a day to let us get out and have some fresh air, remove the dead bodies, get more water, and empty the chamber pots. But we got no more food, and though the weather was nice outside, inside the cars it was always terribly hot and stifling when the train didn't move. When we were traveling, it was fine, since people made small holes in the walls so more air could come in, and as the cars grew emptier, two out of every four prisoners could sit at a time. The mood improved considerably – especially since fewer people died each day. More than ten died the first day, but it turned out that there were several doctors in our car, and after the first several hours of travel they got over their initial shock and started helping those who were ill. So only a few died thereafter.

All along the way, people stood by the window and paid attention to markers that could give a clue as to where we were going. After we entered Germany that first night, the train stopped several times a day because of air raid sirens. We would stay locked in our cars while the Germans would run to protected areas. But we never heard any explosions around our train.

Our trip ended in the train station of a town called Mauthausen, in Austria. When we got out of the cars, we were surrounded by hundreds of SS. They arranged us in rows and we started to march toward the camp. It was beautiful weather, and there were green pastures and flowers all around us as we walked: lots of trees, birds chirping above us, a wonderful smell of flowers and forests in the air. On both sides of the road we saw houses, and all around them were people, children playing, animals. What a surprise: A normal world still existed – and yet, where were we? The world around us looked like a fairy tale and we were in Hell, looking out at it. And yet, we still didn't know what kind of Hell it really was – nor could we ever have guessed.

It was a march of several hours until we got to the Mauthausen concentration camp. We were immediately ordered to undress completely and put our clothes in a pile, and were pushed straight to the showers. For some reason we didn't fear that they were going to kill us. They even gave us each a piece of soap – and the water was warm. It was the first and last time I ever found hot water in Mauthausen... After the shower they shaved us and forced us to go from one station to the next where they sprayed us with various liquids and powders to disinfect us. They then handed out striped prisoners' uniforms (but no underwear), wooden clogs and a cap. Each person was registered, got a number and a symbol to be attached to one's chest. We were then taken to a kind of camp-within-a-camp, which acted as a transition camp for new prisoners. There were several dozen barracks (blocks) in this compound. The one we were put in was clean and neat. There were four rows of beds arranged in triple tiers, with a 2 centimeter "thick" mattress and two blankets on each one. In general, each person got half a bed.

The "clothes" they had given us were made of a paper-like material and were not particularly comfortable, though since it was August we weren't cold. The next morning at 5AM they woke us for roll call. This consisted of exercises like telling us to stand at attention, stand at ease, remove our caps, do sit-ups and lie on the ground on our stomachs, faces pushed into the earth.

The commander of our block was a German prisoner who had a

large staff. He was an old man (over 40...) who was pretty easy-going; he didn't scream or hit people. He had been imprisoned in various concentration camps for over ten years, arrested way back when for being a Communist. He told us at roll call that we would all work in the quarry, except for a few people he'd select and "the three little ones" – referring to myself and two other boys. Our job was to work in the block doing all kinds of cleaning jobs inside and gardening outside, under the watchful eye of one of his assistants. For lunch they invited us to the area where those in charge of the block lived. It was a huge room, almost a hall, which held about ten beds – also in three tiers – a big table in the middle and several closets off to the side. The block commander had his own room. In the corner was a wood stove where one could cook.

We were starving by this point, and when we were given warm soup with rotten vegetables and a piece of bread, we considered it a wonderful treat. The command staff, of course, had all kinds of extra foods – I believe they even had sausages – which looked to me like a meal out of a fairy tale. They did not share it with us...However, we did get a kind of liquid that was supposed to be coffee, and were "honored" with a tiny plate of jam.

The big blow came in the evening, when the prisoners returned from work. It was a scene straight out of Dante's Inferno: The men had been viciously beaten and were dripping blood. They walked like shadows, not talking, carrying on stretchers almost twenty bodies of men who had been murdered at the quarry. I ran straight to my father and couldn't believe my eyes: He had been beaten on every part of his body, was limping and swayed as he walked. He was on the verge of tears.

The quarries, it turned out, were for all practical purposes simply a site for the decimation of the prisoners. They had to carry boulders down a very steep and winding path, with overseers lining the route using their whips and clubs indiscriminately. Whoever dropped his load or fell, was shot. Many toppled over the side of the cliff face as well, falling to their deaths below. They got no food at all during the day, and when they came back to camp in the evening all they received was soup. My father wasn't even capable of eating. It was crystal clear to me that he wouldn't survive another day of this. I decided that I'd go out with him to work and try to protect him. But before I did that, I tried something that really was completely hopeless: I went over to the block commander, stood straight at attention, took off my cap respectfully and asked if I could make a request. He tossed out a laconic answer: "Speak!" I remember that I was very emotional, even though I don't recall exactly what I said. I basically begged for my father's life. To my enormous surprise, it worked, and the next day my father stayed behind in the block to clean it.

On the second day, the men came back in slightly better condition; fewer bodies were brought back. I was extremely worried about the future: Should I go again to the block commander? I was afraid of getting a negative answer. Dad and I decided together to try bribing him, and I did it in a clever way. At a moment when I saw that the commander seemed to be in a good mood, I went over to him, took out from my pocket a $10 bill, told him I'd found it, and said that maybe he could get some use out of it. He took the money, looked at it with interest, and then gave me a very long look that was a bit scary. He looked at the bill again, mumbled something like, "OK," put it in his pocket and walked away. I debated whether I should go over to him again to ask about my father, but didn't dare.

The next day at roll call I stood next to Dad in the front row, in the hope that this way he would remember us. At the end of the roll call, its commander informed us that in addition to "the little ones," another three prisoners would stay behind. He called off their names – and my father was one of them. And until the end of our stay in

Mauthausen[20] ten days later, that's where my father stayed.

Where had I gotten the money for the bribe? In a very complicated and dangerous exercise that had succeeded, my father and I had managed to smuggle into the camp a few hundred dollars and Swiss francs.

---

20   *In Mauthausen, in the approximately seven years of its existence, between 200,000 – 300,000 prisoners of various nations were murdered.* (More about concentration camps and its establishing see Chapter 24, side note 21)

CHAPTER 21

The "Gozen 2" Concentration Camp

When we were at evening roll call on the tenth day, we were informed that the next morning we would be moving to various subcamps. Along with another few hundred prisoners, my father and I were marched to "Gozen 2." This took us a few hours. As our guards were not right on top of us, I felt almost like I was on a nature hike: The birds chirped above our heads, the smell of freshly reaped wheat fields filled the air, and all around us were trees and rivers with all their various aromas and scents. All the people we saw were dressed up, while happy children stood on the sides of the roads and watched our strange procession. For a second time, we got to see that normal life still existed.

The sight we saw upon entering Gozen 2 looked like a new scene of hell: Shells of human beings walked around outside with faces and eyes that radiated despair. Compared to these people we were in excellent physical health... Next to each barrack there was a neat pile of bodies. I found out later that every morning an SS man would come get the results of the roll call and the number of live people plus bodies had to equal exactly the number of people who had been alive the previous day. Only after the morning count would they bring the bodies to the crematorium that was located in Gozen 1.

Dad and I and a few dozen other Krakow Jews were put into Block 20. Each person got half a bed and two blankets; there were no mattresses. The next morning they woke us early for roll call, which was when they also gave out pieces of bread. The SS man came to collect the totals, and then we got onto a freight train for a ten minute ride to the factory.

21.1 – To Save My Father

The train stopped at a small station on the outskirts of a subterranean factory. It was a perfect example of the effort being made by the Germans to survive Allied bombing. It was in a valley surrounded by mountains, and over it all were spread huge camouflage nets so that from above it looked like the continuation of the mountains and forests. The trains and cars would get to the compound by way of tunnels that led straight under the netting, so pilots could not see a single sign of a road or rail leading to the site.

There were several entrances to the factory in the sides of the hills around, with one set aside for a narrow train track through which trucks could enter as well. The factory was in a huge underground area, the size of several soccer fields, where tank, missile and airplane parts were produced. In one part of the factory, production lines worked smoothly, while in other parts people were digging new tunnels to expand the factory. Trains, trucks and small cars continually came and left.

Tens of thousands of people worked there: German and Austrian civilians, forced laborers from the Occupied countries (France, Holland, Poland, etc.), and concentration camp prisoners. The forced laborers wore civilian clothes, with no special insignia, and lived in open camps or the surrounding villages. They lived as free people except that they were being forced to work in certain places. (About ten million people in total were brought to Germany and Austria during the war to work as forced laborers.) The concentration camp prisoners did all the heavy, dirty and dangerous work – digging the new tunnels, in this case. In addition to the difficulty of the work of loading boulders and rocks onto train cars, the ventilation in these tunnels was very poor. Everything had to be done within a huge cloud of dust and it was terribly difficult to breathe.

On that first day, they did a roll call at the factory and divided the prisoners into various work groups. Dad was selected for the tunnels, while the head kapo wanted to give me another job. However, I asked to go with my father, and was allowed to do so. Our group of about eight people started loading the small train cars with dirt and rocks.

An SS man stood next to each work group with a stopwatch, timing how long it took to load the carts. The group's kapo was under constant threat that if his group didn't work fast enough he would be removed from his position and become a regular prisoner again. As for all practical purposes this was usually a death sentence, most kapos would do anything to please their supervisors and tyrannized their workers, screaming and beating them constantly. However, our kapo was clever, and to get the work to go faster he used his brain more than his whip, thereby managing to meet the work quota.

Many SS and Gestapo, Austrian police and others constantly circulated around the factory. The civilian managers and SS never came in direct contact with the concentration camp prisoners, only with the kapos. Even among the kapos there was a hierarchy, with "regular kapos," "head kapos" and the "supreme kapo." For example, if a kapo thought a worker wasn't doing a good enough job, after beating him, he would be taken to a "head kapo" who could order that he be whipped on his bare back and buttocks. This was essentially a death sentence, as nobody survived these whippings. Meanwhile, the supreme kapo could demote regular kapos to simple prisoner status, and even directly order someone's death, whether in the camp or at work. This would be carried out by putting the prisoner's head in a barrel of water and keeping it there until he drowned. Both kapos and prisoners were therefore extremely afraid of the supreme kapo. In short, it simply wasn't worth trying to duck out of working...

That first day was awful – horrific, really – and by the end of it I knew that my father wouldn't be able to survive this for more than a few days. Most of the prisoners were in their twenties, a few in their thirties. Dad was already over forty. Except for the ones who held some kind of position in the camps, no-one of this age survived for more than several days.[21]

As for me, there were no children my age in Gozen 2, but there were many aged 13-17. They were lads who had been caught with the Partisans in Russian, or among the Poles who had revolted in Warsaw, and even some Jewish teens from Hungary who had managed to pass the selection in Auschwitz. In general, the boys got treated better. Some didn't have to go work in the factory, but stayed in camp and did lighter work. As a child, I also got treated well for the most part, even by the cruelest kapos.

Dad and I decided that night that if the kapos gave me different work the next day after roll call, I'd take the first chance I could to speak with the head kapo about somehow helping my father. We did not plan out how exactly I would do this. Indeed, after morning roll call, they put me in a group of seven or eight people that cleaned the camp. Our kapo was an easygoing Frenchman, while a wounded Waffen SS soldier accompanied us everywhere. The soldier didn't interfere with our work; he was there to guard us. We joined dozens of other groups that made up the "cleaning commando," whose mission was to clean the toilets, showers and storage sheds. There was no quota to complete, so we worked without being pressured, but there was definitely inspection to check the quality of our work.

---

21   *The kapos in Gozen 2 were mostly Spaniards Republicans than escaped to France, where they were given political asylum. The Germans arrested these Spaniards and sent them to concentration camps. Some of them became kapos, and apparently they were the only ones of their countrymen to have survived all this time.* (More about the Capos in Gozen 2 see Chapter 24, side note 22)

That first day we spent outside, collecting all kinds of empty boxes and packages.

The whole time I worked, I kept an eye on the head kapo. This wasn't the man who had transferred me to the cleaning commando, but the supreme kapo, the one in charge of all the head kapos. He was a small, fat man – it was obvious that *he* wasn't hungry. At some point, I acted completely on a crazy impulse and asked my kapo for permission to approach the supreme kapo. I lied and said that I had been instructed to go to him. As I started walking toward him, suddenly the SS officer came up to him. I stopped about ten meters away, took off my cap and stood at attention, expecting them to finish speaking soon. He noticed me, and after the German left, I asked him for permission to speak. He raked me over with his scary eyes, but I stood still, with a lowered gaze. Suddenly, he rapped out, "Speak!" I then repeated the same exercise I had tried in Mauthausen: I took out a $10 bill from my pocket and told him I'd found it in our barrack before going out to work. I didn't know exactly what it was, so I'd wanted to give it to our block commander but I hadn't had a chance, so I wanted to give it to him instead. He looked back and forth from the money to me, then put it in his pocket and told me to get back to work. I felt at this moment like I was putting my head in a lion's mouth to ask him not to eat my father... but I didn't dare say another word; what I had done would have to be classified as "sending forth your bread upon the waters."

I didn't go over to any other kapo to request anything for my father; apparently I was simply too afraid. But I made all kinds of indirect efforts in this direction: I asked our French kapo, who was pretty friendly, if he could ask the head kapo for help for my father. I asked the same thing of the soldier who guarded us, as well as a young Polish man who was one of the managers of our block. Nobody promised me anything, and I had no idea how the supreme kapo had interpreted the $10 I had given him.

Several days passed, with me praying every morning that maybe this would be the day that the miracle would occur and they'd transfer my father to a different work group. Finally, it happened. For an unclear reason, they took Dad from the tunneling group and had him join the porters – those who arranged and loaded boxes to be sent out. This was also hard work but it was survivable – and Dad soon managed to become friendly with the kapo who was the head of his group.

Like in Mauthausen, the command staff that ran our block consisted of about ten people who lived in an area that took up about the third of our entire barrack. They had with various rooms for different purposes all to themselves. It was headed by a German criminal who was a very strict, cruel man. However, all the others were good people who tried to help the prisoners as much as they could. The block-master's assistant was a German political prisoner. A young Polish inmate (around twenty years old) was the "schreiber," the one who wrote everything down and took care of the accounting. This Pole was a sweet fellow with a good sense of humor. I liked him very much, and he helped me a lot. There was a Frenchman named Frank, a happy, nice guy who for some reason actually spoke Polish. And there was a Jewish Pole who was a watchmaker. This man had a workshop in the commanders' area, and he fixed watches for everyone – including the SS men who ran the camp. He was a real VIP in the camp, a big "macher" who made deals even with the SS. We were very lucky in that Dad had known him back in Krakow, and every few days he would bring us a little bit of extra food.

All together, the administrative staff in all the blocks and the various kapos numbered a few hundred people. The SS who ran the camp treated them pretty well in order to buy their loyalty. Not only did they get more food, better clothes and accommodations – they were the only prisoners who got any kind of medical attention.

There was no obvious discrimination between the various kinds of camp inmates. The Soviet prisoners of war, mostly Russians, were the biggest group in camp. There were quite a few Jews among them. The second biggest group were Hungarian Jews, then Polish Jews, Polish Christians, Germans, and a few French and Dutch. I learned to speak a little Russian and even a bit of Hungarian... I loved speaking with the Russian POWs, since they told me about what was going on in the war.

It was clear that the war would be over in the coming months, and Germany would be overwhelmingly defeated. American planes flew overhead, dozens and hundreds at a time, and we heard the echoes of their bombardments. Fighter planes accompanied the bombers, and we'd also constantly see the fighters flying quite low, apparently to take pictures and search for specific targets that presented themselves by chance, such as trains, trucks, groups of soldiers, etc. Every appearance of these planes encouraged the prisoners. But it didn't work on my father. I tried so many times to cheer Dad up by pointing out the squadrons flying overhead, fantasizing that soon they'd come to liberate us and we could go meet Mom and my sisters, that we'd go to America and we'd have as much bread as we wanted and could buy chocolate, cakes and bananas...

The Germans were very strict about the sanitary conditions in the camp, as they feared the outbreak of diseases. Their way of doing so, however, was extremely cruel and unbelievably sadistic: Every so often, they would order each block have a "health assembly." We had to get completely undressed, and tie our clothes into a package, with our number prominently displayed. The clothes and blankets would be taken to a "disinfection" point, and they'd spray the barracks. The naked prisoners would be forced to run in the freezing cold to the showers to wash up with cold water, and then be drenched with pesticides. In order to survive in such weather, one had to be in constant motion; if anyone collapsed or even sat down, it automatically meant freezing to death. During these long, terrible hours, I would rub my father's body over and over, to help him survive.

At some point in December, I had come to the end of my rope, both physically and psychologically. It was very hard for me to work. I began having pains all over my body, and started feeling that I just didn't care anymore. Dad's condition just kept worsening, and I made peace with the fact that my father could die any minute of any day. A concentration camp inmate in such condition was essentially dying, and at any moment one of the kapos would help him into the next world.

21.2 – A New Job, Lucky Again

At this point, just as I was about to break down, I was suddenly granted a reprieve: One morning, after we got to the factory and were at roll call, one of the civilian workers came over to me, accompanied by an SS man and the supreme kapo. They looked at me for several seconds, exchanged glances among themselves, and then the civilian asked me a few questions. After that, the kapo told me to go with them. (I'll call the civilian "the manager," because I don't remember his name.) The manager told me that I was going to work with him in the office. The supreme kapo handed me off to a different kapo and gave him some instructions. This kapo took me to a storage room full of clothes and gave me a new suit that was close to being my size. (Until then I had been wearing adult clothes and really must have looked quite funny.) I also got an undershirt and underpants (which was a privilege given only to kapos and those who managed the blocks). The next stop was the shower, where the kapo told me to wash up well. Incredibly, this shower had warm water... When I got dressed again, I must have looked like a prince – with a number still pinned to his chest. Finally, the kapo brought me to an engineer's office. The manager who had picked me out at roll call was there. I was given some kind of symbol to attach to my chest which apparently meant I was allowed to walk around the factory. When the kapo left me, he wished me good luck.

There were two big rooms in the office, with several people working at drafting tables. The manager had his own room. He was the only one dressed in a suit and tie; everyone else was in simple work clothes. A third room held the copying machine for the technical drawings, or blueprints. There was a different machine for copying documents. They put me in this room with a table and chair, and the manager explained that my job would be to make blueprints of the drawings and copy documents. One of the office workers taught me what to do; I think he was a Dutchman brought there for forced labor. After making the blueprint I would cut off the edges of the paper with a special guillotine, roll it up on a cardboard roll, and put a rubber band around it. Under the rubber band I'd attach a note that said who was supposed to get the drawing, with his room number. It was very simple work and I figured it all out in just a few days.

I was very proud of my work and my job and quickly forgot some of my other troubles. The workers would go out to eat for lunch, with a different person staying behind with me every day (who would eat later). They would always bring me back something to eat; usually it was a sandwich with normal bread – a real treat, considering that the 'bread' in camp was awful, made out of spoiled flour and sawdust. They also brought me little extras like a piece of sausage, an apple, or a potato. I would wrap most of the food they brought me in some paper and put in my pockets for my father. For some reason, the pockets in the prisoners' uniforms were big and deep...

There was an internal mail system in the factory. Every so often, someone would come with a little wagon, taking away and returning the blueprints and other pieces of mail. This postman was either a civilian or a soldier (I assume he was a disabled veteran). Sometimes, however, they'd send me with a special delivery, apparently when it was something urgent. It was very simple to know where you were in the factory because all the rooms were numbered. The first digit was the number of the hallway and the second was the number of the office. In a few cases they sent me to the manufacturing area and there the numbering system wasn't as clear, so it was hard to know one's way around.

For the first six weeks of my new job, I didn't talk with the other workers except about things connected to my work. It could have been forbidden for them to have personal conversations with me, but in any case they treated me well. Two of them were relatively young men who apparently had been brought from Holland against their will. The rest were older and were either German or Austrian; in any case, they always spoke together in German. I listened to their conversations, which mostly revolved around their families. Some had sons in the army.

In general, besides food, the thing I lacked most in the camp was sleep. The block smelled horrific, it was hard to breathe, the bed slats were hard, and people snored, sighed, moaned, cried and screamed. I would therefore get up every morning totally exhausted and wanted to sleep all the time. At work, every chance I got I would doze off in my chair – and the manager would catch me at it regularly. Finally, he called me into his office and told me that it was forbidden to sleep at the table. There could be an inspection at any time, and if they caught me sleeping they would punish me severely. The manager then asked me if I knew math, and gave me a few problems to solve as a test. He then gave me the task of totaling up some columns of numbers, seemingly productivity reports. He also said that he'd let me sleep in his room from time to time. So as unbelievable as it sounds, part of my "job" was to sleep with my head on the table next to the manager's room, while he made sure that nobody would catch me... In this way, several weeks passed with my doing easy work, getting extra food that prisoners could only dream about, and having part of the job include sleeping during the day.

February, 1945. It was very cold and snow fell, but I don't remember suffering from the cold, except during the horrible "health assembly." Dad got worse and worse, slowly becoming what was called a "musselman." I would bring him the best food I got in the office, but he could barely eat. He started talking to me as one would before parting, like giving me all sorts of advice, writing down on little notes all kinds of addresses, and (I think) bank account numbers. He also gave me quite a lot of money (in US dollars). Meanwhile, I kept trying all sorts of things in a desperate attempt to save him.

21.3 – I Say Goodbye to My Father

The terrible day finally arrived. It happened during morning roll call. It was still dark; to the best of my memory, a light snow was falling. On that frigid morning at the end of February 1945, they killed my father... And in this time the Soviet army had already liberated Krakow, had already crossed the border into Germany, and was about a hundred kilometers from Berlin. But my father was gone... I won't say here how they killed him, for a simple reason: After they murdered him, I only separated from my father during the day. Every night in my dreams, however, I continued living with him, re-experiencing the traumas of my attempts to save him, seeing him killed again, and fighting with the SS men. It's therefore too hard for me to give a true account of what actually happened.

After my father's death, I started behaving irrationally. I wouldn't go to work and stayed in the barrack. I wanted them to kill me, too – but also fiercely desired to live. At first, I didn't eat. The Polish "schreiber" and block commander's assistant took care of me, tried to encourage me, and brought me things to eat. Two or three days later, the block commander came and said that if I wouldn't go to work he would have to send me to the "hospital." I didn't know exactly what that meant in the camp, though I figured that it was something very bad. But I really felt that I couldn't care less.

Then something completely unexpected happened: Another day

or two passed, and in the morning, after the SS man left the block after the daily count, the block commander's assistant came and said that from now on I'd be part of his staff.

I don't know why I merited receiving such a favor; in essence it meant that got my life handed back to me as a gift.

For another prisoner to be added to the staff that ran the block, the SS man in charge of the barrack had to give his permission. I don't know who took care of this for me; perhaps it was the factory manager who had wondered why I wasn't coming to work. In any case, it was as if I had been granted a pardon that enabled me to live a while longer. However, I did my new job on automatic pilot, as it were, completely disinterested, not taking any initiative, walking about as if I was in a dream.

One of my tasks was to run errands, and one day I was sent to the "hospital" to bring some medicine back to someone who helped run the block. I think it was in Block 15 – and suddenly I found out what it meant to be sent to the hospital in this hell: The block was divided into two parts. Two thirds was for several hundred prisoners who could no longer work – but this "hospitalization" included absolutely no medical treatment, with a bit of soup being provided only once a day. Unsurprisingly, the "patients" died very quickly, with the dead bodies being removed to the crematoria every morning. This would leave room for a new set of "patients." If it got too crowded, they'd open the windows and stop providing any food at all, to free up space even more quickly... Amazingly, in a very few cases, prisoners who had been "hospitalized" actually got well enough to return to work.

The second part of the block was a real clinic and hospital that included nurses and doctors. There was no connection between it and the place where the masses of prisoners lay dying. This was the area where privileged prisoners (mainly Germans) like kapos and those in charge of the blocks got medical treatment. However, it was still primitive. I saw how they would do operations on filthy beds, trying to anesthetize the patient by putting a mask to his nose, while he was screaming the whole time.

Several weeks before my father was killed, we met a young Polish prisoner who became our friend. He tried to help Dad with all his heart; it was clear that he was quite a noble person. At some point he told us he was a priest, but asked us not to tell anyone else. In the days following my father's death, he would come back from work and immediately search me out. He encouraged me and wouldn't leave me for a moment. Perhaps it is thanks to him that I survived those days. After I became a member of the block's command staff and had access to the food, I would give him a little extra every day.

I stayed in this block for only two or three more weeks. Then, for some unknown reason I was transferred to another block, where I also stayed a very short time. This period is very hazy in my memory, as reality and hallucinations got very mixed up in my head and I can't relate anything clear about it. In my dreams I was always fighting the Germans: I was a soldier in the Soviet army, I was a pilot bombing Berlin and afterward going home for the Sabbath to my family. I remember once I even brought a present to my sister, Sarenka, who was going off to school with a big backpack...

Toward the end of March, they made us go through a selection. I think the entire camp was standing outside on that very cold day. We were ordered to undress and march before a group of SS officers, who pointed either to the right or to the left as we passed. When it was my turn, something totally strange happened, but I'm 90% sure it was real: As I started to pass the SS men, I began shrieking at them in German and Polish, "We're cold, we're hungry, you're dressed and warm, why are you doing this to us, you know the war is almost over, why are you so evil," etc. etc. As soon as I began, two SS guards ran over to me, but one of the officers stopped them with a raised hand and let me finish my rant. When I was done, I was told to go to the left – to deportation.

After the selection, we were brought to a kind of small train station and packed into small, open train cars, about 20 people in each one. Everyone was sure that they were taking us some place to be killed. The Christians sang hymns and crossed themselves; everyone prayed. There was no attempt to resist or run away. I am convinced that my little show in front of the SS officers was real since I remember that afterward people spoke to me about it. The ride in this little train took about 20 minutes, and we came to a camp that was about half a kilometer below the main Mauthausen camp, which was at the top of a hill. Although the ride was short, it was very difficult, since we were in the open and besides being cold there was a strong, frigid wind blowing.

Our new camp contained between ten and twenty barracks. Immediately obvious to us all were the piles of bodies next to each one of them. There was a horrible smell of rotting flesh. Shells of human beings were walking around, and wagons were going around collecting the bodies. I was there for several weeks, and not once did I see Germans in any kind of uniform inside. It was all run by prisoners. I was put into a block and lay down on a bunk with no mattress and only one blanket. For several days – I don't know how many – I lay there in a kind of semi-conscious state, with the people around me screaming, crying, and dying. Units of prisoners continually went around the bunks pulling down dead bodies. I think they gave out soup and water every day but I was not in any condition to eat. I really didn't know what was happening to me anymore, and can say that at this point I was slowly dying.

21.4 – My Life is Saved

Suddenly, I felt people moving, and heard screaming. Many people came over to me and tried speaking to me. Then I found myself on the back of a tall, powerful man who transferred me to another part of the block. As I was told later, the following is what had happened in the camp: At the end of March or beginning of April, the Nazis abandoned the camp, just guarding it from outside the fence to prevent people from escaping, and sending in very little food. The prisoners who ruled the blocks set up a kind of autonomy and decided on their own to give the little food the Nazis gave them only to the prisoners whose physical state they thought was such that they had a chance to survive another few weeks. In order to carry out this cruel and daring policy, they divided each block into two parts: One part for those who would be given a chance to live, and the second part for those who would not be able to be saved. According to their private criteria, the men in charge chose the people whom they would help to survive. Children and young people got preference – and even in my state, they chose me as well. Meanwhile, those who were still strong enough to walk had to take care of those who died. They did this by putting all the dead bodies in piles at the far edges of the camp.

All the lucky prisoners were given a piece of bread and soup twice a day. I was barely conscious, I didn't know what was happening to me, I forgot who I was and where I was, and could not eat. However, among the prisoners were also several doctors, and they started trying to help me. One doctor, whose name I unfortunately don't remember, was particularly devoted, caring for me for hours every day, giving me all kinds of liquids, massaging me, forcing me to roll in bed from one side to another, trying to sit me up and get me to talk. Slowly – very slowly – I started to wake up, feel hungry and begin eating. I met Dr. Einhenholz again, the gynecologist from Krakow who treated my mother before the war and in the ghetto. (I also met him again in Israel, several years later, and we reminisced about this camp on the outskirts of Mauthausen and what happened.) And in this "block of the living" I was reunited with Jezyk – not my friend from the ghetto, but the son of Dr. Gross, the head doctor of Plaszow, who survived the war as well.

Among the prisoners being given food was a group of six or seven youths aged 14-17. They were Poles who had been taken prisoner after the failed revolt of the Christians in Warsaw, as well as some Russians who were caught among the Partisans. This group was very close-knit, and luckily they decided to take me under their wing. When I started having an appetite again, they would bring me a little extra food, encourage me psychologically and kept telling me that the war was almost over. The Poles told me about both revolts in Warsaw – the one in the ghetto and the one by the Christians. It took time for me to recover and understand fully where I was and what was happening, and one of these boys helped me a lot by sitting next to me and asking me to tell him all about my family.

I have not managed to find supporting evidence of those last months in Gozen 2. So I don't exactly know what was the reason for the selection at the end of March 1945, what was the official purpose of this small camp I was brought to, or why I was taken there...

CHAPTER 22

Liberation and Return to Life

It was May 5, 1945: Suddenly, I heard the sounds of great excitement in the block. There were shouts of joy and people running outside. I was lying down, still a bit blurry and not completely conscious of what was going on around me. All of a sudden, one of the Polish youths ran over to me, forced me out of bed and dragged me outside. I saw people running excitedly and everyone was looking towards the main camp on the hill. It was a scene straight out of 1001 Nights: Into Mauthausen came a long line of cars and tanks, with dozens upon dozens of prisoners running and jumping around them. We saw this from a few hundred meters away. People started screaming, "Americans, Americans, liberation, it's over!" They jumped and hugged each other in joy. What's going on here? Am I dreaming? Just don't wake me up... For some reason, I became terribly sad. If I'm dreaming, why isn't Dad with me... In this whole celebrating throng of people, I began feeling very alone. I very much wanted to cry, but one must be strong... One of the Polish boys started to shake me, yelling, "Be happy, it's all over, soon we'll return home!" For some reason it was hard for me to burst with joy; I also wasn't feeling well. So I returned to the barrack and lay down again.

22.1 – A Revolution: German Soldiers Serve Me

A few hours after the Americans entered the upper camp, a whole convoy arrived in ours. The Americans were already experienced in entering concentration camps, and had learned how to act. This was already after Germany had essentially surrendered (the official date would be May 8) so the liberators could devote the necessary resources to the camp survivors.

What happened next was almost like a dream: After the various American cars and ambulances came in, a few trucks entered and German soldiers got out... What's going on? Have the Nazis come back?! Yes – they came back, but as prisoners of war, to do all the hard, dirty work for us. The entire camp had to be cleaned. The Germans had to take all the dead bodies and bury them at the edge of the camp, clean and disinfect the barracks, throw away the blankets... Meanwhile, the Americans all walked around with masks. They brought field showers – and suddenly I found myself under a warm stream of water, being bathed by two German soldiers under the direction of an American nurse. I then got new clothes.

The sickest prisoners were brought to proper hospitals. Part of our barrack was turned into a clinic, and a few hours later that's where I found myself, in a proper bed with a mattress and a sheet, and an IV line running in my arm. I stayed there for two to three days, with German soldiers serving me the whole time, even feeding me. My food intake was restricted, and the German prisoner who was mostly my personal servant obeyed the doctor's instructions to the letter. I started getting food I'd forgotten even existed: tea with sugar, meat soup, chicken, white bread with butter – in short, Heaven! One nurse (apparently American) who knew German, would tyrannize the German soldiers, who were constantly cleaning, changing bedpans, and washing the patients. After all the years of horrors and nightmares, this transformation was so dramatic that I would constantly think that I was dreaming. I would close my eyes, shake my head, open my eyes, and see if something had changed...

I asked the German who was taking care of me to take me for a walk outside – or, more accurately, I gave him an order. Suddenly, I am giving orders to a Nazi soldier!! This soldier would do anything to please me. Outside I saw the Germans taking bodies and burying them, with their former prisoners cursing and hitting them. These were Waffen SS, those SS who served in the German army. I also talked a lot with "my" German soldier, but unfortunately do not remember anything that was said. I assume I asked him about his family and what he did during the war; I do know that he was not part of the Waffen SS.

22.2 – The Joy of Freedom; the Fading Urge for Revenge

Several days after liberation, the group of Russian and Polish boys came to bid me goodbye. They were going to leave the camp. I immediately jumped up and said that I'd go with them. All their attempts to convince me to stay for more treatment were useless. I got dressed, said goodbye to the doctors and others, and we left.

It was wonderful weather, and we started walking on paths through fields in the direction of the first village we saw in the distance. We breathed in flower-scented air, heard birds chirping, and I began to feel an extraordinary sense of freedom running to every nerve ending and cell in my body and soul. It was a feeling of unending joy and gladness: Here I am, alive, free! I'm finished with the horror forever. As I walked, I began to yell, to sing, to jump and go wild. All the boys followed my lead, luxuriating in the heady, overwhelming delight of being free.

Suddenly, one of the group yelled, "Let's go kill some Germans!" However, in the intervening days since liberation, much of my urge to take revenge had dissipated. I had always been against hurting living creatures or killing them, so how much more so did I oppose killing people. It's true that during the war I imagined countless scenarios where I would kill and revenge myself on the Germans, but now that it was actually possible, my natural opposition to murder reasserted itself. I started giving religious Christian reasons to my friends why they shouldn't do it – that Jesus and Holy Mary, Mother of God were always against killing, even their greatest enemies, and that according to Christianity it was forbidden to take revenge. After an argument, it was decided that if we catch an SS man we'd kill him, but others we'd only beat up.

Meanwhile, we collected some sub-machine guns on the path, apparently abandoned by escaping German soldiers. Since all these youths had had a military past, they knew how to use the weapons. So we stopped under some tree for them to give me an extremely shortened course of basic training in how to shoot a gun. This took about half an hour... I "graduated" proud and happy, with a cocked Schmeisser sub-machine gun (with the safety catch on) under my arm.

We neared one of the villages and one of the guys announced that the time has come for the Germans to pay for what they did to us. One of the Poles recounted how he had once seen Germans come into a house and demand all the valuables and money, and that we were now going to do the same thing to them. It turned out that I was the only one who knew German well, and suddenly I became a very important person. I agreed to be the group's "spokesman" but on condition that they wouldn't use their weapons. I felt that they would have no problem killing people; one of the Russians had told us how the Partisans would enter villages and kill people who'd collaborated with the Germans.

We entered the first house in the village that looked rich. There was an old couple there with some children. With great politeness, we introduced ourselves, and I explained that the Germans had murdered all our families, and that we'd come to kill them all and burn the house down, but if they behaved nicely nothing would happen to them. I told them to prepare for us a place to sleep in a few rooms, prepare us a festive meal, and collect jewelry and foreign currency (dollars and Swiss francs) for us from their neighbors.

News of our arrival spread quickly through the village. People started bringing us food, money and jewelry. It seemed to me that they had anticipated and feared such a raid. Now, with my feelings of vengeance having cooled so much, every additional collection gave me a slightly unpleasant feeling. The old couple looked wretched and afraid, as did all the other villagers who came to us. Later, a few other old women came to the house and started cooking for us. I heard later that the younger women had apparently gone into hiding because they were afraid of being attacked and raped.

We had a good time in that house, eating and having a party, with the villagers serving us and bringing us "offerings of money and jewelry." The next day, an old, very respectable-looking man came to us with more money and jewelry, and told us that the whole village had been anti-Nazi, that they had suffered terribly from them, that all the young folk had been forced to serve in the army, and many more such lies...

The owner of the house told us about his sons who had died in the war and that the whole village lived in fear because not far from there Russian soldiers and concentration camp inmates had killed people and burned down houses. He said that he was glad that we were good children and wished us that we would get home safely... I remember one slightly funny event, when a woman came with two young children, bringing with her a jewelry box. She told us that her husband had been killed in the war, and she had the engagement ring and wedding band that he had given her that she would ask us not to take from her. Most of the group and I pitied her so we left her almost all her jewelry – except for one gold bracelet and a diamond ring... We also let her keep her watch, as we already had dozens.

After three or four days, we decided to leave the village. Perhaps this will sound strange, but we left these people in friendship. It could be said that we had conquered the place, but their children had also come to us with their balls and we had played with them. Some representatives of the village actually asked us to stay for a few more days and protect them from other prisoners who may attack, offering us a large sum of money for this service. But we decided to go find other, richer villages, and departed. As I said goodbye to our hosts, I looked into this old couple's eyes and remembered how I'd threatened to kill everyone. I couldn't have done it...

We started walking towards some town that was supposed to be very rich. We yelled, we laughed, and as we met people, we didn't hurt them but we did scare them a little. There weren't that many, and they were all terribly afraid of us, raising their hands as if in surrender as they passed by...

Suddenly, my stomach started hurting me. I felt nauseous and dizzy; the rich meals had started taking their revenge. At first I didn't say anything, but soon the group noticed that something wasn't quite right with me. I began vomiting, and soon couldn't walk. We sat under a beautiful, large tree, and another attempt was made to revive me. They gave me some hard liquor to drink (Russians think this is a cure-all...) but it only made things worse.

A short distance away we saw a road that was full of military traffic. My condition grew steadily worse, so they decided to bring me to the road, stop a car and ask the occupants to take me to a hospital. I will note the honesty of these boys, who decided to give me my fair share of the booty we had gathered: I got five watches, a lot of money, two rings, a bracelet and several other things. I had become rich again... Two boys started helping me to the road, but by the time we got there one of them was carrying me on his back.

A short time later I found myself in an American military hospital, which had basically taken over a former German military base, which included a hospital and convalescent home. The American doctors and nurses took devoted care of me. Most of the hospital's hundreds of beds were empty, as a majority of the wounded soldiers had already been sent back to the USA. There were only a few sick or injured soldiers, and victims of concentration camps. In general they kept the survivors in their own areas of the hospital. Another part of it also served as an outpatient clinic for American soldiers staying in the area.

For the first week I was there, I got intravenous infusions all the time. I had tubes running in and out of my arms. They pumped my stomach and gave me enemas more than once. The doctors told me later that I had stuffed myself so much with food that everything had gotten stopped up and my life had been in danger. After several days I started recovering and could eat liquids, like chicken soup. This soup touched me deeply, as it reminded me of my home... I again saw German prisoners doing all the dirty work under the direction of the doctors and nurses. Just like before, a soldier emptied my bedpan and cleaned me, and I kept looking at him, closing my eyes and checking again if I was dreaming, as how could this possibly be? These proud, arrogant, puffed up Nazis, these rulers of the world, are serving me and cleaning me and scouring the bathrooms, doing everything they're ordered to do, with a lowered head and downcast eyes. How we had changed positions in such a flash...

22.3 – Prince of An American Hospital

About two weeks after my arrival I was officially discharged from the hospital. However, I stayed on and got a room to live in. It turned out that a large number of the doctors and nurses were Jewish, and many of them had emigrated from Poland to the United States in the Twenties and Thirties. They spoke Polish and many spoke German, so I could talk to them, and they were very sympathetic and interested in me.

All of them had left family behind when they had emigrated, and my personal story of the Holocaust interested and touched them deeply. Some of them had left children my age at home when they had come overseas, and I reminded them of their family. I remembered a few words of English from my lessons in the ghetto (though mainly the accent), so I also managed to speak a bit with those who didn't know either Polish or German. And so it happened that I was adopted as the hospital's child; everyone knew me and treated me wonderfully.

I had to be very careful about what I ate after my discharge. I could only eat a little at a time, and only when I felt hungry. Soon my appetite returned and I really began enjoying food. I'd eat in the officers' dining room (with the doctors and nurses) five times a day, as they prepared special, small meals for me in a diet that would prevent me from overeating. For breakfast, I got rolls with butter, and a soft boiled egg – after years of not having seen such foods. They also gave me hot chocolate to drink (I'd forgotten that such a thing had ever existed). I won't list here my whole daily menu, with treats that I had long forgotten, but only someone who had been starved for years could understand the fun and ecstatic joy there was in eating.

The Polish doctors brought me books in Polish that had been brought to hospitalized Polish soldiers by their visitors. I also got notebooks and writing implements, so I soon turned my room into a playroom and learning center. I organized a small bookcase and desk for myself, and wasn't bored for a second. I'd also play all kinds of ballgames with the soldiers outside, becoming particularly friendly with some of the African American ones. This was a unique experience for me, since I'd only seen black people in comic books and stories. They'd take me to all kinds of interesting places: I went to big cities, I think even to Vienna, and visited museums. Once I even went with some kind of medical committee to check the sanitary conditions of a German prisoner of war camp. That was amazing – to see German soldiers locked up in a camp, with me coming to oversee them... They were wretched and depressed and sometimes I felt a bit compassion for them.

Since the hospital was actually a big military camp, it also had a club with a movie theater, playrooms, and reading rooms with newspapers and even more books, some again in Polish. So I read, ran around, danced, jumped and sang all day long. I felt that everyone loved me, and was simply in seventh heaven. In short, I lived as if I was in a dream and just wanted it to never end.

My most important daily "task" was to "look after" the German prisoners who worked in the hospital. I was inundated by mixed feelings of revenge, joy, triumph and pity whenever I was with them. I also wanted to learn from these soldiers how they had been capable of carrying out the horrific crimes they had done. What happened, what had they felt, what did they do during the war, where did they fight – I wanted to know it all. I'd walk around the area where the prisoners worked and would talk to them. I loved their war stories because they told of their terrible suffering on the Russian front, and the families they'd left behind who had been killed or died from the Allied bombings.

In every conversation I would emphasize that if they told the truth I wouldn't punish them... I'd walk around as proud and puffed up as a peacock, carrying a British officer's swagger stick. During the first few weeks I ordered every German soldier to stand at attention and remove his cap when I spoke to them or even when I just passed by. I'd introduce myself as a Jew and demand explanations. I pressed the prisoners with questions like, "Why are the Germans so cruel and murderous? Why did they murder all the Jewish children?"

Of course the answer was generally "It wasn't us, it was the SS, we didn't know, we didn't hear..." There were some who admitted to me that they'd heard and saw, but of course they didn't take part in any of it. They would tell me how much they'd suffered from cold, hunger, exhaustion, disease and frostbite; how over the years they buried their comrades-in-arms in Russia and then their loved ones at home, and so they had no energy to deal with anything else. The young soldiers explained that they had been children when Hitler came to power and had never known anything else. They'd learned in school and youth movements (Hitler Youth) about Nazism; Hitler had been like a god to them; and they'd never questioned anything he did.

There were also some officers among the prisoners. According to the Geneva Convention, officers didn't have to do any labor, but one could have them oversee the work of their soldiers. I knew very well that some of these officers did not like at all the fact that I was their superior here. What they most disliked was that I forced them to answer my every question; I would not give them the right to remain silent. I would press them, demand that they think again after they'd given me an answer, and remind them that "a German officer does not lie." I allowed the officers to keep their caps on when standing at attention in front of me, although one particular man continued to take it off, saying he was doing so as a sign of solidarity with his men. (Later, I nullified this particular decree for all the men.) I had many, many conversations with the officers. They were usually well educated, knew a lot, and what they said interested me considerably. With all these conversations, after a short while, I even began recognizing some of the soldiers by name. And I will note that there was not a single case where any one of them broke discipline with me.

The crowning moment of my involvement with these prisoners every day was at the end of their work day, when they would have a roll call before returning to their base. I would come and make them do some drills that were humiliating and a little cruel – just giving them a little taste of what had been done to me and countless others in the concentration camps: I'd order them to stand at attention and at ease, bend over, lie down with their noses pushed into the ground, etc. I would also give speeches, or call out individual soldiers, ask them questions, and force them to answer publicly. Only one time did something go wrong, when during one speech where I was excoriating them for what the Germans had done to my family, I burst into tears.

These drills were the best show in town... There were always dozens – and sometimes hundreds – of American soldiers and hospital staff standing around and watching us. For me, these were moments of real happiness, when I could take out my frustrations and sorrow on the enemy. It was better than my wildest dreams, that I could force German soldiers to do humiliating exercises! In retrospect, it is quite interesting that the Americans let me play this game and not only did they not try and stop me, the military police who were in charge of guarding the prisoners encouraged me further. Meanwhile, the Germans soldiers were very disciplined and there was no attempt to object to what I was doing. They were depressed and despairing and all they wanted to do was go home. This was a period when some POW's were being released, and they were all desperately afraid of being handed over to the Russians. Once, a delegation of Soviet soldiers came to visit the hospital and I was the one who calmed them down, telling them that the soldiers had not come to take them away... What irony, that a Jewish child should be the one to offer comfort to German soldiers.

When I look back on my condition at the end of the war, I see a child who was an orphan, alone in the world, with nobody really taking care of him. One would have thought that I should have been totally miserable. But I didn't feel that way at all. I was in a constant state of euphoria, did not feel sad or lonely, and most peculiarly of all – I did not make any special attempt to find anyone from my family. I felt as if I had just been reborn into a new world and the past did not interest me. I don't remember what was at the root of my knowledge, but I do remember that I did not harbor any hopes that someone of my immediate family had survived. After I had recovered in the hospital, people from various organizations came to me with lists of survivors and registered me on them as well. Not a single relative of mine, either close or distant, ever appeared on their lists – or on any others that I saw in the future.

In the following years, after I'd emigrated to Palestine, I lived and was educated in a kibbutz with many other child survivors. It is worth noting and perhaps interesting from a human point of view, that all the children I was with during those years had undergone a similar process of wanting to erase the Holocaust from their consciousness. We would not talk among ourselves about the Holocaust or what we had undergone. After several years of living together and becoming close friends, I still didn't know a single thing about their pasts. Only many, many years later did we begin telling each other stories of what we had been through, when we got together from time to time.

The only times I would sometimes return to the past would be in my dreams. I'd talk to my father, hug my mother, play with my sisters, travel by train with the family on a winter vacation to Zakopane, and in this way relive my memories...

I never thought of the future when I was in the hospital, of what I was going to do. I lived in a happy bubble, a constant party that I hoped would never end. I grew very close to one of the Polish-American doctors, and he offered to take me with him to the United States. He told me that he had two daughters, one younger and one older than me, and over time, if I so desired, he would adopt me as his son. I don't remember that this presented me with a problem; America was a kind of legendary country to me, one that symbolized hope. I liked his idea, and I assume he talked about me to his wife, who agreed to it. (I would be willing to pay almost any price today to see the letter or letters he wrote to his wife about me...) He also took my picture, and showed me pictures of his family and house, in a little town in western America. But we never got to the stage of planning when and how I'd go.

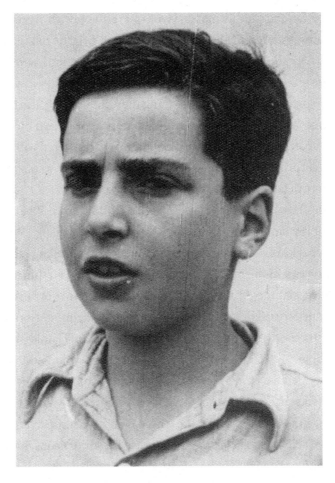

First picture after the war, me, 1946

22.4 – I Become an Ardent Zionist

So the weeks passed happily until one day, when my life changed forever: Soldiers of the Jewish Brigade from Palestine arrived at the hospital. They were searching for Holocaust survivors, and of course found me as well. As all other organizations did at the time, they brought with them lists of survivors that filled several big binders.

(The main organization that were involved in this blessed and holy work of finding and listing survivors were the Jewish Agency, the Red Cross, the American Joint and the Jewish Brigade of the British army. There were dozens of other, smaller organizations as well.) As with the few Jewish survivors who were hospitalized, they invited me to a personal interview. The first thing they did was look through all the names to see if someone from my family appeared in their lists. Unfortunately, not a single relative of mine was registered with them. To my surprise, I found myself on their list, but they wanted me to add more details to the information they had.

After these strange soldiers finished writing down what I told them of my family, I had a question of my own for them: "Who are you? What kind of soldiers are you?" So they started telling me about Palestine and Zionism, about how they were Jewish Palestinian army units that had fought the Germans. They showed me pictures, told me about Jerusalem and Tel Aviv, about kibbutzim and oranges… Their stories stirred long-dormant memories, and I told them in turn about my Hebrew teacher from the ghetto who had a son in Kibbutz Merchavia in Palestine. The soldiers confirmed that there indeed was such a kibbutz in the Jezreel Valley.

Until I met these soldiers, the whole issue of Palestine, Jerusalem and the Hebrew language had been erased from my consciousness. Suddenly, I started remembering what I had learned in the past about it, and connecting all the history to these wondrous men. I listened to their tales with my mouth hanging open, and asked them a torrent of questions. I felt like I was under some kind of magic spell, and the whole thing simply captured my heart. Obviously, the soldiers felt that they were succeeding in gaining another pioneer, so they spent a lot of time on me.

They spoke of Palestine being the Promised Land that we read about in the Passover Haggadah – and I vaguely remembered the *seders* we used to have as a family. I told them about how we used to celebrate the holiday, and they were very interested in all I had to say. My imagination caught on fire when they spoke of how they were going to establish a Jewish state in Palestine, the ancient Land of Israel that had once beheld the kingdoms of David and Solomon. And when they told me that they had weapons there, and were fighting against their enemies – not like what happened in Europe – that was the final, knock-out blow. I was theirs, body and soul. When they asked if I wanted to come to Palestine and join the fight to establish a Jewish state, I jumped up and yelled, "Of course I do!" But I did make one point clear: There was no way I would travel in a closed, canvas-covered truck, for obvious reasons...

And so it was that in just a few hours, these soldiers had managed to convert me into a fiery Zionist. I forgot that I had recently agreed to go to America... The soldiers said they'd return in a few days for me and some of the other survivors in the hospital. So I went to the doctor who had wanted to adopt me and told him I wouldn't be going with him. He didn't try to change my mind. I promised that I'd write him from Palestine and come visit him in the United States...

Now I had a future and a vision to go along with my pleasant, happy present. I was going to go build a new state for Jews, and I'd also fight for it – what fun! Suddenly, I started to feel that this was what I was meant for – building new countries. What a wonderful profession... It wasn't quite clear to me why we'd have to fight for a state, and who would we be fighting against; after all, the Germans had already lost the war.

I suddenly had a crazy idea: I would take with me a unit of German prisoners who had a lot of experience in fighting. After all, they were very obedient to me, so I could be their commander and use them to establish my country... To take it to the most absurd level, I actually went and spoke to them about it! I imagine that for years afterward they told their friends this joke of how a Jewish boy tried to draft them to fight in Palestine for a Jewish state...

In July or August, several big trucks and two jeeps of the Jewish Brigade came to the hospital. I parted emotionally from all my hospital friends, and climbed aboard one of the jeeps; everyone had made peace with the fact that nothing on earth would get me into one of those closed trucks ever again. We went from place to place collecting more Jews from various Jewish Brigade headquarters and other units attached to British divisions. We drove through the Alps through scenery that looked so pretty it belonged in fairy tales. The first city we came to in Italy was Modena, where we were put up in a fabulous castle for several days.

Our last stop was Rome, where they brought several dozen young orphan survivors to a small estate on the edge of the city. It was a kind of agricultural school. Every morning we had regular classes, and the people there showered us with unending love and warmth. One Jewish brigade soldier was our homeroom teacher, and others took us on regular trips to entertain us. We were lucky that the city tram reached us, because I loved going into the city and did it often. I had quite a lot of money, thanks to all the foreign currency and jewelry I had received from the Austrian villagers following my liberation. So I'd always invite other children to come have a good time with me. Meanwhile, in addition to the Jewish Brigade units from Palestine, the entire Jewish community of Rome adopted us warmly. Every weekend we were hosted by Jewish families in the city – in my case, by various people who had emigrated from Poland to Italy in different ways. In this way, about four wonderful months passed by, and then, in December 1945, the Jewish Brigade brought me to the port in Trieste in order to sail to Palestine to build a Jewish state…

CHAPTER 23

Afterword

It is December 1945, we are on a ship on the way to Palestine. It contained mostly children and teens. It was a partial warship, having its cannon still on deck, and we spent several rough days at sea on it before reaching Palestine and disembarking excitedly at the Port of Haifa. I was then sent to Kibbutz Gan Shemuel, which took in a whole group of child survivors from Poland. I spent the next three years learning with these children.

This kibbutz had been established in the 1920s by several waves of Hashomer Hatza'ir pioneers who had emigrated from Poland. Right before the war broke out, it had also absorbed a number of Jewish youths from Germany. Almost every member of the kibbutz had left family and friends behind in Poland, and they were very interested in hearing what had happened during the Holocaust from me and the others. I therefore spent the first few months there repeating my story to hundreds of kibbutz members, until one day, after a certain incident, I decided to stop talking about it.

About three months after our arrival in the kibbutz, we made an internal decision to stop talking Polish, and started trying to imitate the kibbutz-born children. During this period of time, society in general and the kibbutz in particular was united in its battle to drive the British from the country and establish a Jewish state. All our thoughts and actions served to further this goal. Our whole past in the Holocaust became ancient history that was not to be discussed. We worked and learned in difficult conditions - with the emphasis being on work. On this kibbutz, labor was considered holy, and a person was judged first and foremost according to how much he contributed through his work. My love for learning never ceased, but I mainly expressed it by learning by myself. I continued being a "nerd"; it wasn't a great honor, but I still managed to gain some respect for my knowledge.

I am a driver at the age of 17, in my first year at the kibbutz, 1950

A short time after our arrival, we began pre-military training; the purpose of all our sports practices and hikes was to prepare for our battle to establish the State. In June 1948, during the battles of the War of Independence, I took an advanced basic training course that lasted a few weeks, with an eye to joining the Palmach together with my group. I was not even 16 years old. But in the end, instead of drafting us into the Palmach, they transferred us to Kibbutz Gat, which was an army position on the front line that faced the Egyptians. The kibbutz was about 1,500 meters from an Arab village called Iraq al Menashia, with Fallujah lying close by, to its west. Together, they were a military base that contained a full Egyptian brigade. Our transfer took place in July 1948, after the second cease-fire of the war. We were transported suddenly, in the middle of the night. With no advance notice whatsoever, we took tearful and emotional leave of Kibbutz Gan Shemuel's members; it was all quite dramatic.

Kibbutz Gat became a military base that contained a whole system of underground bunkers with communication trenches running everywhere. We spent all our time underground. The fighting was basically a standoff, with the Egyptians constantly shelling us with cannon and mortars as well as bombing us from the air. A number of attempts were made to conquer the "Fallujah pocket", but they only resulted in many sacrificed lives on our side and heroic fighting on the part of the Egyptians. This part of the war continued on and off for almost a year until the final ceasefire in the spring of 1949, when the Egyptian army was allowed to retreat. For all practical purposes, this ceasefire set the borders of the State of Israel. I can't point to any particular heroic deeds on my part during these battles... I spent 90% of the time in the bunkers and in fortified positions, using the time to learn and read books.

In December 1949, together with about 60 friends, I established Kibbutz Nir Yitzchak on the border of the Gaza Strip, opposite Rafiach. This kibbutz is part of what is currently called the settlements of the Gaza Envelope. For the first five years, my main job was being the kibbutz driver. I first drove kibbutz cars and trucks, and then represented the kibbutz in the Negev Cooperative, driving heavy vehicles. I began my driving career at age 16 1/2 and loved my job very much, since it allowed me to travel throughout the country, meet many people, and to a large extent satisfy my adventuresome spirit. In 1954 the kibbutz remembered that I was the kind of person who loved to learn, and they sent me to be trained in a teachers' seminary in Jerusalem within the framework of Aliyat Hano'ar. I also completed my matriculation exams while learning both math and physics in Hebrew University with some of the best teachers there. These were two very happy years for me, where I studied with an excellent group and didn't have to worry about supporting myself. I then returned to the kibbutz as a certified teacher and, together with three more teachers, taught a group of teens from all over the country for about four years. I managed to instill in them a sense of the importance of their studies and a love for learning.

In general, those first years were difficult ones, and we lived very modestly. Despite this, I loved kibbutz life very much and was not only very content with my life, I was extremely proud of being a full partner in the important mission of developing the land and establishing its borders. We developed a unique and honorable way of life in which everyone was equal, living by the well-known dictum, "Each giving according to his means and taking according to his needs." We felt proud to be an example of a just and high-quality lifestyle, and perhaps, according to Jewish tradition, serve as "a light unto the nations."

During the time I lived in the kibbutz I took on many different jobs. These included several months of putting up and maintaining field latrines, as for the first seven years of its existence, the kibbutz did not have indoor bathrooms. I also spent several months taking my turn in the kitchen and dining room, working in the orchards, the cowshed, and even as a shepherd. I found something to interest me in everything I did, and each job gave me a sense of fulfillment and satisfaction.

After twelve years of living on the kibbutz I reached a turning point in my life. There were several reasons for this, but one of the main ones was that all my friends had married around the age 18-21, when we first established the kibbutz, while I was by now 27 and still single. Social life in the kibbutz largely revolved around the family and raising children, and I felt alone and different. I had had girl-friends starting at age 14, but it was hard for me to imagine having a family of my own. It was a very difficult crisis for me, as I had spent the last 15 years with these friends, overcoming the challenges of integration in the country, establishing the State, participating in the War of Independence and creating a new kibbutz. I was bound heart and soul to my kibbutz friends and the pioneer mission. When I left in the end, I suffered pangs of conscience and felt a bit like I was betraying these people with whom I had traveled a long and hard road.

I am travelling 1955

I made the decision to leave the kibbutz in the summer of 1962. I parted from my friends on a positive note and have remained on excellent terms with them ever since. I went to live up north, in Haifa, to learn in the Technion, which at that time was the only technologically-oriented university in the country. The courses were on an extremely high level and the pressure of my studies was intense. This whole period of study was difficult and challenging, but it was also a very happy time. I had to work very hard for my living while keeping up with my classwork, but luckily I had the stamina to do it all. Three nights a week I worked as a porter in the Port of Haifa, finishing at 2 AM. I would go home to sleep for four hours and then go to the university. Twice a week I would ride my motorbike to teach in a kibbutz in the Jezreel Valley. Devoted to my job, I would go no matter how much rain was pouring down. To my surprise, I earned a lot more than what I needed to live on, and despite not having any family supporting me I was considered a wealthy student...

Me on the motorcycle, 1964

Speaking of family, as mentioned in the Introduction, my father's cousin, Gina Wimisner, arrived in the country in 1946. She settled in Kibbutz Avuka in the Beit Shean Valley together with her good friend (and future husband) Shmuel Milgrom. Gina and her two brothers were the only surviving remnant of my family, and while her brothers emigrated to England, I was in constant touch with Gina and

Shmuel from the moment they landed. Thankfully, I also became very close to their children: Miriam, Tziki, and David. All three became very successful and to date have seven children between them. Unfortunately, Gina passed away before her time in 1994, and her husband died several years later as well. We all mourned them deeply. When I decided to go on my first trip back to my roots in Krakow in 2003, it was natural for me to take Miriam and her sister along. Then, when we made another trip in 2010, we took both second and third generation "survivors" as well: my daughters, Orit and Liat, and Miriam and her husband Meir's children – Michal, Eran and Einat.

I graduated from the Technion in 1966 and started working for the Ministry of Defense in a company called Rafael. For 25 years I did weapons research and development. The work suited my personality perfectly, as it demanded that I keep learning and investigating. I loved every minute of my job and considered myself very lucky indeed. I retired in 1990 and then took upon myself the task of managing and developing the computerization of engineering firms. I mainly oversaw the transition from working on drawing boards to using computer programs. Although this was being done all over the world, I saw it as my mission to accomplish this in my small corner of it.

Regarding my personal life: In 1967, following the Six Day War, I met 21-year-old Ariella Pollack, who in my opinion was the most charming and prettiest girl in the entire state... We were married within months, and are currently (as of 2014) celebrating our 47th wedding anniversary.

Ariella my wife 1968

Since Ariella is 13 years my junior, I have had to keep myself young – which is all to my benefit. To this day we are like a young couple, walking around arm in arm if not hand in hand… Ariella is a second generation survivor, born immediately after the war ended. We were very lucky and for decades we at least had one set of parents. Ariella's mother died in 2011 and her father died in 2006. Even though they died at a ripe old age, as they say, we were heartbroken at their loss. They were a downtrodden couple, as their experiences during the Holocaust hurt them badly, but they dedicated their lives to raising their children, grandchildren and even great-grandchildren.

Our wedding 1967

We've also raised two wonderful daughters: Orit Share, who married David Share and is raising two of our grandchildren – ten-year-old Shelly and eight-year-old Ben, who are naturally extremely talented and beautiful… Our younger daughter, Liat Adler, and her husband Eran, are raising two boys and a girl: Tom (14), Liran (11) and Itamar (6). Of course, they, too, are wonderfully talented and good-looking grandchildren!

Children, grandchildren and great- grandchildren of Gina and me, 2012

Ariella and me with all our grandchildren, 2012

This is just a short summary of my post-Holocaust life. Perhaps I will yet manage to write a detailed account of this period... in just a few hundred pages...

THE END

CHAPTER 24

Historical look on the events

Side Note 1: The Jews of Krakow and the Kazimierz Neighborhood

Krakow became the capitol of Poland in 1038. In 1535, the town of Kazimierz was established nearby specifically for the Jews, by King Kazimierz the Great. It was separated from Krakow by the Visula River and was under the direct protection of the king. Jewish life flourished there for the next 400 years, both culturally and religiously. At the end of the 19th century, the course of the river was changed, Kazimierz became physically attached to Krakow, and the Jews were given permission to now live in the capitol. The whole region was called "Galicja" in the second half of that century, and was part of the Austro-Hungarian Empire. Being very tolerant of minorities, people were allowed to go to either Polish or German schools; both were official languages of the realm. When World War I ended in 1918, Galicja became part of the re-established country of Poland. When World War II began, nearly 60,000 of the 300,000 residents of Krakow were Jewish. The vast majority – over 80% – lived among the Christians in Krakow, not in Kazimierz, and was part of the upper and middle class of the city.

The few Jews who survived the Holocaust and returned to Krakow did not live in Kazimierz. The neighborhood was neglected by the Communist authorities, who even planned to destroy it and build new housing there. After Poland was freed in 1990, the new national and local governments made great efforts to rehabilitate and preserve the neighborhood. These efforts are very praiseworthy. All the synagogues, ancient cemeteries and old houses have undergone and are yet undergoing repairs. The place has become a tourist attraction, full of coffee houses and hotels. Many of the stores – most of which have become restaurants – have preserved the original signs and displays dating back to when they were Jewish-owned businesses.

Side Note 2: The Judenrat

From the start of the German Occupation until the ghetto was liquidated, a Jewish administration called the Judenrat ran the Jewish community. All its members were appointed by the Germans. The first head of the Krakow Judenrat was Dr. Biberstein, who was one of the leaders of the community even before the war. He was a man of principle and did everything he could to ease the lives of the Jews. When he was arrested on suspicion of bribery, Dr. Rosenzweig was chosen to replace him. He, too, was a man of principle and conscience, just like his predecessor. Dr. Rosenzweig was fired during the deportation of June 1942, and his place was taken by David Gutter. This last leader was completely uneducated and had no conscience whatsoever. Like the head of the Jewish Police, Spira, he served the Germans loyally and helped them kill Jews.

Side Note 3: Testimonies Regarding Life in the Ghetto

Thousands of books have been written and tens of thousands of testimonies have been given regarding life under German Occupation in general and life in the ghettos in particular. But even if the same things are being described, each testimonial has its own character. This writing is just another one of many such witness accounts. By nature I am quite optimistic and in general I try to reflect upon life in a slightly humorous fashion. There is no doubt that these two traits have, and will, come through in my writing.

In my opinion, one of the best testimonies ever written about the Krakow Ghetto is Tadeusz Pankiewicz's "Apteka w Getcie Krakowskim" (A Pharmacy in the Krakow Ghetto). He was a legendary pharmacist who ran his business in Zgody Square the entire time and of the existence of the ghetto and witnessed all the deportations. I believe that his memoirs are the most interesting and important books ever written on ghetto life. Another excellent source on the life in Ghettos is a movie made by the Germans themselves in 1942 of the Warsaw Ghetto, which parts of it are shown in many documentary films and lately was produced as a full documentary film under the name "The Silence of the Archives"; it is an incredible film.

The original purpose of the Nazis was to present this film to the German populace as an evidence of the filth and degeneration that marked Jewish life: rats, mice, lice, fleas. Jews dying on sidewalks from disease, befouled children dressed in rags begging for charity, wagons continually passing by and collecting bodies. The Germans wanted to convince their own people as well as the Christian population in the countries they'd conquered, that Jews must be kept far away from any contact with the Aryan race, and then the "natural" next step would be to annihilate them. But when this film was shown to select target audiences in Germany, it turned out that they aroused more pity and questions than hatred and revulsion. Therefore, a propaganda piece that was supposedly educational was put away in an archive. Today, of course, they are an authentic, filmed testimonial to the Nazi atrocities in the Warsaw Ghetto.

Side Note 4: Gestapo Collaborators

In general, the Jewish informants and collaborators were the dregs of society and criminals who engaged in extortion, theft and acts of fraud even before the war, who now found a way to express their true selves, make a wonderful living and rise to greatness. However, there were also a few normative souls who simply thought that this would be the way to survive the war easily and save their lives. Part of the Jewish Police also collaborated with the Gestapo and SS.

Among others, the informants turned over to the Germans many who tried to organize a Resistance in the ghetto. They would walk around the ghetto without anything denoting that they were Jewish, although everyone knew who they were; they didn't try to hide their connections to the Gestapo. (I assume that there were also collaborators who were better at being undercover and who didn't stand out in any way.) These informants would try and get friendly with other people, and through them, one could get all sorts of papers and leniencies – usually for pay. It wouldn't have been much of a problem to hurt them, but for some reason this wasn't done inside the ghetto. Only at a later stage, after the ghetto was liquidated, when they started hunting Jews down on the Christian side and informing on Poles who hid Jews, did the Polish Underground close accounts with some of them. Their criminal treason didn't help them save their own lives, either. The second the Gestapo didn't need their services, they would be executed, along with their families.

Side Note 5: The Jewish Police in the Ghetto

I used to love walking in the area around the building of the Jewish Police that was on the other end of our street. There was always something interesting going on, like the bringing in of suspects, the arrival of SS and Gestapo agents, the departure of those under arrest. I would gaze with both wonder and hatred at the sparkling clean uniforms and shiny boots of the SS. They always wore leather gloves: The SS officers had white gloves and the Gestapo wore brown or black ones. I recognized many of these men, even by name. They treated us children nicely, even giving out candies – yet these same people were the lowest of the low, cruel murderers who killed even toddlers and infants, as I shall describe below.

Near the police station one could also meet the commander of the

Jewish Police, Symche Spira. He was dressed like a South American general, all polished and sparkling, full of decorations on his chest and shoulders. He would get off his personal carriage, full of his own self-importance, but whenever he met a German officer he'd spring to attention and salute. The officer would look at him with scorn and not respond. I wondered to myself if this was how the king of the Jews once looked, or maybe how the royal jester dressed for court? This Spira was a great example of what happens when "a servant becomes a master." He had been a very religious man, unlearned, who spoke a broken Polish and German. He then exchanged his belief in (and loyalty to) God for a belief and fidelity to the Germans, who saw in him the perfect type who would serve them best. Indeed, he gave his heart and soul to their service. There was nothing he would not do to fulfill their wishes. Later on, as I will note, I witnessed his execution at his masters' hands.

The Jewish Police had different badges, according to their jobs: As I described above, one part of the force was in charge of public order. Not only did they oversee tax collection and sanitation, but they also were in charge of giving out housing and taking care of disputes between neighbors. Another department, which was called the "civilian police," was used as the arm of the Gestapo and collaborated fully with them. They would arrest those suspected of "security crimes" like listening to the radio, spreading rumors, hiding foreign currency and the like. They would either gather the intelligence that would lead to arrests or get it from informants, who cast terror wherever they went. It was not a good thing to get into trouble with them, so if you had the means, they could be bribed. To ensure the safety of your family it was enough to pay off one or two of the informants and they would make sure that your names never got to the Gestapo. Every one of this gang of criminals and traitors got rich from the numerous families that bribed them.

I assume that my father paid them off as well, as I heard my parents speaking about it. Dad had a friend who was the commander of one of the departments in this civilian police force. (I will say more about him later on as well.) I believe they really were friends, as our two families hosted each other for meals. They lived in one of the grander apartments in a newer building, and their son was my friend

Side Note 6: Abbreviated History of Polish-German Relations

As soon as the Germans attacked the Soviet Union, a strong propaganda machine went into action. In newspapers and notices, the country was plastered with calls for the Aryan Polish nation to join the war against "the Bolshevik-Jewish Satan." Every piece of propaganda tied Bolshevism to Judaism, with the theme being "Jewish Bolshevism aspires to enslave all enlightened nations."

The German call to the Polish nation to "join us in our war against the Bolsheviks," was extremely significant, because for hundreds of years Germany had seen Poland as a bitter enemy and fought against it. The German nation had never forgotten their terrible defeat at the hands of the Poles in the Battle of Grunwald in the 15th century. And on the Polish side, this victory was one of the greatest legends in their history and took pride of place in the saga of their national honor.

More recently, after Germany lost World War I, the Poles annexed tens of thousands of square kilometers of Germany that included some major cities, which was one of the reasons Germany invaded Poland in 1939. The Germans then tried to set up a puppet government that would cooperate with them, just as they did successfully in most of the other countries they conquered. (I refer to collaboration on a governmental, political level, not to individuals, who could be found everywhere, even among the Jews.) For example, in France they set up the Vichy government; in Norway, Quisling headed their puppet regime; while in Belgium and Denmark the kings were allowed to stay in their positions and Denmark was given a broad mandate for self-rule. In contrast, in Poland the Nazis couldn't find a single Polish political figure who was willing to collaborate with them.

Before our move to the ghetto, the German lady who boarded with us maintained that Germany was actually still in a state of war with official Poland, because the government never surrendered or signed a cease-fire agreement with Germany. The Polish government went to London, and parts of the Polish army went abroad to join Britain in its fight against the Nazis. The Polish air force flew missions out of the British Isles. In North Africa, the Polish army fought together with the British forces against the Italians and Germans. In 1941, volunteer units from the occupied countries of France, Holland, Norway and Belgium joined the Germans in their invasion of the Soviet Union, but not a single one did from Poland. It should also be noted here that Poland was the only country in Europe whose army continued fighting in a serious and significant manner against the Germans during the entire war. Perhaps the only others who could be compared to them would be Tito's partisans in Yugoslavia.

Side Note 7: Going into Hiding

At this point in time, on the beginning of 1942 year there was no suspicion – let alone knowledge – of the Nazis' intentions to carry out the total annihilation of the Jewish people. The Jews in the ghetto treated rumors of a slaughter in the Ukraine and the Baltic countries as just that – exaggerated rumors. But the tension and fear was intense, and attempts were continually being made to hide among the Christians with a false identity or get to another country not under German control. There were many ways to buy a false identity, but one of the most common was to buy the real identity of an existing family, get all their authentic documents, and make exact copies of them. The Christian family would get the copies, and the Jewish family would move to a distant town and live on the original papers. Of course, it was best if the Christian family didn't have many relatives or a wide social circle. It was also very common to give children to be adopted by non-Jews, or put in orphanages or convents. Many Jewish children were saved this way.

Side Note 8: The Village Jews

It's worth noting that in pre-war Poland, about 1 million out of the 3.5 million Jews lived in the big cities. The rest lived in thousands of small towns and villages, most of which had been established hundreds of years ago by Jews as service and business centers for farms in the area. (One has to remember that Poland was an agricultural nation, with over 80% of the population involved in farming.) The Christians who lived in these small towns and villages actually came as a result of the Jews' presence. In these villages, Jews lived pretty much as their ancestors had, dealing in the same trades and businesses they had been in for centuries: shoemaking, blacksmithing, tailoring, carpentry, etc.

Side note 9: Deportation of 1-4 June, 1942 by Tadeusz Pnkiewicz

"The night after the first of June, after 2,000 Jews had been deported":

On that terrible and tortuous night, not a single person in the ghetto closed their eyes. The insecurity of those who were left, the fear over what the next day would bring, and the feeling of total helplessness, is breaking everyone. Friends who came to visit the pharmacy keep peeking at the clock to check when daybreak would finally come, with whatever it would bring. Some of the people who hadn't received the longed-for authorization to stay in the ghetto had not reported for the deportation and were trying to get their hands on these papers at any price. The whole ghetto is making phone calls to anyone they can. Those without papers are trying to get their German employers to intercede for them, as this tactic often works.

During all of June 2nd and 3rd, hundreds of German police and their helpers, accompanied by the Jewish Police, went from one house to the next, checking papers and searching for people in hiding. Whoever doesn't have the right papers or is suspected of having forged documents is taken straight to the square, with no chance to take anything with him, and he is put straight onto the trains. The examination of papers takes place amidst curses, kicks and beatings. Machine guns are placed all around the square.

A stream of people begins flowing into Zgody Square. Everyone is being shoved along with sticks, fists and the kicks of the Germans. They move like shadows, with quiet and slow steps, faces serious, keeping their self-respect. Others give the impression that they don't know what's happening and are running in groups or alone. The Germans are hitting and shooting people; many die or are injured. The Germans shoot insanely; the sight of blood heightens their cruelty.

New groups of families, children and the aged keep passing the pharmacy. I see an old lady who looks like she is in her seventies, white-haired, walking slowly and proudly in a dress and house slippers, with no packages, not even a handbag. She holds a small dog close to her chest. A girl of about 13 walks by with a wave of her hand, smiling. She looks mentally ill, so happy, with not a clue as to what's going on. People walk by in their pajamas or underwear, just as they were dressed when they were thrown out of bed. The Germans look on, hit and push, shoot and laugh.

Out of one house not far from the pharmacy comes an old blind man, with his black eyeglasses and stick. He had lost his sight as a German soldier in 1914 on the Italian front. He walks with head held high, accompanied on one side by his son and on the other by his wife. On his chest is the Iron Cross he received for his courage fighting for Germany. Following him is an elderly man who is lame. Several Germans come up to these old men, one of them showing off some dance steps. He goes up to the blind man and screams in his ear: "Run! Run!" This awakens the desire of the other Germans to have a personal little game. One yells "Run!" in the lame man's ear. When the two start to hurry, one of the Germans hits the lame one in his bad leg with his rifle and when he falls down the Germans go wild with laughter.

After they satisfy their sadistic lust with the lame Jew, they go over to the blind one. They separate him from his wife and son, trip him to the ground, and every time he gets up they throw him down again, or rain blows upon him until he falls down. The son and wife stand on the side, crying, shocked and helpless. It's not clear what amuses the Germans more – the sight of the old man getting up and falling down or that of the son and wife who have to watch this torment. This type of torture is happening every step of the way, along with beatings and kicks. Sometimes they shoot people's legs and sometimes they just shoot them to death.

The blood all over the sidewalks and street attests to the Nazis' crimes. It's terribly hot, it's like fire is pouring down from the sky. People are also falling and fainting from heat and thirst. A small truck stands near the pharmacy and every few minutes the SS bring over suitcases filled with precious objects they have stolen from the Jews in the square. Some SS officers are also standing near the pharmacy and I overhear their conversation. They are still not pleased with the tempo of deportation. One gives a signal to a group of Jewish Police who are standing by with Spira at their head. They run up to the Germans and salute. The police get an order to bring over Dr. Rosenzweig, the head of the Judenrat. A few minutes later, Rosenzweig appears. They hit him, and tell him that he is immediately relieved of his duties as all the blame for the deportation not going as planned is on his head. He is to bring his entire family to the square to be deported. On the spot, a man named David Gutter is appointed as the new head of the Judenrat.

The Jews are either loaded onto trucks or made to run while the Germans yell at, kick or beat them, down the length of Lwolska Wieliczka Street to the train station in Plaszow. They kill anyone who falls down. At the station, they push 120 people into each train car, which were built to carry animals. They are shoved in without food or water, and the heat is awful. Each car has one small, barred window.

In the two parts of this June "Action", about 7,000 people were deported; this was close to half the population in the ghetto. They were all taken to the Belzec death camp; there were no survivors from this *group. (In Belzec, the Jews were murdered via carbon monoxide from a motor of a tank. This kind of death takes a long time and causes terrible suffering.) A number of people managed to cut the bars on the windows and jump while the train was on its way, and some of them did manage to survive. A few of them even returned to the ghetto.*

Side note 10: the "Action" of October 1942 According to Tadeusz Pankiewicz:

As I did regarding the June "Action", and for the same reasons, I will quote a few passages from the book by Tadeusz Pankiewicz about this "Action":

October 28th, a beautiful day without a cloud in the sky, that reminds one of the deportation back in June. People gather near the exit gate close to the Judenrat. Many are taking their children to work with them. All the Nazi figures active in the ghetto start arriving at 6 AM. SS Sturmbannfuhrer Haase arrives to take charge of the "Action". He's about 30 years old and looks older; he's tall and thin, with gray hair, never smiles, is married and has three children.

In addition to the uniformed Nazis come dozens of managers of factories in which Jews work, to try and save their employees. Although they are acting in their own interests, it really seems that they care about their workers. The men of the SS were making a 'selection' at the gate, going solely by people's looks. Sometimes the factory managers manage to change the SS men's decision. Everything is taking place with the screaming of the SS men, who also beat the Jews with their sticks. Gutter, along with his clerks in the Judenrat, and Spira with his policemen, are running around among the SS to get their orders. They don't allow children to leave. Police units and units of Polish, Lithuanian, Latvian and Estonian collaborators all enter as well. They excel in their cruelty!

The order comes that all Jews have until 10 AM to leave their homes and report to Juzefinska Street, and that everyone who stays at home will be shot on the spot. People run in the street, constantly being pushed with sticks and rifles. Suddenly, Haase, who's standing on a raised platform, raises his hand and says, "All Jews should return quietly to their houses and take their most important things, because the ghetto is going to be cleaned of Jews; not a single one will return to the ghetto." It was a trick to get people to leave their hiding places. The first shots are heard, the victims falling in their apartments, the corridors and yards. There are many wounded and we hear the victims' crying and shouting. A lot of blood is spilled. The Hitlerites are gazing at the terrible suffering of the wounded and laughing with pleasure. It's impossible to describe what those going to work were thinking, especially the men whose wives and children had stayed in the ghetto.

Around 12:00, the SS enter the main hospital on Juzefinska Street, shoot all the patients, and expel or murder the entire medical staff. A woman who was in the middle of labor was thrown on a wagon standing outside. I see SS men in the square cursing people for no reason. They especially love to mock old men and women, whose begging causes them to burst out laughing.

The shooting gets worse every minute. More and more people are being pushed into Zgody Square. Nobody has anything with them; when you're going to your death, what's the use of carrying a suitcase? The people are under no illusions.

After 10 AM, the Sonderdienst police go from house to house in groups of four to search for Jews who had remained home or in hiding. Those people are herded with blows to the square or are shot on the spot.

In the square, people are passing me by with whom I'm very friendly and have spent hours in conversation. Some are optimistic and some, pessimistic. Doctors, lawyers, engineers, industrialists. I see Dr. Leon Glick with his wife and daughter. At the last minute they take Dr. Glick out of the square, while his wife and daughter are deported. I especially notice dozens of doctors who until now had been safe from deportation. It's too hard on me to name them all.

Thousands of people are sitting and standing in the square. A few meters away stand a group of SS and Gestapo officers in brilliant, beautifully sewn uniforms and sparkling boots, holding all kinds of sticks in their hands. They're laughing all the time. Sometimes they go over to a group of Jews to give expression to their sadistic streak. A woman with a baby in her arms goes over to the head of the Judenrat, Gutter, who's standing next to the Germans. She falls on her knees and asks him to save her life. He pushes her away from him and the woman faints.

Many sick and crippled people are murdered in the October "Action". Their liquidation of the old age home is particularly cruel: They roll the crippled and sick down the stairs to the laughter of their Nazi torturers.

Many people I know commit suicide during this "Action", killing themselves along with their families, giving poison to their elderly parents.

An SS man named Pilarchik appeared at that "Action" who especially excelled in his cruelty and desire to kill. He even dared hit the head of the Jewish police, Spira, and the head of the Judenrat, Gutter. Later he calmed down and became friendly. He explained that he had come to the "Action" straight from the special school the SS had for training people to deal with Jews, and was trying to put into practice all that he had learned. However, he reached the conclusion that his actions were not becoming and he was sorry for what had happened.

Side note 11: The best places to hide outside the Ghetto

The Germans couldn't permanently station their people in all the small towns and villages of Poland – there were thousands of them. They relied on instilling fear by raiding them every so often. Many villages, however, were dominated by the various Undergrounds who would kill collaborators or force them to work for the Resistance, so the Gestapo had no intelligence regarding these places. These small towns and villages were therefore good places for Jews to hide or impersonate Christians. When the Gestapo would swoop down, all the people in the Resistance would run to the nearby forests to hide.

But in the big cities like Krakow, Gestapo rule was ironclad and it was very hard for the Jews to hide. During this period, the searches and checks on the roads became much tougher and whoever tried escaping without help and good organization was caught very quickly. Unfortunately, our former German tenant, Gerta, had left Krakow by now, so we were too late to take her up on her offer to help us. As I already mentioned, the percentage of survivors among those who escaped was infinitely greater than those who stayed under the Germans. This was especially true of the children

Side note 12: The Under ground Resistance In the Ghetto

There was a high-quality, wonderful Underground in the Krakow Ghetto which was mainly organized by the religious Zionist youth movement. Many books have been written about their courage and deeds. Since I write here of my memories, and at the time I didn't know anything about the Resistance in the ghetto, I won't go into great detail about it. However, I do want to express my opinion about it, with the benefit of 20-20 hindsight: The main goal of all the Jewish Undergrounds in all the ghettos was to die with weapon in hand and not be led like sheep to the slaughter. Other goals were to catch the attention of the world, get revenge on the Germans and join the war against them. In my opinion, all these resistance movements are worthy and even sublime - but there should have been only one primary aim of these Undergrounds: to save as many Jews as possible from extermination. First of all, it would have been possible to do this by bringing to the attention of the Jews over and over and over again that all the deportations were going to lead to death, that the goal and plan of the Nazis was to destroy us, and that this would never change. That all their periodic promises that "this is the last deportation" were lies and the only way to be saved was to escape and hide. The Undergrounds should have also concentrated on giving practical aid to enable the Jews to run away and hide, and they could have done a lot on this front.

Side Note 13: The German Forces that Operated in the Krakow Ghetto

SS-Sturmbannfuhrer Haase was the highest ranking officer of the SS in the Krakow District. He organized and actively carried out all the "Action"s and murders in the Krakow Ghetto, coming to the ghetto for every "Action" with his staff, which consisted of several officers. During the "Action" he would stand like a frozen statue in one of the central areas, usually Zgody Square, surrounded by his staff, and give out orders. He was considered extremely cruel, murdering people without batting an eyelash. After the war he was jailed in Poland, judged in Krakow and hung. I tried to get the protocol of his trial but unfortunately have not succeeded as yet.

The officer whom I called Mayer, who saved us from the October deportation, could have been Obersturmfuhrer Theodor Heinemayer, who was one of the Gestapo officers in the ghetto, but I'm not sure.

Regarding the various police forces that were active in the ghetto: First of all there were about 10 SS and Gestapo officers who administered the ghetto on a permanent basis. Each of these officers had a small staff consisting of lower ranking officers. Those several dozen Nazis would come into the ghetto on a regular basis. The ghetto was surrounded by a ring of Polish police as well as the Sonderdienst – the general German police force of Occupied Poland.

For the various "Action"s in the ghetto, the Germans used armed units of the Sonderdienst, and special units of the SS called the Einsatzkomando, who were specially trained to deal with Jews and went from one place to the next in Poland, as needed. SS volunteers also participated; they were nationals of Ukraine and the Baltic countries, Lithuania, Latvia and Estonia. They also used the special Polish police force that had sworn allegiance to the Third Reich, as well as the Schutzpolizei – members of the Volksdeutsche community. (It should be noted that after the war, all the Volksdeutsche left in Poland were banished to Germany in cattle cars with only the clothes on their backs.)

I'm not sure that I've mentioned here all the various police forces, let alone the civilian forces. Of course, the Gestapo and SS led them all.

Side Note 14: Street Kids

During the war in Poland, about a million Polish soldiers were killed or escaped abroad. In addition, approximately another million were grabbed by the Germans for forced labor in Germany. Add to that close to a million Polish Christians who were murdered by the Germans (mostly men), and you had hundreds of thousands – if not millions – of Polish children who were orphaned, mainly of their fathers. So the phenomenon of orphaned street kids was a common one. The orphanages that were set up throughout the country were only a very partial solution. Therefore, my appearance as a street kid who had run away from an orphanage was not an unusual one.

Side Note 15: Activity of the Jewish Underground in Krakow

At the end of 1942, a unit of the Jewish Resistance that had a hiding place in an apartment outside the ghetto attacked the Cyganeria night-club (near Rynek in the center of town) with automatic weapons and grenades. The attack was very successful, killing and wounding dozens of Germans – mainly officers. Right after they returned to their hideout, they were surrounded by Germans and after a short firefight they were all killed. It had been an oversight on the part of the Germans, as they had known about the unit and where they hid but in order to collect more intelligence they had only followed them but not arrested them. The Poles in the city knew very well what had happened.

Side Note 16: Plaszow and its Commandant, Amon Goeth

Plaszow was defined as a labor camp and was administered by the region's SS commander. The Jewish prisoners belonged to the SS, and the factory owners who employed them paid the SS for their labor. It differed organizationally from the concentration camps in the Third Reich, which were under the authority of a single central body, and the camp commandant was supposed to act according to that body's regulations. In contrast, a labor camp commandant had almost limitless authority – in our case, SS Hauptsturmfuhrer Amon Goeth. He answered to the SS commander of the Krakow region, whose name was Sherman. As they were close friends Sherman let Goeth have a free hand in the camp. Goeth was Vienna-born and an educated man – as well as a psychopath, sadist and cold-blooded killer. He was also a hedonist, and would regularly host parties and banquets in his house for high-ranking SS officers. He kept many horses and several prostitutes, as well as having a regular mistress – and a wife and daughter as well.

Goeth's greatest pleasure was to kill Jews with his own hands and torture them. He would go around the camp hunting for victims almost every day. Another pleasure he enjoyed was to hang Jews in the roll call yard and force all the prisoners to watch. In his trial in Poland immediately after the war he was convicted of the murder of 8,000 people, and according to the detailed testimonies at the trial, he had killed over a thousand of them himself. Indeed, over 90% of all deaths in Plaszow were caused by Goeth, as very few died of hunger or overwork. (It should be noted that Plaszow was also used by the Gestapo as an execution site for Polish Christians.)

One of the most fascinating books about the camp is "Process Ludobujcy Amona Getta", which is the 500-page protocol of Goeth's trial. Hundreds of camp survivors testified, so this book is an extremely trustworthy and authentic record of what happened there, because their memories were very fresh. Several dozen pages in the book are devoted to the testimony of one Mieczyslaw Pemper, then a 22-year-old man who specialized in German, Polish-German translation and German shorthand. He worked for Goeth personally and had access to all the camp documents. I consider this the most important and instructive witness account in the book.

During the trial, Amon Goeth would cross-examine the witnesses himself, trying to prove that they contradicted themselves. He knew every detail of what went on in the camp and remembered the names of everyone who held a position there. His eventual sentence: Death by hanging – in the same place in Plaszow that he had hanged his many victims.

In comparison to concentration camps I was in later, conditions in Plaszow were reasonable (except for the fact that at any moment one could fall victim to Goeth's lust for killing). The vast majority of the block commanders, work overseers and kapos (all Jews) were decent people who just wanted to survive the Holocaust. They did not mistreat the prisoners. The German administrative staff was also easygoing for the most part; when they killed or beat anyone as a punishment, it was always on Goeth's direct order. Most of the Ukrainian guards had been bought off by the prisoners. Many would even come to the barracks to have a good time – and get more bribes.

Side Note 17: Children's Compound in Plashow Camp

Since the Jews in the ghetto who helped build Plaszow convinced many that the camp was a safer place for their children, many were smuggled in. Even on the day the ghetto was liquidated, people managed to get their children to Plaszow in one way or another. But the special children's houses that had been built stood empty; not trusting the Germans, the Jews preferred to hide their children. Through the Jewish Police, Goeth tried to convince the prisoners to transfer their kids to the children's houses. There was excellent care there, with many nannies, pre-school teachers and instructors; the food was good; there were many toys and books; and they built a fully equipped playground as well. The parents were even allowed to go visit their offspring once in a while. Over time, many parents were convinced to put their children there, and when I got there, about 150 kids were in this special area of the camp.

When I came, I had the option of going there or staying with my father and going to work. My parents decided that I should work, since they considered the children's houses to be a trap. It flourished for over a year, and in the beginning of 1944 they even brought in German nannies. The legend of the children's camp in Plaszow lasted until its terrible end in May 1944, which I will speak of below.

Side Note 18: Role of Jewish Police in the Ghetto's Liquidation

When the news spread in the camp about the murder of the entire special Jewish Police force, no-one shed a tear. Now, over 60 years later, I still see in my mind's eye the dozens of families with children standing in a circle surrounded by all those Nazis, and the time has come for me to be horrified and mourn for them. Perhaps not for the policemen who "sold their souls to the devil," who aided the Nazis to kill Jews – which I witnessed personally – but for the children, the families...

I found the following information in the book "A Pharmacy in the Krakow Ghetto":

The Gestapo and the SS promised that all the special units of the Jewish policemen that collaborated with the Nazis would receive citizenship in a South American country, that they would all be taken to Hungary and be allowed to continue on to their new homes. They also promised that until they could be taken to Hungary they'd be allowed to live in another section of Krakow. This latter promise was not kept, but they and their families were allowed to walk around the city freely even if they had to still keep living in the ghetto. During the whole period of liquidation and that which followed, they enjoyed very close relations with the SS and Gestapo officers. When valuables were found in the emptied apartments, they were shared by all; when Jewish possessions were sold on the black market, the proceeds were split evenly. The Jewish families were to go to South America quite wealthy indeed... There were several policemen who didn't believe the Germans and managed to escape with their families. What naivete it was to think that the Germans would let the people who helped them and witnessed the ghetto's liquidation and horrific murders go abroad to speak of the hideous acts committed by the Nazis. Happy is he who believes....

During the post-liquidation period, the head of the Jewish Police, Spira, married off one of his daughters to one of his officers. He made a magnificent wedding, inviting all the Gestapo and SS officers who ran the ghetto. After this, the Germans notified everyone that they should get ready for their trip to Hungary, pack, etc. It isn't known if the policemen's families suspected anything. On that fateful day in December, several trucks came to collect them, supposedly to take them to the train to Hungary. Instead, they brought everyone to Plaszow, to be executed in Hujowa Gurka.

Side Note 19: "Children Action" in Plashow of May 1944

The most terrible part of the "Action" was seeing all those wonderful small children and knowing they were going to murder them. I saw no brutality; even when we began escaping the Germans didn't use a lot of force to catch us. Those who were caught were simply put back in line, with minimal violence. The horror I still feel is connected to how these wonderful children were being taken to their deaths with music, gently, in an attempt to make them happy – as if they were being taken on a great trip.

One of the accounts about this "Action" appeared in Spielberg's movie "Schindler's List." I assume that Spielberg investigated this subject and relied on eyewitness accounts, but even so there are several mistakes in the movie...

Once more, I found the most important source regarding this "Action" to be Pemper's account during Goeth's trial. In all Nazi war crime trials, the defendants argued that they just obeyed orders to kill. It turns out that in this case the initiative to kill all the children belonged solely to Amon Goeth. Pemper had managed to read a secret letter that Goeth sent to the High Command in Berlin, where he asked for authorization to send "unproductive elements" to the gas chambers, and following that he'd be able to take in other prisoners, as he'd been asked. His generous offer was accepted and he was directed to coordinate the murder with the commandant of Auschwitz. In his letter to the latter, Goeth requests that the clothing of those who are killed should be returned to him. Since the SS was very well organized financially, the commandant of Auschwitz was paid by the commandant of Plaszow for getting rid of these "unproductive elements." Pemper says that in addition to the 280 children aged 3-10 in the children's houses, another hundred were brought from the adult roll call, out of whom 25 managed to escape.

Amon Goeth had a young son and daughter. At his trial, when he claimed that he would get orders and as a soldier he had to obey, and that even in the future he didn't think a soldier could judge those who are giving the orders and refuse to obey them. One of the judges then asked, "If you would get an order to kill your two children, you also wouldn't judge the order and you would carry it out?" Goeth sank into thought for long seconds, and then answered that no, he wouldn't carry out the order...

So what happened to my friend, Jezyk? I never met him again, but I do remember knowing that he had managed to run away and was saved from this particular "Action". I know that some of the others had managed to hide in the cesspools for several hours. Some I managed to meet again in the camp, later on. But after this "Action" I was mainly involved with my own survival. Who of them survived the war? Unfortunately, after the war I made no special effort to search for them. Perhaps I will do so now?

Side Note 20: Hilowitz and the Jewish Police in Plashow

The Jewish Police force in Plaszow was established even before the Krakow Ghetto was liquidated. Some of the men came from the ghetto. Hilowitz was appointed its head, with Finkelstein his deputy. All the policemen got extra food, but only the senior officers got better living accommodations. Hilowitz got a magnificent apartment in a block, where he lived with his wife. Another block housed other higher-ups, like Dr. Gross, the chief doctor of the camp. They lived with their families in modest apartments. For some reason, Hilowitz was considered a good and fair man. At the last stage of the camp's evacuation, in September 1944, he and all his senior staff – along with their families – were executed on the order of Amon Goeth. In order to get permission to do so, Goeth claimed that they had tried to organize a revolt. The truth was that they were collaborators in all his corrupt activities, like stealing food meant for the prisoners and selling it on the black market in Krakow. Goeth suspected that they would become witnesses in his prosecution, so he had them killed.

Side Note 21: An Introduction to Concentration Camps

According to the research and the evidence presented in war crimes trials of those who ran Mauthausen, in the approximately seven years of its existence, between 200,000 – 300,000 prisoners of various nations under German occupation were murdered in this camp. The Nazis had established it in Germany along with several other concentration camps after burning down Germany's Parliament in March, 1933. The Nazis had used this act as an excuse for making mass arrests of Communists, Jews and other anti-Nazi opponents. Since the numbers reached hundred of thousands, the existing jails couldn't hold them all and these camps were where they put the overflow.

At a second stage, the camps were made official and defined as places for opponents of Nazism to be destroyed physically, spiritually and psychologically via starvation, beatings and hard labor. After the war broke out, when millions inhabited the concentration camps, it was decided to take advantage of their ability to work in order to supply slave labor for the war effort. Mauthausen was an administrative center and a transit and sorting camp from which prisoners were sent to dozens of camps in the region which were set up right next to the factories where the inmates worked. All internal administration was taken care of by the prisoners themselves.

The block commanders, who were the highest ranking prisoners in this hierarchy, were always German prisoners, who were usually there for criminal offenses. Every block had several hundred inmates, and each member of the staff that ran it (about ten in all) had a specific duty. The overseers were in general the SS. There was one more administrative "rank" in the camp: the kapos, whose main job was to manage the work done by the prisoners. All inmates who were attached in some way to the camp's administration got better conditions. The inmates were marked according to the type of "crime" they had committed that led to their incarceration: A red triangle was used for political prisoners, a black one for criminals, an orange one for Jews, etc.

Side Note 22: "Kapos" of Gozen 2

The kapos were mostly prisoners of war from Spain, who had fought in the Republican Brigades against Franco's fascists in the great revolt of 1936. After Franco's victory, the Republicans escaped to France, where they were given political asylum. Then, when the Germans conquered France in 1940, they arrested these Spaniards and sent them to concentration camps. Over time, some of them became kapos, and apparently they were the only ones of their countrymen to have survived all this time. They had begun as intellectuals and idealists, but over the years they became beasts and the cruelest kinds of killers. If one of them looked at you and for some reason he decided he didn't like you, you could immediately begin preparing to leave this world... A very few kapos were Polish or French prisoners, and they still kept in touch with their humanity. All kapos were well compensated for their terrible work, mostly with extra food, clothes and better accommodations.

Side Note 23: War News

How could we get the news: There were official news of the war from German newspapers like "Nowiny Krakowskie" (The Krakow News). They were full of lies, but we always knew how to read between the lines. For example, "battles full of glory" meant that they had suffered heavy losses. Via the BBC, Radio Free Poland managed to broadcast throughout the country, though it was completely illegal to listen to it, and the punishment was certain death.

The Polish Underground also published a newspaper. I saw with my own eyes how Polish children would toss these pages onto the ground in the middle of a movie being shown in a public square, as well as slip them into people's pockets. The many Gestapo agents who stood in the square would immediately arrest anyone who picked the paper up, so the people refrained from doing so... I once saw a Polish kid put the paper in a Gestapo agent's pocket, and he was instantly arrested. The Polish resistance did something else sophisticated: They would print their paper in the exact same style as the Germans used their own newspapers, and would then insert them into the stack of official German papers.

Made in the USA
Middletown, DE
10 October 2021